Voices of Latin America

Resistance + Land   P6-7

Extractivism P8   →   ↑I foreign investment

Reduce labour costs   & attractive

Argentina - The Ministry of Agriculture

now called the Min of Agribusiness

CEOs in power   ownership (government)

P13-14 Extractivist model

P16 Land concentration

P18 Territory Resistance

Praise for this book

'This is a wonderful X ray of modern Latin America, a vision of the continent's struggles and potential futures through the eyes of its social movement leaders and intellectuals. Read it from end to end, whether as an introduction or an update, or mine it for quotes from inspirational figures across the region on a range of contemporary issues. Latin America (or most of it) has come to the end of its progressive 'pink tide' years of the early 2000s. For the coming years, social movements will provide the grains of resistance and future directions. Tom Gatehouse has assembled an unparalleled set of views and insights from the leaders and intellectuals of that movement.'

Dr. Duncan Green, Senior Strategic Adviser, Oxfam

'*Voices of Latin America* gives expression to the rich diversity of the social movements of the region. The book's chapters cover a wide range of human experience, public and private, from gender and sexuality, to indigenous peoples, state violence, struggles in education, the media and culture, as well as the environment and urban life. In each area we find a need to secure past achievements, often associated with the governments and popular movements of 'The Pink Tide', and to resist new and varied challenges, usually associated with 'neoliberalism' and the interests of the powerful. The voices collected here register not only resilience and determination but also a social and cultural originality that defies the headline messages of an uncontested right-wing advance.'

James Dunkerley, Professor of
Latin American Politics at Queen Mary, University of London, and
the former Director of the Institute for the Study of the Americas and
the Institute of Latin American Studies of the University of London

'This is a book of hope. Against the backcloth of a return to right-wing governments across Latin America, the growing power of extractive enterprises, the rise of intolerant religious movements, and rampant consumerism, *Voices of Latin America* gives voice to those involved in a wide range of social movements. Indeed, it provides a refreshing and personalised view as to how social movements come into being, how they are organised, and how they tackle the many obstacles that they confront. It is a tale of rights, how to establish them and how to defend them. Here the people involved recount their experiences, analyse their present predicament, and tell of their dreams.'

Dr John Crabtree, Research Associate,
Latin America Centre, School of Global and Area Studies, University of Oxford

'An inspiring and thought-provoking book that gives voice to the courageous Latin American activists who speak out against violence to women and LBGT activists, the indigenous communities who stand up to multinational mining and oil companies, the students who have fought for free education, the shanty-town residents who have fought for decent homes and human rights activists who have shone a light on the abuses of US-funded military forces. As well as exploring the tensions between social movements and the left-wing Pink Tide governments, this book gives crucial insights into how activists will confront the new right-wing governments in Latin America from the neoliberal austerity of Argentina's Macri to the authoritarian extremism of Brazil's Jair Bolsonaro. This book is a must read for anyone interested in Latin American politics.'

Grace Livingstone, affiliated lecturer at
Centre of Latin American Studies, University of Cambridge, and
a visiting research fellow at the Institute of Latin American Studies,
School of Advanced Studies, University of London.

'*Voices of Latin America* is a very distinct sort of book. While it deals with the types of issue that one might expect to encounter in other textbooks or pieces of investigative journalism on Latin American politics and social change, it addresses these themes primarily through the words of the people who live them. The key voices in this collection are not those of the authors or the editor but rather of the seventy or so people who were interviewed in the course of preparing the book. Here the reader listens to activists, community authorities, public intellectuals, popular journalists, NGO workers and movement leaders as they talk of issues about which they care passionately and that affect their everyday lives and being. *Voices of Latin America* reflects the human experience of everyday oppressions, struggles, resistances, and hopes that animate so much day to day conversation and grassroots politics in the region. It will be tremendously helpful for teaching as well as being an important and inspiring read in its own right.'

Anthony Bebbington, Higgins Professor of Environment and Society,
Graduate School of Geography, Clark University, MA, USA
Member of the Board of Directors, Oxfam America
Professorial Fellow, Global Development Institute, University of Manchester

'*Voices of Latin America* is a gem. At its heart are extensive excerpts from powerful interviews across multiple subjects with Latin American activists and scholars such as Alicia Cawiya, vice-president of the Huaorani people, Ecuador; Tania Montalvo, Animal Político, Mexico; and Eva Sanchez, director of the Lenca Women's Rights Organization, Las Hormigas (The Ants), Honduras.

Editor, Tom Gatehouse's introductory essay lays out the political terrain for readers unfamiliar with contemporary Latin American politics and social activism. The format of organizing interview excerpts around ten themes allows for comparisons across themes and across fourteen countries. Activists everywhere will find much to learn from this readable text. It will certainly be a significant addition to courses on social movements, political ecology, gender, indigeneity, and development.'

Louise Fortmann Professor Emerita of
Natural Resource Sociology, University of California at Berkeley

'While much attention focusses on the return of the right in many countries of Latin America, this book reminds us of the vibrant resistances and activisms for democratic change in Latin America. Far from disappearing from the political and social landscape, this book gives us deep insights into their ongoing presence and new manifestations. While not uncritical of the left in government nor ignoring its redistributive contribution, this book shows us rather, the creativity at the grass roots, organised around land, social, cultural, sexual, environmental, educational and urban city rights. It thus brings together in a highly readable text, the learning from Latin America for all those interested in transforming the world.'

Professor Jenny Pearce, Research Professor,
Latin America and Caribbean Centre, London School of Economics

'*Voices of Latin America* brings us urgent dispatches from the front line of struggle against the violent, racialized and gendered forms of dispossession that characterize the continent today. From the mothers of the disappeared in Mexico's cartel wars fighting against state impunity, to indigenous and afro-descendant leaders organizing to defend their territory against the predations of global capital, to women resisting policies that criminalize them for exercising their reproductive rights, this book provides a vital overview of contemporary social movements in Latin America. Essential reading.'

Rachel Sieder, Senior Research Professor, Centre for
Research and Graduate Studies in Social Anthropology (CIESAS), Mexico City

Voices of Latin America

Edited by
Tom Gatehouse

Published by Practical Action Publishing Ltd in association with
Latin America Bureau

Practical Action Publishing Ltd
27a Albert Street Rugby, Warwickshire, CV21 2SG, UK
www.practicalactionpublishing.org

Latin America Bureau, Enfield House, Castle Street,
Clun, Shropshire, SY7 8JU, UK
www.lab.org.uk

ISBN 978-1-90901-424-4 Paperback
ISBN 978-1-90901-423-7 Hardback
ISBN 978-1-90901-421-3 Library PDF
ISBN 978-1-90901-422-0 Ebook

Since 1974, Practical Action Publishing has published and disseminated books
and information in support of international development work throughout
the world. Practical Action Publishing is a trading name of Practical Action
Publishing Ltd (Company Reg. No. 1159018), the wholly owned publishing
company of Practical Action. Practical Action Publishing trades only in support
of its parent charity objectives and any profits are covenanted back to Practical
Action (Charity Reg. No. 247257, Group VAT Registration No. 880 9924 76).

Latin America Bureau (Research and Action) Limited is a UK registered charity
(no. 1113039). Since 1977 LAB has been publishing books, news, analysis and
information about Latin America, reporting consistently from the perspective
of the region's poor, oppressed or marginalized communities, and social
movements. In 2015 LAB entered into a publishing partnership with Practical
Action Publishing.

A catalogue record for this book is available from the British Library.

Gatehouse, Tom (2019) *Voices of Latin America*, Rugby, UK: Practical Action
Publishing <http://dx.doi.org/10.3362/9781909014213>.

Picture editing by Marilene Cardoso Ribeiro
Cover design by Fiona Macintosh & Brian Craig
Printed in the United Kingdom

Contents

http://dx.doi.org/10.3362/97817909014213.000

Acknowledgements

This book would never have been possible without the wonderful team of volunteers who took part in the Voices project. Linda Etchart, Tom Gatehouse, Nina Meghji, Louise Morris, Ali Rocha, and James Thackara travelled to Ecuador, Argentina, Chile, Bolivia, Guatemala, Honduras, Brazil, and the United States to collect interviews. Emma Banks (Colombia), Francesco di Bernardo (Mexico), Eliane Brum (Brazil), Gwen Burnyeat (Colombia), Carol Byrne (Mexico), Marilene Cardoso Ribeiro (Brazil), Jennifer Chisholm (Brazil), Roberto Navarrete (Chile), Rachel Simon (Belize), and Kary Stewart (Peru) all contributed additional interviews . Sue Branford and Antonia Burchard-Levine contributed distance interviews collected via Skype or similar channels, as did several of those already acknowledged.

Sadly there were some interviews for which there was no space in the printed book, but we are equally grateful to those who contributed them: Álvaro José Aburto Gadea (Nicaragua), Dan Baron Cohen (Brazil), Eliana Barrera (Chile), Thaís Borges (Brazil), Camille and Julio Etchart (Uruguay), Danielle House (Mexico), Ainhoa Montoya (El Salvador), Loehrl and Robert Pillers (Nicaragua), Bert Schouwenberg (Honduras), and Lena Schubmann (Bolivia). Some of this material will be posted on the Voices website (https://lab.org.uk/voices).

Nine authors contributed the eleven chapters of the book, selecting and editing interviews, explaining their context, and writing the analysis for each chapter theme. They are acknowledged at the start of each chapter.

Special thanks to Pierre Fromentin and Julien Jatobá Karl, who took beautiful photos for the project, and Marilene Cardoso Ribeiro, our photo editor; to our dedicated team of volunteer translators, whose work is acknowledged at the end of each chapter; and to our meticulous copy editor (and former LAB author) Mandy McDonald, who did her utmost to ensure style and consistency throughout a very complex book.

LAB editors and council members Sue Branford, Nick Caistor, Mike Gatehouse, David Lehmann, Grace Livingstone, Marcela López Levy, Shafik Meghji, Linda Newson, and David Treece all provided valuable guidance and support to the Voices team throughout the project.

We could not have completed the research or written the book without generous funding from Christian Aid, the estate of David Slater, and the Lipman-Miliband Trust, as well as everyone who contributed to the 2017 crowdfunding campaign and the follow-up appeal in 2018. They included a very generous donor who twice provided substantial match funding, and two donors who volunteered to fund the additional cost of printing the entire book in colour, to show the photographs to full advantage.

Special patrons of the appeal were: Stephen and Bryn Allpress, Pauline and Francisco Alvarez, Alicia Bastos, Bill Lamme, Richard McColl, Sandra Morris, Ulrich Oslender, and Matthew Wright.

Other donors included: Vanessa Baird, John Barker, Oscar Barlow, Clare Bolton, Fred Branson, Antonia Burchard-Levine, Anne Burke, Steven Busfield, Jonathan Casey, Alistair Clark, Gail Critchlow, Simon Deeley, Jane Freeland, Bruno Guillaume, Natalie Harris, Jahn Harrison, Danielle House, Malcolm Jones, Sioned Jones, María Fernanda Lanfranco, Fabiana Lopes da Cunha, Mandy Macdonald, Julia McNaught da Silva, Jean Meghji, Shafik Meghji, Martin Nathan, Danny Nemu, Adam Padel, Dominic Power, James Purcell, Jackie Reiter, Simone Ruotolo, Apolo Santana, Jessica Sklair, Russell Slater, Susie and Gary, Gui Tavares, Marilyn Thomson, Christine Toomey, Marcia Tosta Dias, Nadia Tottingham, Trevor Tucker, Daniela Vieira dos Santos, Lucy Whitman, Claire Williams, Ron Witton.

Many others helped in different ways to make this project a reality, including Alberto Acosta, Natalie Alem, Stephen Allpress, Leonardo Batista's partner Antonia, Paola Bayle, Patrick Boulet, Javier Burchard, Patricio Bustamante, Ines Castillo Muguerza, Leo Cerda, Maria Helena Chagas de Almeida, Maria Dalva Chagas de Almeida Costa, Ann Chaplin, Alejandra Corvalán, John Crabtree, Clare Dixon, Freddy Ehlers, Nikki Evans, Mari-Carmen Falcon-Aide, Melissa Fitch, Gustavo Fuchs, Jeremias Goransky and family, José Gualinga, Gerardo Gualinga, Elif Karakartal, Maria-Olga Levine, Valerie Mealla, Mario Melo, Verónica Menargues Soriano, Tania Montalvo, Jen Moore, Sorrel Moseley-Williams, Denise Maria Moura da Silva Lopes, Pablo Navarrete, Victoria Neyza, Paola Onofa, Sergio Onofrio, Maria Pacheco Fernandes, Maria Rosa Pessoa Piedade's partner Jaime, Jon Polo Iturregui, Dulce Ramos, Romina Rivera Bravo, Leila Salazar López, José Serra Vega, Leslie Villapolo Herrera, and Saúl Zeballos.

Our thanks to the following institutions and organizations for their support: Alborada, Amnesty International, Citizens' Group for the Decriminalization of Abortion (El Salvador), Guatemala Solidarity Network, Human Rights Watch, Institute of Latin American Studies, London Mining Network, Mongabay, Movement of People Affected by Dams (Brazil), Movimento Xingu Vivo para Sempre (Brazil), National Council of Scientific and Technological Development (Brazil), National Science Foundation, The Pachamama Alliance, Peace Brigades International, Royal Geographical Society, Socioenvironmental Institute (Brazil), The University for the Creative Arts, and War on Want.

Special thanks are due to the team at our co-publishers, Practical Action Publishing, who gave enthusiastic backing to the Voices project from its inception and who will take care of the production, printing, and distribution of this book. US publisher Monthly Review Press gave a generous advance to help us complete it.

And last but not least, a very special thank you to all of our interviewees, their families, and communities. They are the real stars of this project.

Preface

In 2015, the team at Latin America Bureau (LAB) were thinking of the best way to update or replace our very successful book *Faces of Latin America* by Duncan Green, now in its fourth edition. LAB author Marcela López Levy observed that our unique contribution across 40 years had been to report on the 'voices' of the less powerful, the poor, and the marginalized of Latin America.

We concluded that perhaps the best way to do this would be to begin collecting these voices and creating a new book in which we would give them as much space as possible to 'speak'. We found funding to send four volunteer researchers to Honduras, Brazil, Argentina, Chile, and Bolivia in late 2016, with a mission to find those with important stories to tell and collect extended interviews. Other friends sent us interviews from Mexico, Guatemala, Nicaragua, El Salvador, Belize, Cuba, Colombia, Venezuela, Ecuador, Peru, and Uruguay.

Over the following two years we translated these interviews, selected key passages, and organized them by theme into 11 chapters, in which the interviewees are introduced, their particular situation set in context, and relevant parallels drawn with other countries in the region. But the objective was always to allow the interviewees to speak for themselves, and, indeed, many of the interviews are so powerful and engaging that very little context or explanation is required.

Most of our 70 interviews (spanning 14 countries) are with active members of social movements involved in campaigns to improve life for themselves, members of their groups and communities, and their fellow citizens. As we explain in the Introduction, we wanted to see how these diverse and vibrant movements fit into the current social, economic, and political scenario in Latin America, how much they are able to exchange ideas and link up with one another, and ultimately what the future might hold – to what extent their visions for other types of society are likely to become reality.

Voices of Latin America is not just a collection of essays with testimonies. It is the product of a carefully planned collaboration between many different people: LAB's editors, our researchers, in-country contacts who suggested and arranged interviews, translators, photographers, the nine different authors who wrote the chapters, and above all our interviewees, who trusted us to transmit their voices faithfully.

The Voices website

Alongside this book we are creating a website: www.vola.org.uk. This will not only carry material for which there was no room in the book, but also additional material of interest to the reader, particularly multimedia content.

Organized by chapter, it will include: all the references in the book, most of which will be conveniently accessible via a clickable hyperlink; full text PDFs of selected interviews; photos; and videos and additional reports related to the chapter theme.

We will add to this material in the coming months and years to create a steadily expanding collection of voices from the region. Readers will be encouraged to send us additional material, to post their own comments, and to engage in debate – in short, to add their own voices.

We very much hope you enjoy both book and website. Please send us your comments and suggestions to contactlab@lab.org.uk.

Stop press: Brazil elects a far-right demagogue

On 28 October 2018, just as this book was going to print, hopes for social progress in Latin America's largest nation received a major setback. Former army captain Jair Bolsonaro (see Chapters 3 and 8) was elected president and will take office from 1 January 2019. The most prominent face of the Brazilian far right and a member of Congress since 1991, Bolsonaro had spent most of his political career on the fringes, flitting from one minor party to another and showing little interest in running for high office. He has never held any position in government and is known more for his violent rhetoric than any legislative achievement, having over the years made a string of offensive statements about women, Afro- and indigenous Brazilians, and the LGBT community. He explicitly defends torture and praises the Brazilian military dictatorship (1964-85), criticizing it only for failing to kill enough of its opponents.

The Workers' Party (PT), which governed Brazil from 2003-16, saw its reputation diminish rapidly during the two administrations of Dilma Rousseff (2010-16). Rousseff, who lacked the charisma and political skill of her mentor and predecessor Luiz Inácio Lula da Silva, was unable to arrest a period of economic decline which set in soon after she took office, culminating in a two-year recession from 2015. From 2014, this economic crisis was accompanied by constant news of Operation Car Wash – a police investigation into a massive corruption scheme at the state-controlled oil company Petrobras. Car Wash exposed a political and economic elite up to their eyeballs in sleaze and has resulted in prison sentences for dozens of politicians of various parties and executives from some of Brazil's biggest companies.

Rousseff was impeached in 2016 for alleged budgetary irregularities and was replaced by her vice, Michel Temer, of the PMDB (now MDB), arguably the most corrupt of Brazil's major political parties. Temer limped to the end of his presidential term with single-digit approval ratings, and could have been impeached himself – there is evidence of his involvement in Car Wash and he is accused of crimes far more serious than those for which Rousseff was removed. Most dramatically, Lula was convicted of corruption and money laundering and was sent to prison in April 2018. His supporters argue his prosecution was designed to prevent him from standing in the 2018 elections, which polls predicted he would win comfortably, and many legal experts have questioned the legitimacy of his trial. Sérgio Moro, the judge who nailed Lula, has accepted the job of Justice Minister in Bolsonaro's incoming administration – reinforcing accusations of judicial bias.

With the PT haemorrhaging support and right-wing movements increasingly vocal, Bolsonaro's moment had come. He seized on righteous public anger at economic mismanagement and corruption, widespread loss of faith in Brazilian democracy, and rejection of the political status quo. He also gave voice to the concerns of millions of socially conservative and religious Brazilians who feel that the country is suffering from a 'moral crisis', following an extended period of relative social liberalism from the mid-1990s onwards. Finally, like Donald Trump, Bolsonaro circumvented the mainstream media via an aggressive social media strategy and an avalanche of fake news. With more Brazilians now consuming news online than from television or newspapers, this strategy proved effective.

The gravity of Bolsonaro's election cannot be overstated. He plans to modify Brazil's anti-terror laws, in order to criminalize activity by social movements and left-wing political groups (Truffi, 2018). He has stepped up his attacks on the press (Sögur Hous, 2018). He looks set to appoint at least four current and former military men to positions in government (Martins, 2018), and implement a reckless, trigger-happy security policy (Cerqueira, 2018). He has pledged to slash environmental protections and open up the Amazon to miners and loggers (Watts, 2018a). On the world stage, he is already cosying up to Trump, promising to move the Brazilian embassy in Israel from Tel Aviv to Jerusalem, which would make Brazil only the third country to do so (The Guardian, 2018). His appointee for foreign minister has called climate change 'dogma' and a plot by 'cultural Marxists' to promote Chinese interests (Watts, 2018b), and there is concern he may withdraw Brazil from the Paris Agreement.

Bolsonaro is not only an immediate danger to ethnic, religious, and sexual minorities in Brazil, but an existential threat to Brazil's young and fragile democracy. And by committing the world's most biodiverse country to such catastrophic environmental policies, he poses a real threat to the future of life on our planet.

References

NB: All web references were checked and still available in November 2018 unless otherwise stated. All references are listed, with web-links, on the page for this chapter on the Voices website www.vola.org.uk

Cerqueira, D. (2018) 'Por que a política de segurança pública do Bolsonaro seria uma tragédia?', *El País*, 24 October, <https://brasil.elpais.com/brail/2018/10/24/opinion/1540336594_761394.html>

The Guardian (2018) 'Brazil president-elect Bolsonaro says he plans to move embassy to Jerusalem', 1 November, <https://www.theguardian.com/world/2018/nov/01/bolsonaro-brazil-embassy-jerusalem>

Martins, L. (2018) 'Veja os ministros já anunciados para o governo Bolsonaro', *EXAME*, 21 November, <https://exame.abril.com.br/brasil/veja-os-ministros-ja-anunciados-para-o-governo-bolsonaro>

Sögur Hous, D. (2018) 'Ataques de Bolsonaro à imprensa ameaçam a democracia, dizem associações de jornalistas', *Folha de S. Paulo*, 22 October, <https://www1.folha.uol.com.br/poder/2018/10/ataques-de-bolsonaro-a-imprensa-sao-descompromisso-com-a-democracia-dizem-associacoes-de-jornalistas.shtml>

Truffi, R. (2018) 'Proposta de Bolsonaro, votação da ampliação da lei antiterrorismo é adiada no Senado', *Estadão*, 31 October, <https://politica.estadao.com.br/noticias/geral,proposta-de-bolsonaro-votacao-da-ampliacao-da-lei-antiterrorismo-e-adiada-no-senado,70002576840>

Watts, J. (2018a) 'Our planet can't take many more populists like Brazil's Bolsonaro', *The Guardian*, 24 October, <https://www.theguardian.com/commentisfree/2018/oct/24/planet-populists-brazil-jair-bolsonaro-environment>

Watts, J. (2018b) 'Brazil's new foreign minister believes climate change is a Marxist plot', *The Guardian*, 15 November, <https://www.theguardian.com/world/2018/nov/15/brazil-foreign-minister-ernesto-araujo-climate-change-marxist-plot>

CHAPTER 1

Introduction: living life on their own terms

Tom Gatehouse

Abstract

Since the fall of the Cold War dictatorships, social movements have thrived in Latin America and have been some of the most important and effective agents of change. However, with the recent end of the 'pink tide' – a wave of more or less socially progressive governments that held power across the region from the late 1990s – these movements now face tougher conditions and an uncertain future. Five experts assess the current regional panorama and the role of social movements within it.

This is a book of many voices: of anthropologists and archaeologists; urban planners and architects; artists and musicians; journalists and politicians; women and LGBT people trying to halt gender-based oppression and violence; indigenous activists fighting oil drilling on their territory; residents of favelas resisting evictions; students staking their claim to a free, universal, and high-quality education; and many more.

What do these voices tell us? Almost all of our interviews were conducted between 2016 and 2018 and they testify to an extremely sensitive and uncertain moment in the history of Latin America. The so-called pink tide of more or less socially progressive governments that came to power across the region in the late 1990s and early 2000s is in retreat. Though there were major differences between them, these governments all shared a commitment to eliminating or at least reducing some of the egregious extremes of poverty from which the region has long suffered. As the Chilean journalist and sociologist Raúl Sohr comments:

> Perhaps the outstanding government of the pink tide period was that of President Luiz Inácio Lula da Silva in Brazil, which over the course of its two terms achieved the biggest redistribution of wealth ever seen in Latin America as a result of state policy, a real landmark achievement. As well as Lula's government, there was the Proyecto Nacional y Popular in Argentina, part of the Kirchner phase of Peronism, and in Chile we had the Concertación and Nueva Mayoría coalition governments, as well as the Bolivarian governments in Ecuador, Venezuela, Nicaragua, and Bolivia. So there were several countries across the continent that carried out redistributive and generally progressive policies, relying

http://dx.doi.org/10.3362/9781909014213.001

on a favourable economic situation that allowed them to do so. This redistributive phase, however, came to an end, generally coinciding with the fall in the prices of commodities, a reduction in available resources, and an over-reliance on certain commodities.

This redistributive phase was based on what is known as the extractivist model of development – the large-scale extraction and exportation of raw materials such as oil, natural gas, minerals, and soya. While Latin America has depended on the export of raw materials since colonial times, during the 1990s and 2000s governments of all political stripes across the region expanded this model, taking advantage of high demand from emerging markets, particularly China. When the Chinese economy began to slow, the knock-on effect on Latin America was decisive. Since 2012, every major Latin American economy has underperformed in comparison with the previous decade, while Brazil – the region's biggest economy – went into a recession lasting two years, its longest on record.

It is no coincidence that this economic downturn has been accompanied by the return to power of right-wing governments and traditional elites. Much of the progress of the pink tide period is now under threat – not least as regards poverty and income inequality, but also in the spheres of environmental regulation, workers' rights, pensions, and the representation of women and ethnic minorities. On top of this uncertain political climate, Latin America finds itself in the midst of some extremely acrimonious culture wars – similar to those across much of Europe and the United States – in which the far right appears increasingly emboldened and hard-line religious movements are especially vocal and influential.

But the social movements that have flourished throughout Latin America since the end of the dictatorship period remain strong and dynamic. These range from very small, single-issue campaigns at the local level to national and even international mobilizations for change. And in certain countries – such as Honduras and Chile – recent social movements have led to the formation of new political parties and coalitions. So, can Latin America's social movements continue to influence national politics and articulate a vision for economies and societies that differs from the ones currently being put forward by those in power?

To answer this question, we spoke to five regional experts.

Achievements of the pink tide

The term 'pink tide' – or the progressive cycle, as it is also known – is a problematic one, given that it refers to governments of very distinct political instincts, policies, and discourse, from the soft left administrations of Michelle Bachelet in Chile (2006–10 and 2014–18) to the more interventionist Bolivarian administrations like those of Hugo Chávez in Venezuela (1999–2013) and Evo Morales in Bolivia (2006–present). For the Argentine sociologist Maristella Svampa:

> Leaving aside the differences between the more moderate and more radical governments of this period, they shared a number of common

Maristella Svampa

features. The first was a challenging of the neoliberalism of previous decades. The second was the introduction of more unorthodox economic policies. The third was the development of a series of social policies aimed at the most marginalized sectors of society, which implied an increase in salaries and, above all, an increase in consumption. The progressive governments managed to increase their legitimacy by expanding the model of consumption ... Fourthly, we must remember that from the very beginning of the progressive cycle there was a push for the creation of a Latin American regional space, of an anti-imperialist nature, which led to the creation of a strong regional bloc. These are the four elements that bridged the differences between the more radical governments, such as those of Venezuela, Bolivia, and Ecuador, the more moderate ones in Argentina and Brazil, and even more centrist governments as in Chile. They established a common language that became almost hegemonic in Latin America, defining a new political climate and rethinking the relationship between state, society, and economy.

The pink tide governments achieved some impressive outcomes. Ten million Latin Americans joined the middle class every year between 2002 and 2012, while the proportion living on less than US$4 a day shrank from 45 to 25 per cent between 2000 and 2014 (Encarnación, 2018). Meanwhile, the percentage of young people aged 18–24 enrolled in courses of higher education nearly doubled between 2000 and 2010, from 21 to 40 per cent, progress being particularly strong amongst low- and middle-income groups (World Bank, 2017).

These gains occurred throughout the region but were greater in countries with pink tide governments.

One interesting case in point is Bolivia. Though it remains one of the poorest nations in the region, Bolivia has more than halved extreme poverty since 2006, when Evo Morales took office. It has also made major progress on inequality: while the richest 10 per cent in Bolivia used to earn 128 times as much as the poorest 10 per cent, by 2017 this was down to 38 times as much, the biggest fall in inequality in the region. These gains have been achieved while Bolivia still managed to run budget surpluses every year between 2006 and 2014, reducing public sector debt from 83 per cent of GDP in 2003 to just 26 per cent in 2014 (Toro, 2017). Morales' economic policies have drawn plaudits from even the World Bank and the IMF – organizations of which he is highly critical.

As Raúl comments:

> Perhaps the most important and successful example of a government that has refused to toe the American line, and which is fighting the changing political currents in Latin America, is that of Evo Morales in Bolivia. Without a doubt, in Latin America this has been the most successful left-wing government, with the most interesting model. They've had a broad vision in terms of governance and the national project: not only did they declare Bolivia a plurinational state, engage with the indigenous communities, and carry out social reforms for the elderly and the poor – there has been a process of redistribution – but they have also focused on the diversification of exports. Bolivia had never experienced meaningful economic growth like it has under Morales. I think it's a profoundly interesting government.

But in terms of regional significance, the most important government of the pink tide era was undoubtedly that of Luiz Inácio Lula da Silva in Brazil (2003–11). A former metalworker, trade unionist, and the seventh of eight children of two illiterate farmworkers from the arid and poverty-stricken north-east, Lula shattered existing perceptions of what was possible. For the Brazilian journalist Eliane Brum:

> Under Lula, Brazil saw a real increase in the minimum wage, a significant reduction in extreme poverty, greater access to university education, important improvements to the SUS national health system, racial quotas [in higher education] – a timid but essential affirmative action policy – and access to financial credit for the poorest. This is no mean feat. Really. The effects will be felt in Brazil for many decades. Today's main voices of resistance from the urban peripheries emerged from this experience and gained access to worlds from which they had hitherto been barred.
>
> The fact that a worker could take power by means of the vote in a country like Brazil has had an impact on the lives of Brazilians which is

Eliane Brum

hard to gauge exactly, being so subjective – but it has undoubtedly been immense. Lula did this – and no one can take that away from him.

Brazil under Lula also increasingly took the lead at the regional level, reflected in the creation of the Union of South American Nations (UNASUR), an intergovernmental organization based on the EU model, which brought together the Mercosur trade bloc (Argentina, Brazil, Uruguay, Paraguay, and Venezuela, though the latter has been suspended since 2016) and the Andean Community customs union (Bolivia, Colombia, Ecuador, and Peru). The aim was to promote greater regional integration, with the eventual creation of a continental free trade zone, a South American passport, and a single currency. For Maristella:

> We shouldn't underestimate the importance of UNASUR to the progressive cycle. It was formed at the Mar del Plata Summit [Fourth Summit of the Americas in Mar del Plata, Argentina, 2005], where Latin America rejected the Free Trade Agreement of the Americas (FTAA). The Summit was characterized by the strong links between anti-neoliberal social movements from Paraguay, Brazil, Argentina, Uruguay, and Bolivia – which had been preparing for the rejection of the FTAA – and their political leaders.
>
> It also provided the opportunity to develop the Initiative for the Integration of the Regional Infrastructure of South America (IIRSA), later renamed the South American Infrastructure and Planning Council (COSIPLAN). This involved big infrastructure projects, such as

waterways, ports, and mega-dams, linked to the process of extraction, to transport raw materials to the ports for export.

Raúl adds:

> UNASUR was an initiative of Brazil's, the aim being that it should serve as a counterweight to the Organization of American States (OAS). It was based on the idea that Mexico is tied to the US, Central America is another region completely, and Brazil is the engine of South America. It has played a positive role: it contributed to the resolution of the crisis in Bolivia when some parts of the country, namely Santa Cruz, were voicing separatist ambitions, which was a major headache for Evo Morales' government. UNASUR intervened and managed to re-establish the government's authority over the country.
>
> Under the Lula administration, Brazil positioned itself very clearly as a regional leader, and this was largely accepted. The other countries were more or less happy to follow Brazil's lead. There was a change with Dilma [Rousseff; Lula's successor], who turned her back on foreign policy a little as she was more concerned with internal issues, and Brazil's presence in the region diminished noticeably. This roughly coincided with the death of Hugo Chávez, and in the period since there has been a lack of leadership by any particular country or political figure in Latin America.

The pink tide period also saw a proliferation of social movements across Latin America. In some cases, these social movements had a direct relationship with political power. Lula's and Dilma's Workers' Party (PT) in Brazil was originally a coalition of artists, intellectuals, journalists, and especially trade unionists, which came together in the late 1970s and early 1980s as Brazil's long military dictatorship began to loosen its grip on power. Similarly, in Bolivia, Evo Morales was a leader of the *cocaleros*, the coca leaf growers' movement, which defends indigenous and campesino coca farmers against the criminalization of the crop. In other cases, while the relationship with power has been less direct, the pink tide governments did allow for some dialogue with social movements and were receptive to their demands, to a certain extent. As Raúl comments:

> Social movements for health and education, environmentalist movements, as well as landless workers' movements and agrarian reform groups in other parts of the continent, are extraordinarily important and have been able to achieve significant social change. In Chile I'd say the strongest and most innovative groups in society have been social movements, and they're the ones bringing about big change. Perhaps the most important landmark here is the year 2011, when we saw the emergence of massive student movements. This really changed the country, it was a decisive step in which we saw the emergence of a post-dictatorship generation of young people with no fear, who took to the streets en

masse demanding change and concessions. We have seen movements of this kind in various places and they have achieved very important, clearly defined objectives, such as stopping certain projects. In Bolivia, it was the social movements, not any political movement, that propelled Evo Morales to the presidency, especially the demonstrations against the privatization of the water supply, which had generated a great feeling of indignation and had mobilized many people across Bolivia.

While the pink tide governments were widely criticized for abandoning their bases and making alliances with precisely the sort of forces they were elected to oppose, such as transnational companies and local oligarchies, their links to social movements and the cultural shift they have brought about has undoubtedly broadened the scope of historically limited Latin American democracies.

The ebbing of the tide

With the narrow election victory of Mauricio Macri in Argentina, 2015 marked the year that the pink tide finally began to roll back. The following year Dilma Rousseff was impeached in Brazil for alleged budgetary irregularities and was replaced by her vice president, Michel Temer, of the Brazilian Democratic Movement (MDB – formerly PMDB), a 'big tent' party with links to local interest groups including militias, evangelicals, and the old *coronéis* – powerful rural oligarchs – of the Brazilian interior. In Chile, the right-wing billionaire Sebastian Piñera won his second presidential election in 2017. Most dramatically, the once-untouchable Lula was convicted of corruption and money laundering and given a nine-and-a-half-year prison sentence in July 2017. By April 2018 he had exhausted his appeals process and was finally sent to prison, where he remains at time of writing. He was therefore unable to run for president in October 2018, despite comfortably leading the polls.

One feature of the right's return to power has been the use of extraordinary parliamentary or judicial mechanisms to depose democratically elected governments. As Maristella comments:

> The first was the removal of Manuel Zelaya in Honduras in 2009, then Fernando Lugo in Paraguay in 2012, and the most scandalous, the impeachment of Dilma Rousseff in 2016. So while conspiracy theories tend always to blame the Evil Empire [the United States], it's true that there were parliamentary coups, which showed the resurgence of conservative sectors in the region in a climate of polarization. The impeachment of Dilma was followed by the conviction of Lula, which we can also agree was very suspicious, to say the least. The speed with which the Brazilian courts managed to convict Lula, despite a lack of evidence, was very suspicious.
>
> So yes, I believe that we are seeing a tendency of deploying coups d'état. However, they are not openly military coups, involving troops on

the streets. They are carried out in a more 'institutional' way, and this is very worrying. I think that we need to consider them carefully, without falling into the same old pattern of conspiracy theories. We need to consider them in their complexity. How is it possible that the tools of the democratic system can be used to bring about a parliamentary coup d'état? This is an important question.

What are the characteristics of the new right-wing governments? Maristella continues:

There is more extractivism and more abuse of human rights, while on the social level, governments like those in Argentina and Brazil are implementing blatantly regressive policies which reduce social rights. In terms of democracy, this is very worrying.

In Argentina, we have clearly seen a policy of encouraging foreign investment, alongside heavy borrowing. It's worth noting that the Kirchner administrations also sought credit but couldn't secure any because of their problems with the vulture funds [international finance companies which bought up Argentina's external debt as a speculation and then used the courts to embargo new loans and impede trade until the debt was paid]. It wasn't that they didn't want to borrow, they couldn't. However, Macri is introducing a new cycle of borrowing, of which neoliberal governments have a long history. It opens the country up to foreign capital, which never materializes, seeking above all to develop a short-term policy of speculation. Nobody wants to invest in Argentina!

And there are other classic neoliberal policies such as reduction of labour costs. In Brazil, this is happening thanks to a labour reform that is dragging the country back to the stone age. In Argentina, such a reform wasn't possible, but a series of measures have been introduced that clearly aim to reduce the cost of labour, blaming the workers for Argentina's economic problems while maximizing the profits of large corporations. It's very clear whose side the government is on. The government is trying to encourage the investment of big capital at all costs, especially by lowering salaries and reducing the cost of labour.

What's worrying about the situation in Argentina today is the presence of CEOs and directors of big companies in government. When you consider that what used to be called the Ministry of Agriculture is now called the Ministry of Agribusiness, and that the minister is the former president of the Sociedad Rural Argentina [the association representing Argentina's big landowners], it's very shocking. The Argentine Workers' Left Front (FIT) says the country is being governed by those who own it. [Juan José] Aranguren, the minister for energy, used to manage Shell in Argentina. Every one of the government ministers and officials has a clear relationship with big business. This never used to be the case in Argentina; or at least, not so blatantly. In the early days of Carlos

Menem's presidency it was attempted, and it didn't work. They had to resort to mediation.

Politics is subordinated to the economy, in the neoliberal sense of the word, without any concern as to whether the whole of society is included. Those excluded from the economy are expendable. This limited understanding of the economy is fundamental.

How did this happen? For Raúl Sohr:

Latin America's history is cyclical. It has had cycles of dictatorships and military regimes, followed by transitions to democracy. In this wave of transition to democracy, which, in general, started for most countries on the continent during the 1980s, there has been a big proliferation of social movements, which also coincided, especially from around 2000, with a huge rise in the price of commodities. The export revenues of most countries in Latin America depend on a single product. Venezuela gets more than 90 per cent of its export revenue from oil, and in Chile more than 50 per cent comes from mining, especially copper mining, and these countries are therefore heavily dependent on the prices of these products.

[Over-reliance on a single commodity] happened especially in the case of Venezuela, which had a huge sphere of influence, in part thanks to exceptionally high oil prices – let's not forget that the price of oil got as high as US$140 per barrel. It's now [in late 2016] around $40–50 per barrel, which is a really brutal collapse in value. The prices of different commodities have behaved differently in the market, but Venezuela is particularly emblematic of this commodities boom because it was, perhaps, the country most reliant on a single commodity – oil. When the oil price collapsed, so did the political support for the government and Venezuela's influence on the rest of the region, because *chavismo* really was very influential.

To a certain extent, the pink tide governments were also victims of their own success, as Raúl explains:

The fall in commodity prices meant that the Bolivarian and progressive governments' ability to satisfy people's demands was limited. On top of this, a parallel phenomenon occurred, whereby a lot of these governments started to become victims of their own success, in the sense that when you raise people's living standards their expectations start to rise too. This is manifest in education, for example, where suddenly there is a much stronger demand for the improvement of the education system and a lot of people no longer accept such a basic state education. They want better possibilities from a professional perspective too, and this has led to the emergence of large student movements across most Latin American countries, demanding better education, better pensions, better healthcare; and this pressure generates an expectation of change.

René Orellana is a Bolivian politician and academic. He has served in several ministries in the Morales administration and was Bolivia's special ambassador to the UN on the environment and development. At the time of interview, he was minister for development planning. He echoes Raúl's idea:

> In Bolivia, for example, the middle class has grown by at least two million people in the last 11 years. This is evidence of a country that is changing, and it also means the emergence of a generation of young people who haven't grown up with the problems caused by neoliberal economic policies in our country and haven't witnessed the damage they can do. Therefore, they have new expectations. These expectations are embodied in the new social movements that are emerging, and we must be in dialogue with these movements in order to strengthen our democracy.

Raúl continues:

> The most interesting example for me is Brazil, with Bolsa Família [the PT's flagship conditional cash transfer social programme], which has been an extremely successful programme in many ways. Though it remains very important in the north-east of the country, elsewhere people have other demands which are no longer necessarily the basic demands of poverty alleviation as addressed by Bolsa Família, but rather the expectations of an emerging middle class that is looking for another kind of social inclusion. When this sort of thing occurs, as in the case of Brazil or Argentina, the right comes up with a proposal for change based on more individualistic values, with a closer link to consumerism, and this sort of platform has met with approval.
>
> Of course, you have to take into account the unique circumstances of each situation. With Brazil, as with Argentina, there has been the whole issue of corruption, and therefore you get calls for the change of governments which, while they were successful in the fundamentals with regard to social issues, weren't so successful in managing the political situation. So, what happens is that you reach a point of saturation, and this is normal: power gets worn out.

As Raúl says, corruption has been a major factor. In Argentina, former president Cristina Fernández de Kirchner faces charges of corruption and money laundering. In Chile – traditionally considered one of the most transparent countries in the region – Michelle Bachelet's reputation took a major hit thanks to a series of corruption allegations which touched not only her political allies but also members of her family. In Brazil, the PT governments became caught up first in the *Mensalão* – a vote-buying scandal that did serious damage to the first Lula administration in 2005 – and later in Operation Car Wash, the investigation into a massive system of corruption at the oil company Petrobras, in which the Brazilian State has a controlling share. For Maristella Svampa:

> We mustn't forget that, aside from the institutional corruption entrenched in contemporary politics, political candidates need billions of dollars to run their political campaigns. We need financing laws for

political campaigns, to democratize the political playing field. But this is a long way off. We must keep in mind that the commodities boom produced strong economic growth of extraordinary profitability, the likes of which had never been seen in Latin America. There had never been so much money sloshing around, it was unprecedented. The temptation to just continue milking this cash cow, rather than diversifying economies or taking on major economic interests, was intense. No Latin American country managed to carry out fiscal reforms that would have had an impact on the most powerful sectors, nor did they even really try. But the response of the powerful has been to take back control.

Now, at the end of the cycle, they blame 'populist' governments for shared acts of corruption. In Argentina it is proven that Macri's relatives benefited from public works during the Kircher administrations. They were involved in the Odebrecht [Car Wash] case in Brazil. Evidence of their complicity is everywhere. However, the involvement of the so-called progressive governments in corruption has been a tough blow for all those on the left. The right being corrupt is nothing new, but the left being systematically involved in corruption and this kind of corporate cronyism was very damaging for progressive politics in Latin America. Why? Because now, it's very easy for the right to reduce the progressive governments to a context of corruption, downplaying their achievements and their tendencies towards more democracy and greater integration.

I have been critical of the progressive governments, of course, but we can't look at the problem from just one perspective ... We can't reduce it to pure democratization or pure corruption ... All Latin American governments, whether progressive, conservative, or neoliberal, have been systematically involved in corruption, a problem which has been aggravated by the economic boom and the huge profitability that came about from the high value of raw materials.

Prospects for further integration

The Car Wash investigations have affected not only Brazil, but several other countries in the region, most notably Peru, where Pedro Pablo Kuczynski was forced to resign as president in 2018 over his links to the Brazilian construction firm Odebrecht, one of the major players in the scandal. Kuczynski is not alone: the scandal has engulfed the Peruvian political elite, including former presidents Ollanta Humala, Alejandro Toledo, and Alan García, as well as 2016 presidential candidate Keiko Fujimori. At the regional level, Car Wash casts a shadow over the whole integration agenda of the pink tide era, which now appears inextricably linked with corruption. For Maristella, this is one factor behind the decline of UNASUR:

UNASUR turned into something very different. It became a space for the various leaders of progressive governments to assert their leadership and develop a rhetoric based on personal charisma. Effectively, it became a soapbox for the leaders of the progressive governments, to the detriment of the social organizations. This is very important. UNASUR was the stage for a concentration of leadership.

Brazil had a very important role with its National Development Bank (BNDES), and this was the context for the whole Odebrecht scandal. I think that the progressive cycle can be understood through UNASUR and what it became, the process of leadership concentration, extractive projects, and corruption. I'm not suggesting we should celebrate the end of the progressive cycle, not under any circumstances, but in UNASUR we can see the problems that were at the heart of it. UNASUR is practically defunct nowadays.

Indeed, in April 2018, half of UNASUR's membership – Argentina, Brazil, Chile, Colombia, Paraguay, and Peru – announced that they were suspending their participation in the organization for a year. Its future now appears uncertain at best.

What are the prospects for regional integration now, post–pink tide? For Raúl Sohr:

We are in a sort of interregnum – it is unclear who is going to come forward and lead the continent. Macri shows little interest or ambition to do so. Smaller countries like Chile don't have the size, capability or political will. Neither is there currently on offer any particularly attractive political-ideological project to follow. Macri is concerned more with administrative proposals than grand ideas. Temer even less so – he's just an accident of history who is trying to survive the tail end of a mandate he snatched off someone else by foul means. He's an embarrassment; he can't appear in public without being booed and is incapable even of governing his own country. In the sense of being the driving force, or the country offering a vision for the continent, Brazil has completely disappeared. And don't even get me started on Enrique Peña Nieto. With all the damage he's done, the mistakes he's made, the highly precarious economic situation, and a downright disgraceful domestic situation – Mexico is a source of shame. It can't possibly aspire to be any sort of role model [However, on July 1 2018 Andrés Manuel López Obrador (AMLO) won an outright majority in the presidential elections on a progressive platform].

Despite recent political developments, René Orellana argues that integration remains a priority – not only between Latin American countries, but between Latin America and other emerging economies, in what is becoming an increasingly multipolar world:

We're going through a new cycle, one where the new administration in the US is turning its back on Latin America and the Caribbean by building both physical and political walls between the two regions, and this is going to create a new international context. From what I can see, this could mean the start of a potential process of integration between Latin

America and the Caribbean. This is where we have to see whether a new regional leadership emerges that is intelligent and progressive in terms of formulating a forward-looking agenda, capable of creating this new centre of regional gravity, and recovering our project for regional integration. As well as the political will, this will require economic and commercial efforts towards productive and technological integration, as part of a progressive approach in a world where climate change is a reality and where technology plays an increasingly crucial role in processes of production and communication. This must have the capacity to interest and engage the Caribbean, Central America, and South America. But I observe similar processes in other developing countries.

You also have the growing relationship between China and Latin America and the Caribbean. In this new international context that I mentioned, the US is not only building walls between itself and Latin America, but also between itself and China, and a consequence of this is that the relationship between China and Latin America is going to grow stronger. Nowadays, China doesn't just have commercial ties with Latin America and the Caribbean, but political ties too, which are becoming increasingly well established.

This relationship with China is of fundamental importance. As Raúl adds:

China is Latin America's main economic and commercial partner. For example, most of Chile's copper is bought by China and the price of copper, as a raw material, is determined by Chinese demand. China is a crucial partner for the region. It is behind several mind-bogglingly large-scale projects, though it's hard to know whether they'll ever be completed. What's certain is that the Chinese are making a lot of noise, and important noise at that. For example, they are involved in a project to build a new interoceanic canal in Nicaragua. This has already been approved, the studies have been done, but it's still not certain that it'll go ahead. There is another project involving the construction of a rail link between Brazil and Peru – another enormous mega-project. If this project goes ahead, the Chinese will be at the heart of the development and exploitation of huge swathes of Latin America. China is investing more and more here. In Mexico, and particularly in Peru, we have seen the arrival of Chinese mining companies, and these companies are especially interested in projects relating to infrastructure – road and rail networks.

Extractivism and climate change

However, for Maristella, the expansion of the extractivist model, fuelled by new capital from China and elsewhere, is highly problematic:

Chinese capital has invested heavily in extractive industries in Latin America – in oil and mining. They also own Syngenta, the seed company, as well as railway infrastructure, dams, and renewable energy projects. This is all part of a big package that clearly demonstrates the role of China in Latin America and this process of hegemonic transition.

If we look at the way things are going with regard to economic policies and development models, we obviously see the continuation, aggravation, and exacerbation of the extractivist model throughout Latin America. The end of the commodities boom implies an exacerbation of the extractivist model because, as profits are lower, projects are multiplied to cover the trade deficit. This issue is fundamental. You might think that the crisis, or the fall in commodity prices, would create the possibility for thinking about other models, but this isn't the case. On the contrary, we've seen an exacerbation of extractivism apparent in the advance of the frontiers of exploration. This includes, for example, extreme energy sources such as fracking; offshore and pre-salt oil exploration, which has been tested in Colombia; and tar sands – which are the most polluting energy source – in the Orinoco Belt, like those in Alberta, Canada.

In light of the socioecological crisis, Latin American governments need to rethink their entire energy policies. Instead, they are starting to include some renewable energy, just to be politically correct, while simultaneously consolidating the use of extreme energies. The latter, in terms of their social and economic impact and the higher risk of accidents and contamination, are much worse than conventional energies.

A related point is the relaxation of environmental regulations, incursions into protected areas, and attempts to revoke laws which were passed to protect the environment: forests, glaciers, and so on. This is happening with the government of Evo Morales, which is advancing the hydrocarbon frontier into protected areas, in spite of protests by indigenous groups. It is also happening violently in Argentina, where the government is encroaching on Mapuche territories, which have earning potential for fracking and large-scale mining projects, as well as tourist and residential developments. This exacerbation of the extractivist model is very worrying.

Indeed, while many of the pink tide governments introduced new environmental regulations, adopted a rhetoric of reverence for Pachamama (Mother Earth), and, in the cases of Bolivia and Ecuador, even wrote the rights of nature into their national constitutions, the expansion of extractivism has resulted in further environmental degradation and grave human rights violations. Marcos Orellana, a Chilean, is director of the Environment and Human Rights Division at Human Rights Watch:

Back in 1992, the Earth Summit, which was at the time the biggest gathering in human history concerned with the environment, promulgated what was known as Principle 10, [which promotes public participation in environmental decision-making] and the concept of sustainable development. This has been manipulated since and used to justify all

Marcos Orellana

kinds of rhetoric and propositions. But at its origin, its heart, was the notion that decisions would be taken with the informed participation of those who were affected. It effects a fundamental devolution of authority back to the local level. It abandons the mentality of bureaucratic decision-making by technocrats in a nation's capital, conceiving of sustainable development as a process of dialogue where those who are affected at the local level participate meaningfully. And yet the distance between the promise and the reality that we see in the region is so grave, we are witnessing a trend of proliferating environmental conflict. This is resulting in environmental defenders being harassed, attacked, and murdered.

In this context, the proposal to integrate the rights of nature into [national] constitutions, as Ecuador and Bolivia have done, is quite welcome. It signifies a paradigm shift, where we abandon a purely anthropocentric approach, recognizing nature in its own right, and yet this can't be seen as a panacea. It doesn't act in isolation to safeguard the right to a healthy environment for present and future generations. That's because rights of nature can only be effective if accompanied by a vibrant civil society that defends them and what we're seeing in Bolivia is a total crackdown on environmental NGOs. When the government persecutes environmental activists, the rights of nature provision in the constitution are basically a dead letter. Similar situation in Ecuador, which has criminalized indigenous leaders for defending their lands and their territories. So there is a divergence of positions: on the one hand, recognition of the rights of nature, but on the other, harassment and persecution of those who make these rights a reality. For the region to have real hope, the work of environmental defenders needs to be embraced and its importance recognized. There must also be respect for basic rights, such as freedom of expression and assembly. These are the basic democratic pillars of social dialogue, which are at the heart of the promise of sustainable development.

And Maristella adds:

Global Witness revealed in a recent report that Latin America is the most dangerous place in the world for environmental activists. And this doesn't even take into account all the murders resulting from socioen-vironmental conflicts. Activists are killed by *sicarios* or in 'traffic accidents', but the murders get covered up, when the killing was clearly intentional. We're at breaking point today in Latin America. We've entered a new cycle of human rights violations. Finally, Latin America is also the region with the highest concentration of land ownership in the Americas. This tendency is a problem all over the world, but in Latin America land conflicts, related to extractive projects, are more extreme. In these cases, the winners are those with the most capital, such as agri-business, while indigenous and campesino communities lose out.

It's a very complex panorama that clearly shows the withdrawal of the frontier of democracy. At the beginning of the progressive cycle, we saw this frontier expand in terms of social, collective, and individual rights. Now, at the end of the cycle, we can clearly see the intrinsic relationship between more extractivism on the one hand, and weaker democracy on the other. We can see this now under the conservative governments.

In a context of climate change, this is all of enormous concern. The reality of climate change is already apparent in Latin America, as René Orellana comments:

Bolivia is already suffering from serious impacts of global warming – the drought we're currently experiencing is the worst we've had in 22 years. Over the last 11 years we've made key investments in our water supply and water system of over $2.8 billion, especially in rural areas. This focus on rural areas has been important, as it has meant that food production has remained largely unaffected by the drought ... This is a big achievement, but if we don't continue to invest in our water sources then we're going to have major issues, and you can see this in what is currently happening – this [2016] is the third consecutive year of record temperatures worldwide, and it is affecting us here in Bolivia. If global warming continues at its current rate, our glaciers are going to disappear, which is why we need to make predictions about the levels of water catchment, water accumulation, and harvesting, especially in urban areas, and push forward with policies that seek to increase agricultural production in rural areas.

And for Eliane Brum, criticizing the PT governments in Brazil:

> It became clear that the country's development project was a 20th-century one; in some ways, even 19th-century. The urgent issue of climate change was ignored, partly because neither Lula nor Dilma Rousseff understood it, along with a large part of the left. Nowadays, no leftist project can be taken seriously if it doesn't take into account the exacerbating impact of climate change on inequality. It is the poorest who suffer and will suffer first with the destruction of the planet. The serious drought in São Paulo beginning in 2014 [when the city almost ran out of drinking water and draconian rationing was imposed, mainly on poorer, peripheral communities] showed this very clearly. But even then it wasn't fully understood.

For Marcos, climate change obliges Latin American countries to rethink their attitudes towards the environment found within their borders; in particular, towards the forests and the people who live in them:

> One solution to this problem is the recognition of indigenous people's rights over their lands and territories, because protecting indigenous people's rights to their forests doesn't only further their human rights, culture, livelihoods, and their right to life and self-determination; it's also a way to contain the increasing emissions of carbon dioxide and other greenhouse gases into the atmosphere. While scientific evidence of this has been established through the work of international agencies, deforestation in the region remains rampant. Something needs to happen to reduce deforestation to zero. That's both a political and an economic commitment.
>
> When administrations in the region are in political crisis, environmental laws suffer from very lax enforcement. The institutions for the protection of indigenous peoples are underfunded and weakened. Areas that have been created for the protection of biodiversity and indigenous peoples are often a reality only on paper. It's also sometimes the case that areas are protected for their aesthetic or environmental beauty while excluding the people who were relying on the resources in these areas. Finding common ground between human rights and the environment requires that conservation is done on the basis of community engagement, where access to cultural resources and sacred lands isn't curtailed by the creation of protected areas.
>
> I think an example could be useful. In the state of Maranhão in Brazil, we have seen reports of indigenous leaders being murdered by illegal loggers. Indigenous communities have been organizing to defend their last patches of rainforest in the state. These are traditional territories.

They have organized monitoring patrols and have been targeted by illegal loggers as a result. The government has completely failed to investigate these cases adequately. When this impunity penetrates the fabric of society, then environmental rule of law begins to weaken. With such weak governance, the environment and human rights suffer, deforestation goes on, and climate change continues unabated.

The future of social movements

What role will there be for social movements in this new scenario? For René:

> I believe Latin America's social movements possess great strength, and this strength persists despite the difficult context of a political offensive which seeks to revive and rebuild neoliberal economic models across the continent. This political-ideological spirit can clearly be seen in the workers' movements in Brazil and Argentina and, of course, in the indigenous, trade union, and campesino movements in Bolivia, Ecuador, and other countries. History has taught us that there are cycles in which innovative, creative social movements and important leaders emerge with projects which aim to influence and shape society. The conditions for a return to neoliberalism are ever present, and here in Latin America we've lived through long, repetitive cycles of nationalization and privatization. Nevertheless, what has been present throughout, in the very essence of the continent's social movements and state-building projects, is a transformative, revolutionary current which is emboldened when major social achievements are destroyed by neoliberal economic processes. In such conditions, social movements are strengthened and come to the forefront, and this is what will happen if governments that are currently carrying out 'legal' political coups in the region persist in their desire to reintroduce orthodox neoliberal policies.

This reaction may already be under way. For Maristella:

> [The social movements] are stronger in small- and medium-sized cities, especially in marginalized areas. These range from large organizations to small collectives, including indigenous organizations, and are using a new language about territory. This characterizes the current tendency of different social movements to defend land, territory, biodiversity, and the environment. They are developing a different language for the relationship between society and the environment, which aims to preserve life cycles. This is part of the new emancipatory language in Latin America that I believe also has an important place in the new political grammar of anti-globalization movements all over the world. Autonomy, environmental rights, *buen vivir* [see Chapter 5], and the ethics of care are all issues which recur in language globally, not just in Latin America.

They have a basis both in theory and practice. There are alternative economies and other fields of experience which highlight, for example, the increasing importance of agroecology as an alternative model for development. Under the agroecological model, territory is valued differently, based on use value and respect for common assets rather than exchange value, thus marking a shift towards decommodification. There are many examples of campesino and social economies, based on tradition and agroecology, which are the basis for these other models. How successful will they be? We don't know. We know that they exist. We know that they face increasingly extreme hostility and brutal repression.

But socioecological crises are going to become more and more significant, in my opinion. It's a very paradoxical situation. On the one hand, regardless of the introduction of renewable energy policies, there is a move in Latin America towards the consolidation of an energy framework based on fossil fuels, and a series of extractive policies that benefit the business sectors and the big corporations. On the other hand, there are a multitude of social, ecological, and territorial struggles in Latin America that aren't going to go away, in spite of repression. They are going to keep moving forward.

For René, young people, aided by technology, will be at the centre of this process:

If there's something that characterizes these new movements emerging across the region, it's that for the most part they are youth movements in which long-standing issues such as access to land and natural resources are still important, but there are also new expectations and demands, which tend to be linked to issues such as education, technology, and employment opportunities, as well as entrepreneurship and the possibility of carving out new sectors of the economy such as microenterprise. This reflects a young population that is increasingly well informed about the international debates going on from their perspective. The role of more participatory media platforms such as social media is also important in this, as young people are more able to express their opinions and incite change, and this can clearly be seen not just in the urban youth movements in the big cities, but also in neighbourhood movements in towns that lack services and suffer from limited access to education. This is something that we are seeing not just here in Bolivia but across many developing countries.

New agendas are emerging: indigenous farmers' movements are searching for increased participation in the market and better prices for their goods, as well as improved access to education, technology, and credit. These are the new demands, and if the state, in its mission for society, doesn't think about the distribution of wealth, strive for the construction of a fairer society, or consider the democratization of production and access to credit, technology, and innovation, then people simply won't listen. We're no longer talking about the old way of thinking about society and the economy, in which small groups of business interests had control of the production processes. Now, young people, associations, and cooperatives from different social groups are seeking increasingly to participate actively and play a leading role in the production processes of the economy and society. This is our new reality.

For Maristella, there are four thematically and geographically disparate types of social movement in Latin America at present:

The first is the eco-territorial struggles, which are increasingly visible, but don't appear on the public agenda, even though they are at the centre of this model of accumulation: indigenous people, campesinos, assemblies of various kinds, anti-extractivist movements in general.

The second type of struggle is the union movements. They are very heterogeneous and are experiencing a retraction of their rights, but they often don't have a narrative for change. They challenge neoliberalism, but they aren't anti-capitalist, as the anti-extractivist movements can be. These are the movements that are most visible on the public agenda and they occupy large spaces in the city because they represent a huge number of people.

The third type of struggle is the socio-territorial urban movements, which aren't linked to formal workers' associations but to neighbourhoods, with the strong presence of the popular classes. In Argentina, the *piqueteros* [the unemployed workers' movement] and their successors, who are once again present in the public sphere, are subject to unemployment and informal labour, as well as gang violence in their neighbourhoods. This is a huge problem in Latin America. The struggle is totally asymmetric. They are fighting against conservative governments on the one hand, and narcotraffickers on the other. They were represented by the progressive governments and were very involved in the progressive cycle. Today, in countries like Argentina and Brazil, they are on the streets. In Brazil, they are the Landless Workers' Movement (MST) and the Homeless Workers' Movement (MTST). In Argentina they are the Confederation of Workers of the Popular Economy (CTEP), the Movimiento Evita, Class Combat Current (CCC), and Free of the South. They have a narrative of change and they are involved in some big struggles, but they are completely disconnected from the extractivist problem.

Lastly, the fourth type of struggle is the women's movement, which has been increasingly important in Latin America on various fronts. The fight against extractivism, the identification between the female body and territory, and the defence of the environment has led to ecofeminism and other popular feminisms in Latin America. These movements are both original and powerful, criticizing not only extractivism but also the patriarchy. There is also the fight against femicide, above all in the urban environment, which has generated a new anti-patriarchal narrative that is very strong among young women.

The environmental, popular, anti-neoliberal, and anti-patriarchal narratives should all, at some point, come together. Above all, we must rethink the big problems of the progressive cycle that have had such a strong impact on the crisis of the left. In Latin America there are multiple lefts, and the progressive cycle demonstrated the hegemony of one kind of narrative: the populist, or national-popular, at the expense of the indigenist and environmental narratives. Nowadays, we can't think about the future of the left in Latin America without articulating the environmental narrative, together, of course, with the indigenist and anti-patriarchal narratives. The Latin American left will either be environmentalist and anti-patriarchal, or it won't exist at all.

There are some signs that these types of alliance are beginning to form, as Eliane Brum says in the case of Brazil:

> Marielle Franco, the city councillor from Maré [a favela complex in Rio de Janeiro] who was murdered on 14 March 2018 [see box in Chapter 8], has far more in common with a *ribeirinho* [traditional riverside dweller] like Chico Caititu, from Montanha e Mangabal on the Tapajós river, whose life is in danger, than either of them do with anyone from the Zona Sul of Rio de Janeiro or the Zona Oeste of São Paulo [affluent and fashionable areas].
>
> This dialogue between geographically distant peripheries is emerging. It's still very slow, but it is happening. The emergence of Guilherme Boulos – who represents the homeless of São Paulo, one of Brazil's most dynamic social movements – as a pre-candidate for president, with Sonia Guajajara, one of the country's main indigenous leaders, as his running mate, indicates that this idea has been put into motion in various ways. The pre-candidacy was launched by the left-wing Socialism and Liberty Party (PSOL), but both Guilherme and Sónia find their identity in their own movements and can extend them by means of this alliance.
>
> This is the context in which the path to rebooting the Brazilian left may lie. A left capable of providing answers at this moment in history, in which climate change is such a challenge, not least because of its impact on inequality. With these new alliances we can think about the world not only with new ideas, but via new thought processes, borne out of different experiences of living and being on this planet, such as those of the different peoples of the Amazon rainforest.
>
> The experience of the Workers' Party (PT) in power, especially during Dilma Rousseff's government, failed to recognize this wealth of cultural diversity, by prioritizing a model of development which invaded the Amazon in order to produce commodities. Faced with a vision of the country which saw the forest as merely a body for exploitation and extraction, the forest as merchandise, unprecedented alliances have begun to form out of survival instincts. Indigenous people and *ribeirinhos*, who had previously been strangers to each other, began to realize

they had things in common: in the middle Xingu, in the fight against the Belo Monte hydroelectric dam complex; and in the Tapajós, to stop the construction of dams such as São Luiz and Jatobá.

These alliances seek to survive a model of development which is common to both the right and the left, blurring the political lines.

It isn't just survival which mobilizes these populations, but living life on their own terms – on other terms.

* * *

This is where Latin America stands today. Although there is much cause for concern, there are also some grounds for cautious optimism. For Raúl Sohr:

This is what has happened, and yes, we are at the end of the pink tide. However, this doesn't necessarily mean a return to the kind of neoliberalism that we experienced before. I don't think Macri is a neoliberal in the classical sense, in the same way that Sebastián Piñera wasn't in Chile – they are right-wing governments, but really, in Latin America, pure neoliberalism is an economic project that you can only impose via a dictatorship.

And, referring to the process of globalization as it has unfolded in Latin America:

If the philosophy is that everyone competes at the same level, what will clearly happen is that the strong get even stronger and the weak even weaker. And this is exactly what has happened. A polarization of society has taken place and we are left with colossal levels of inequality within countries, not only between countries. In fact, globalization has worked better between countries, as a lot of countries like China and India have improved their standing in the world; but the internal situation within these countries, in terms of social equity, has deteriorated. The outcome is a situation like the one you have today in the US, where the richest 20 per cent of the population own 84 per cent of the national wealth, and the poorest 20 per cent of the population own 0.1 per cent. This kind of inequality is intolerable, socially speaking, and that's expressed politically.

The same thing is happening in Latin America. It isn't that the poor are getting poorer, in fact the poor are becoming less and less poor, but the rich in society have become immensely richer. The process of accumulation of wealth and inequality in Chile, for example, is completely brutal. Poverty has been falling in Chile. There are fewer poor people than before. But jobs are insecure, wages are low, and quality of life is the absolute bare minimum when compared to economic groups and families that are among the very richest in the world. In a country like Chile! In the long run, this just isn't viable.

Indeed, there does not appear to be a decisive or widespread appetite for a return to conservative and neoliberal programmes of government across the region, reflected in the fact that the right has in some cases had to resort to underhand and unconstitutional tactics in order to take power. Neoliberal models brought in by dictatorships, which were maintained – and in some cases, expanded – following the return to democracy, are no less discredited than they were at the turn of the century. Meanwhile, more or less progressive governments have survived in Ecuador, Uruguay, and Bolivia, while the centre-left Carlos Alvarado won a convincing victory in the Costa Rican presidential election in April 2018. Most significantly of all, Andrés Manuel López Obrador won a landslide victory in the Mexican presidential elections in July 2018 and will become the first leftist president of Latin America's second-largest economy in modern history.

And while Latin America's social movements may face tougher conditions in the current climate, they are better organized, informed, and connected than ever before. They have greater regional and global awareness than in the past, with far more ability to transcend their immediate circumstances – aided, of course, by advances in communications technology, particularly social media and WhatsApp. One recent example is the feminist movement Ni Una Menos. It emerged in Argentina in 2015 in response to the brutal murders of two teenage girls but has since spread all over Latin America and even as far as Spain, uniting women and girls fed up not only with macho violence but also economic insecurity, scant or non-existent sex education, and restricted reproductive rights.

The genie is out of the bottle, and as Raúl says, without a return to the coordinated state terror of the military dictatorships, orthodox neoliberal policies will not go unchallenged. For René Orellana:

> Essentially, I think that if there is something that history has taught us, it's that the harshest and most ruthless forms of neoliberal capitalism create and strengthen their own adversaries. It's precisely the most severe crises caused by neoliberal policies, the crises most aggressive towards social rights, from which alternative models to build new societies have emerged and re-emerged. So we can expect the leaderships of social movements to strengthen and we can also expect to see new political and social leaders emerge. I think this is the way things are going to go.

And, as is made clear by many of the voices in this book, it is possible to effect change. LAB heard stories of success in the most desperate situations and against the most improbable odds. As Marcos Orellana says:

> Is there hope for the continent? Is there hope for the region? The question takes me back to when I was working with the indigenous community Mapuche-Pehuenche a few years ago, in southern Chile. They were threatened by a big dam in their territories that was going to flood their ancestral, sacred lands, disrupting their culture and their ability to conduct their semi-nomadic lifestyle. When I was up there with a woman leading the struggle, she used to get up very early every morning, saying,

'We have to get up early, or the devil is going to come and get us. And we cannot give up hope, we cannot give up hope.' That phrase stuck with me, because this woman, that community, were facing bulldozers coming into their lands, a hostile press, a whole bureaucratic government set on displacing them. It was a World Bank project, so the international financial architecture was there. From the outside, it looked like the whole world was impending upon them. And still she was saying, 'We cannot give up hope.'

About the author

Tom Gatehouse is a writer and translator who has lived in Argentina, Spain, and Brazil. He holds an MPhil in Latin American Studies from the University of Cambridge. He has written for LAB and Red Pepper and his translations have appeared in *Folha de S. Paulo*, Agência Pública, and *Tales and Trails Lisbon*, a recent collection of short stories and other writings. He lives in London.

Interviews

Eliane Brum (journalist, writer, and documentary film-maker): interviewed via email on 1 May 2018 by Sue Branford. Translated by Hugo Moss.

Marcos Orellana (Human Rights Watch): interviewed in Washington DC on 22 December 2017 by James Thackara. Transcribed by Tom Gatehouse.

René Orellana (politician and academic): interviewed in La Paz on 5 December 2016 by Tom Gatehouse. Translated by Matty Rose.

Raúl Sohr (journalist and sociologist): interviewed in Santiago de Chile on 22 November 2016 by Tom Gatehouse. Translated by Matty Rose.

Maristella Svampa (sociologist): interviewed in London on 25 April 2018 by Tom Gatehouse. Translated by Theo Bradford.

References

NB: All web references were checked and still available in May/June 2018 unless otherwise stated. All references are listed, with web-links, on the page for this chapter on the Voices website www.vola.org.uk

Encarnación, O. (2018) 'The rise and fall of the Latin American left', *The Nation*, 9 May, <https://www.thenation.com/article/the-ebb-and-flow-of-latin-americas-pink-tide>

Toro, F. (2017) 'As socialist Venezuela collapses, socialist Bolivia thrives', *Washington Post*, 5 January, <https://www.washingtonpost.com/news/global-opinions/wp/2017/01/05/as-socialist-venezuela-collapses-socialist-bolivia-thrives-heres-why/?noredirect=on&utm_term=.213385c7c228>

World Bank (2017) 'Higher education expanding in Latin America and the Caribbean, but falling short of potential', <http://www.worldbank.org/en/news/press-release/2017/05/17/higher-education-expanding-in-latin-america-and-the-caribbean-but-falling-short-of-potential>

CHAPTER 2

Fighting machismo: women on the front line

Louise Morris

Abstract

Women in Latin America have made significant advances in every social and institutional field, being at the forefront of fights for justice. Yet cultural values have not caught up. Ingrained sexism permeates almost every aspect of daily life, so that women in the region face extreme forms of oppression and inequality. This is manifest in some of the highest rates of femicide and sexual violence in the world, as well as draconian anti-abortion laws.

Women in Latin America have always been active in social struggles, but they are becoming more engaged and increasingly confident about asserting their rights, making significant advances in every social and institutional field. In the past quarter of a century, the proportion of women in the workforce has risen more in Latin America than in any other region in the world, and women now spend more years in school than men. In addition, Latin America currently has the second-highest level of female political representation in the world, surpassed only by Scandinavia. Women have been elected president in Argentina, Brazil, Chile, Costa Rica, Nicaragua, and Panama.

At the grassroots level, women across Latin America have been stepping to the forefront of social struggles, not only for women's rights, but also in the fight for land, the environment, and indigenous rights. Patricia Gualinga is an indigenous Kichwa activist from Sarayaku, Ecuador. She is part of the Women's Earth and Climate Action Network and a leading figure in the struggle against oil drilling in the Ecuadorian Amazon. She testified at the Inter-American Court of Human Rights in 2012, in the landmark Sarayaku vs Ecuador case. The court ruled in favour of Sarayaku, finding Ecuador liable for breaching international standards on free, prior, and informed consent when it granted concessions for oil drilling in Sarayaku territory. As she says of the indigenous movement:

> Women were always behind the men, supporting them, in some ways sustaining the system. But we were not at the forefront. It was much more difficult in the past … The men's voices, though still valid, have ceased to have credibility, have lost their power to defend our territory. Now it's the turn of women, ordinary women, with simple words, untainted by political discourse.

http://dx.doi.org/10.3362/9781909014213.002

It is notable that many of the female leaders gaining recognition are indigenous. Despite facing the double stigma of being female and indigenous, and often belonging to the poorest sectors of society, they are confronting some of the worst inequalities in the region. Alicia Cawiya is vice president of the Huaorani people of the Yasuní National Park in eastern Ecuador, and a steadfast opponent of oil drilling in their territory. 'Women have more of a long-term vision,' she says. 'The men are more willing to negotiate with the oil and mining companies, but the women are the mothers of the land. They can say no.'

Women have also played significant roles in fighting for justice post-conflict. During Guatemala's decades-long civil war (1960–96) – which pitched the government against various leftist rebel groups – the military, police, and intelligence services embarked on a brutal campaign of state terror against the civilian population, in which 200,000 people were killed or disappeared. The brave testimonies of Ixil Maya women were instrumental in securing the conviction of former dictator Efraín Ríos Montt for genocide and crimes against humanity in 2013. This was a historic moment, the first time a former head of state had been convicted of genocide by a court in their own country, though the judgement was later overturned and Ríos Montt died before a second trial could be completed. Similarly, Peruvian Andean women have exposed the brutal forced sterilization campaign of Alberto Fujimori's authoritarian presidency, though they are yet to be compensated.

Mothers often lead campaigns for justice for the disappeared and fight to preserve their memory; from the Chilean mothers combing the Atacama Desert for the bones of the victims of Pinochet's regime, to the Mothers of the Plaza de Mayo in Buenos Aires, who still stoically circle the Plaza every Thursday, nearly 35 years after the end of the dictatorship. This tradition continues today with organizations like the Mães de Maio and Mães de Manguinhos in Brazil, groups of mothers from favelas and the urban *periferia* fighting for justice for their sons and other family members killed by police. Likewise, in Mexico the Caravana de Madres takes Central American women around Mexico in search of their missing loved ones, most of whom were vulnerable migrants persecuted by police and criminal gangs (see Chapter 8).

Nonetheless, women continue to face some of the most extreme forms of oppression and inequality in the region. Entrenched sexism permeates almost every aspect of daily life, with women in general having less secure employment, worse pay, scant reproductive rights, and little or no access to family planning information, as well as facing frequent violence and harassment. Just under half the female population receives an income, and while overall poverty in Latin America has decreased, women's poverty has increased. A 2014 Gallup survey found that Latin Americans are the least likely people in the world to say that women in their countries are treated with dignity and respect, with Colombia and Peru being the worst offenders. Only 35 per cent of adults across 22 Latin American countries said women are treated respectfully, half that of any other global region.

In the world of politics, sexism also persists. There is a 'power pyramid' in which 'the greater the power, the lower women's presence' (Tello Rozas and Floru, 2017), while female politicians are frequently denigrated on the basis of their gender. The former Costa Rican president, Laura Chinchilla, endured sustained sexist attacks she says aimed to 'present her as a weak person' (Goudreau, 2011). Former Argentine president Cristina Kirchner was colloquially referred to as 'Botox Evita' and 'Bimbo', while her Chilean counterpart, Michelle Bachelet, was called *'La Gordis'* (the fat woman) not only on the street but even by her fellow politicians. During the impeachment of Dilma Rousseff in Brazil, many officials in the male-dominated Chamber of Deputies celebrated by holding up posters displaying the derogatory slogan 'Tchau, querida!' ('Bye, love!').

Clearly, there is still much work to do. Despite women's increasing participation in public life, cultural beliefs have not caught up. Conservative attitudes that consign women to the home, raising children and being submissive to their partners, remain widespread.

Cultural machismo

Nicaraguan writer and activist Gioconda Belli defines machismo as dividing women into two categories: 'sexual beings to be conquered and possessed, and mothers as authority figures that embody everything that is virtuous, gracious, and worthy of praise in female nature' (Belli, 2016). Yet machismo is not limited to men. Often it is other women who continue to enforce the belief in male superiority, from the insidious extreme of believing that women who are raped deserve it, to mothers saving the best food for boys. About 38 per cent of women in Ecuador say wife-beating is justified for at least one reason, while the percentage of women who agreed that a wife should obey her husband, even if she disagreed with him, ranged from just over 25 per cent in urban Paraguay in 2008 to nearly 75 per cent in rural Guatemala in 2008/9. Substantial proportions of women in these World Health Organization surveys did not agree that outsiders should intervene to help a woman who was being abused by her husband or that these issues should be discussed with anyone outside the family (WHO, 2012).

As Patricia Gualinga comments:

> For me, as a woman, the greatest challenge is ourselves. I know what the men are like. I know their weaknesses, their tendency to try and dominate. But women's reluctance to change is a structural problem. We find ourselves within a social and cultural structure that has been reproduced over many years. Many women don't understand this, and therefore it's difficult to change it.

Indeed, machismo is so socially ingrained and institutionally reinforced that even women's rights campaigners like the Argentine journalist Hinde Pomeraniec, who co-founded the Ni Una Menos (Not One Woman Less) campaign, has to remind herself not to ask her daughter to help with domestic chores before she asks her sons.

Eva Sánchez is the director of the Lenca women's rights organization Las Hormigas (The Ants), located in the town of Intibucá in western Honduras. This is the indigenous Lenca heart of the country, an area known for its fertility. Guns are omnipresent here, but not as visible as in the cities of Tegucigalpa or San Pedro Sula. It is one of the few places in the country where it is considered safe to walk the streets at night. The violence here is a hidden one. Intibucá has some of the highest levels of alcoholism in Honduras and corresponding levels of domestic violence. The office of Las Hormigas is a lilac-painted building, tucked away down a dusty lane, a bastion of security and solidarity for the women and families who visit. A common joke from locals when referring to the organization is 'Be careful they don't bite you!' But it is said with huge respect.

Eva has had to confront machismo in her personal life:

> My father rejected me, so I grew up with my mother and grandmother. I believe this made me see the injustices that there were for us women. I always said that I was going to get married at 25, because here what's normal is that after 21 you get married and have kids. I enjoyed my youth very much! I liked dancing a lot, so my grandmother – who was very radical in some ways – would always give us permission to go to

© Pierre Fromentin 2016

Eva Sánchez

parties, because they were safe and wholesome. When I was 25 I got pregnant and got married. My husband knew that I worked, and I said that I would never stop – I was very clear on this point – but he came from a traditional family, where the mother has to attend to the father the moment he arrives. If he arrived at 8 p.m. that would be the hour she served dinner; the tortillas would have to be piping hot and she would have to attend to him like a king.

I remember when I had my first daughter. He said to me, 'I'm not a woman!' I said to him, 'I'm not saying that you are; I'm telling you to be a father to your child because I'm busy!' It's been 22 years of managing, dialogue, thinking, and changing relationships. If you go out with a sexist it's very, very difficult at times, but little by little we have built things up. We have two adult daughters, the eldest is studying law and the youngest sociology. The youngest seems to want to do what I do, which sometimes scares me given the current situation. I also have a son who's seven and another girl who's five. They were born at the time of the campaign against femicides. When my son was born, he came with me to the meeting in Tegucigalpa so I could breastfeed, and he marched in the protests. My two older daughters used to say he was famous because he was all over the newspapers and on TV. When we came home, he was shouting the slogan 'El silencio mata!' ['Silence kills!'].

My husband has to look after the kids and cook when I'm not at home. Sometimes he too is scared about the work I do, because we don't know who I'm confronting when we speak out. [Because of impunity], we are asking for justice for murders and we don't know who the perpetrators are.

Sometimes they say that we are in the feminist fight because we are lesbians or frustrated women, but I believe that we're all independent – some of us are divorced, others are married. But the most important thing is that if we don't achieve changes at a personal level, we're not going to convince others. First, we have to fight at a personal level.

In school it's still taught that women have to stay at home whilst men are social. Men are the owners of cars and land, whilst women are owners of stoves and hormones. Games teach children that boys are strong and girls are weak. There is no form of education which promotes respect for human rights and educates boys and girls about shared responsibility and non-stereotypical gender roles.

We teach our children not to be violent but, for example, if they tell us they are being bullied and we go to the school or church and tell the teachers, often they tell us that we have to teach our children to defend themselves. There's no question of trying to teach them that there are differences you have to discuss until you reach an agreement. No, you have to get stronger, defend yourself, defeat the opponent! This is replicated in every social environment – at home, at school, and even at church, where they teach that the man is the head of the home and the woman has to be submissive to him.

Such cultural machismo has a number of harmful consequences, perhaps the most common of which is gender-based violence – one of the main problems that Eva and her colleagues at Las Hormigas have to confront.

Gender-based violence

Luis Almagro, chief of the 34-nation Organization of American States (OAS), said in November 2017 that 'progress on combating widespread gender violence in Latin America risks backsliding', and that 'violence against women is driven by an entrenched patriarchal culture and a lack of justice for women, with few criminals punished' (VOA, 2017). The rate of non-partner sexual violence against women in Latin America is the highest in the world, while within relationships, one in every ten women has suffered sexual violence from her partner. Between a quarter and half of women report experiencing domestic violence, with the highest rates in Bolivia. A Pan American Health Organization report (Bott et al., 2012), found that most women tend not to seek help – in 2004 just 8.2 per cent of women in Ecuador sought help from an institution, and 36 per cent in El Salvador in 2008. The reasons given for not doing so were diverse, but included shame, fear of retaliation, not knowing where to go, and not believing that anyone would help.

One of the most powerful and prominent regional social movements in recent years has been Ni Una Menos, which started in Argentina in 2015 in response to the brutal murder of Daiana García and has spread to several other Latin American countries, as well as Spain, as women have become increasingly angry with high levels of gender violence and impunity. Ni Una Menos is paralleled by the long-running Mexican protest Ni Una Más (Not One More [woman murdered]). These calls to action led millions of women to take part in the International Women's Strike on 8 March 2017 against macho violence, both in Latin America and globally.

García's death is far from an exceptional case. The term 'femicide' – referring to the murder of a woman based on hatred for her gender alone – first became widely used in Latin America, sparked by an epidemic of murders in the Mexican border town of Ciudad Juárez. Around 400 women and girls were murdered in Juárez between 1993 and 2008, and hundreds more disappeared. Femicides account for two out of every three women murdered in Central America, and a recent report by several international organizations revealed that seven out of the ten countries with the highest female murder rates in the world are in Latin America (Waiselfisz, 2015). Eva explains:

> A femicide is motivated by great anger and hatred towards women in general, because they're not just murders committed by friends or partners, but also by strangers. They mutilate the body. For example, they cut off their breasts and often the femicide is combined with anal or

vaginal rape. The body is left exposed and semi-nude in public as a message of hatred. That's what we typify as a femicide here in Honduras. Over the last ten years, more than 5,000 women have been murdered in Honduras, and the violence of these murders is increasing. Now they are frequent, and it seems that people are losing their sensitivity – they see it as something normal.

I don't believe that there's any woman in Latin America who hasn't experienced violence at some point. We have all experienced it, even if it was psychological. Our rights are often violated in the street – they make comments about our body, about our style of dress. We confront this day-to-day – a situation of violence at any moment.

At Las Hormigas our primary objective was to have an office to provide free legal advice for women who needed representation but couldn't pay for it. Sometimes, if they come from other communities, they have to walk for three or four hours to where the bus is. They have to queue and if they don't get seen that day, the woman has to return home to the aggressor and continue suffering.

Fear also prevents women from reporting violence. Even when they manage to file a report the process is difficult, as the police can only detain a man legally for 24 hours. After 24 hours he can leave, unless the woman reports it again, in which case the judge can implement a restraining order. But as no one enforces it, he returns to the house. Sometimes things improve, but usually the violence is worse than before. He'll say, 'If you report it, I'll kill you', so she won't return, or he'll convince her to reconcile. There's no effort on the part of the authorities to monitor this and sometimes the judge will arrange the date for the hearing eight days later. This is when she's at most risk. The aggressors see that there's a weakness in the system and the violence just gets worse. This happens in most cases.

Another difficulty can be with the police. We train them how to work sensitively with women, but then they're sent elsewhere and new agents come in, who have a *machista* attitude. It's much harder being a Lenca organization with the authorities. If a Lenca woman and a *ladina* [non-indigenous woman] went to the authorities, then they would first attend to the *ladina* and use more formal language, but with the Lenca it's just 'you, wait', 'sit here', and so on. When dealing with reports of violence, the police will even say, 'Are you sure that you served food at the right time?' or 'What did you do to make him treat you like that?' Or they'll say, 'We can't help you because we're only helping with cases of machete injuries.' So she has to turn up with machete wounds to be taken seriously! If the women have only been verbally threatened, they'll say, 'But he hasn't done anything to you.' The Honduran law against domestic violence does actually refer to psychological violence, but the police don't recognize that psychological violence is the first step leading to other acts of aggression.

On top of all this, there isn't a space where women can come and take refuge temporarily while the violence is ongoing, where they can receive all the legal and emotional support they need so they can return home again. Sometimes they have to leave in the middle of the night and can't find anywhere to go because their families or friends are too scared of the aggressor to give them shelter. So Las Hormigas want to build a refuge, called La Casa Matriz Hormiguero, which will be a safe space for women to come to. Our dream is that at the same time they can get occupational therapy and learn something, as well as receiving counselling, because often it's economic dependency as well as emotional dependency which traps women in these cycles of violence. We have the land and the plans, but we don't have enough money to continue – we need around $300,000 to do it. We will collect money, lempira by lempira, and little by little we will be able to build it. We've tried asking for support from two different governments, but they've not given us any response, so we put no faith in them.

Not everyone supports our work. It's quite difficult because the term 'women's rights' implies empowering women and men don't want to lose their privileges. They want to maintain this control over women and this power relationship, controlling their bodies, decisions, resources – everything. But we do have cases when women successfully demand child support from the father. Almost always they both end up satisfied and the man changes his attitude towards the organization. We don't want to get men arrested, what we want is for them to stop being violent and take responsibility for their children.

We have achieved some positive changes with Las Hormigas. There was a case of a woman whose husband went to the US and left her with their two children at her in-laws. Her brother-in-law became violent and there came a point when she couldn't take it any more, so she tried to leave, but they wouldn't let her take the children. The law in Honduras says that only one or other of the parents can keep the children, but in this case, without any investigation, the Department for Childhood, Adolescence, and the Family (DINAF) gave custody to the mother-in-law – just because she came and said their [the children's] mother had left the house for no reason. Our lawyer had to make a legal case, but the court said they couldn't return the children to their mother because she sold alcoholic drinks and was a bad example to the little girl, and that she couldn't provide for them.

We had to administer a lot of support. A sister gave her a little house. She got a job as a community teacher and continued studying. Finally, they gave back her children and she returned to Las Hormigas with them. To see her reunited with her children! That happy face and her children playing with her! This touched our hearts. It's not just ten women that we can help every week, it's ten life stories that we can change for the better with one little action. These are the cases which help us to go on.

Mural at Las Hormigas: 'Before it kills you, alcohol will kill everything you love.'

> There are others that are very bitter and difficult, but we are encouraged by these life stories.

Alongside cultural machismo, another major factor contributing to violence against women in recent years has been the growth of organized crime, which is rife across Latin America. The worst-affected countries are Brazil, Colombia, Venezuela, Mexico, and the Northern Triangle of Honduras, El Salvador, and Guatemala. Misogynistic power structures in gangs and criminal groups reinforce male power over women, at times forcing them to participate in criminal activity (Yagoub, 2017). Women who resist gang recruitment or romantic advances from gang members are subject to extreme violence, including gang rape. Women are also targeted for gang reprisals and extortion threats – being raped, beaten, abducted, and murdered – to intimidate them and their partners or families. As Eva Sánchez says, 'Within organized crime, the body of a woman is used for taking revenge. It's said that if you murder a woman it settles the account.' This has led to an increase in emigration among women and children – from Central America in particular – who seek asylum in other countries, principally the United States.

The Honduran district attorney for women, María Mercedes Bustelo, argues that organized crime hinders progress on preventing violence against women: 'Lots of women experiencing domestic violence are involved with gang members, so there is no way they will report it,' she said. 'They can't ask for help because it would be a death sentence' (BBC News, 2017). In addition, some studies have indicated a vicious circle of crime and domestic violence, in which children exposed to violence between their parents are more likely to become violent themselves and engage in criminal activity. This was a stronger indicator of later violence than the neighbourhood the children lived in (Yagoub, 2017).

To combat endemic violence or organized crime, Latin American governments have tended to implement militarization policies (see Chapter 8). However, though these policies may be popular, especially with middle- and upper-class voters concerned about rising crime, they often have the opposite result to the one intended (Clavel, 2018). They also reinforce the idea that conflicts can only be resolved with violence, and this influences domestic disputes. Militarization policies also fuel the easy availability of firearms. Over 75 per cent of all homicides in Latin America are committed with a firearm, compared to a global average of about 40 per cent (Phillips, 2018). As Eva says:

> The politicians incorrectly believe that violence can be countered with violence. Instead of investing in preventative education programmes, they believe it's better to militarize the country and increase the budget for this. This has increased violence at every level, affecting women the most, as the majority of murders are committed with firearms and those who have access to firearms are men. There is a law which supposedly regulates the control of guns, but it is not implemented in practice. They give guns to men who have been reported for violence and those who have psychological problems. There are a lot of guns and no real control.

When Rio de Janeiro city councilwoman Marielle Franco was assassinated on 14 March 2018 (see box in Chapter 8), less than a month after the military assumed responsibility for security in the city, a defamation campaign on social media immediately followed, attempting to connect her to narcotraffickers. For the authorities – both the police and elected officials – the presence of organized crime can provide a convenient smokescreen for their own failings, allowing them to victim-blame murdered women. This is common in Honduras, as Eva says:

> There is a 98 per cent impunity rate in femicide cases. When the law is not applied, it's an invitation to keep committing these crimes. They don't investigate, because it's assumed that if she's murdered it's because she was a criminal. There's nothing to justify it, and later the woman's family deny what the police say in the press – really, the woman worked selling tortillas, has left behind six kids, and had no real connection to any illegal activity. But what emerges is that she was killed because she was outdoors when she shouldn't have been, because of the way she was dressed, or because she was with people she shouldn't have been with. These accusations are based on stereotypes which dictate that women should remain inside, wear long dresses, and behave traditionally, if they know what's good for them.
>
> There's a big feeling of impotence, because we fight and fight but it seems that things don't advance the way they should. Investigations

aren't handled properly. Often there are cases where the police don't cordon the area off and as a result the crime scene is contaminated and the evidence lost. Who is responsible? The state.

Femicides affect indigenous communities even more because of their [limited] access to justice. In Tegucigalpa or San Pedro Sula the responses are more immediate, the body can be taken straight to the pathologist – but out here, the people who recover the body don't have the experience. There are cases where the bodies of the murdered women have to be transported to Tegucigalpa for an autopsy, which is four hours away. By the time they arrive a lot of evidence has deteriorated because the bodies are put in nylon bags and then they can't identify the killer.

The other thing is that if a woman is murdered here, the impact of her death on her family isn't noticed. There are women who sometimes have five or six children and these children are left with their grandparents, women who are physically incapable of looking after them all, but the state doesn't examine this. It's a double pain: the loss of their loved one, not getting justice, and the extra burden that the family assumes because of the absence of the woman.

I am sometimes scared for my own safety. The coup d'état was accompanied by the criminalization of the feminist struggle and much stronger repression of women. Women who marched against the coup d'état were captured, raped, and tortured.

The Honduran constitutional crisis

At dawn on 28 June 2009, the Honduran army stormed the house of President Manuel Zelaya, acting on orders from the Supreme Court. Zelaya, of the Liberal Party, was bundled onto a plane bound for Costa Rica. Later that day, Speaker of Congress Roberto Micheletti was appointed as his replacement. The official justification was that the intervention was necessary to prevent Zelaya from convening a constituent assembly, the aim of which was to rewrite the constitution and allow him to stand for re-election, though in practice this was legally impossible to achieve before the end of his presidency.

Critics of Zelaya's removal suggested that it was motivated by the Honduran oligarchy's objections to Zelaya's progressive reforms, such as raising the minimum wage, and to his joining the Venezuelan oil alliance, Petrocaribe. Zelaya's removal was internationally condemned, with the United Nations, the Organization of American States, and the European Union all describing it as a military coup.

Since the coup Honduras has been governed by the conservative National Party, a period which has seen increasing militarization and a huge surge in human rights abuses, as well as dramatic increases in poverty and extreme poverty. In 2015 the Supreme Court removed the restriction on sitting or former presidents from running again – supposedly the reason for which it had ordered Zelaya's removal – allowing Juan Orlando Hernández to run again in 2017 and to win in elections widely criticized as fraudulent. At least 31 people have been killed in protests against the election result.

What's more, women aren't only being murdered in situations of abuse, but also in targeted assassinations, as in the case of Berta Cáceres. She was the coordinator of the Council of Popular and Indigenous Organizations of Honduras (COPINH), a strong activist organization focusing on indigenous land rights and protesting big dams and mining. I studied with her. I think we don't believe they're actually evil enough to order a murder. But they do. The fight isn't just about one person, and the death of Berta has served as a seed to make the struggle much stronger. I'm not going to say that we're not scared. We are scared – terrified sometimes – but if we let our fear overcome us, then who is going to fight?

I believe it's important to focus on young people. If we can promote a new mentality amongst young people, where they know their rights and are able to establish relationships between men and women based on respect, then we'll have achieved a lot. When they're adults they will teach their children, and little by little we can alter the social construction that we have. This is what we hope for.

Our dream is that Las Hormigas would no longer need to exist, because there wouldn't be any violations of women's rights! [*Sighs*] But the future is very uncertain. There are a lot of very, very difficult situations, but I also believe in what we are doing. It's the work of the ants [*las hormigas*] – tiny animals, but they can carry great weight and achieve a lot. I think that what we have done, with very scarce resources, has made a big difference to the women who come here. So I say yes, little by little things are going to improve – above all if we work with the young to make a different world.

Reproductive rights

Proof of ingrained machismo and a dominant conservative worldview at a national level is reflected in attitudes to reproductive rights. The strong presence of religion, mainly Catholicism and Evangelical Protestantism, has manifested itself in extremely tough anti-abortion legislation throughout the region. Of the eight countries in the world where you can go to prison for having an abortion under whatever circumstances, six are Latin American (the Dominican Republic, El Salvador, Haiti, Honduras, Nicaragua, and Suriname). Argentina, Belize, Costa Rica, Ecuador, Dominica, Guatemala, Honduras, Paraguay, Peru, and Venezuela all ban abortion even in cases of incest or rape. Three-quarters of all abortions in Latin America are performed illegally, and it is the second-highest cause of death for women in South America. These draconian measures enforce women's secondary position to men in law, with less choice over how their bodies function and less sexual freedom.

Latin America has the highest rates of non-marital childbearing in the world, and while this does not necessarily mean children are raised by single mothers, it is common. Laws on parental responsibility and child support often go unenforced, leaving women in a much more vulnerable economic position. The lack of adequate sex education, access to contraception, or legal abortion mean that women often do not have full freedom of choice when considering the best time to start a family, further jeopardizing their financial security and opportunities in life.

The country which most aggressively enforces its abortion law is the tiny Central American nation of El Salvador, nestled between Honduras and Guatemala. It is estimated that between 1998 and 2013 more than 600 women were jailed for up to 40 years after being accused of having had an abortion. In many of these cases they had simply had a miscarriage. Those still serving such sentences have been nicknamed 'Las 17', although in reality there are more (Sherwell, 2015). Three out of every eight maternal deaths in El Salvador are suicides by pregnant girls under 19, and in July 2017 a 19-year-old who became pregnant after she was raped was sentenced to 30 years in jail after suffering a stillbirth (Lakhani, 2017).

It was only in August 2017 that a 23-year-old law was overturned which allowed pregnant girls under the age of 18 to wed with parental approval. This often enabled rapists to marry their victims, avoiding prosecution by doing so. Just a month previously, a 12-year-old girl who had been raped by a 34-year-old was forced to marry him (Driver, 2017). The parents, usually in poor, rural areas, would allow their daughters to be married off for fear of social stigma and the girl having to raise the child alone. Currently, more than 22,000 minors are married or cohabiting, according to Salvadorean government data,

Some of Las 17 y más, with their psychologist and one of their lawyers

while UNICEF estimates there were more than 25,000 births by underage mothers in 2015. The Guttmacher Institute, a US organization that works on reproductive health issues around the world, has estimated there are 35,000 illegal abortions a year in El Salvador. Roughly 11 per cent of those result in the death of the woman.

Abortion was not always illegal in El Salvador. It used to be permitted in cases of rape, incest, where a foetus was injured, or if the life of the woman was in danger. However, reforms to the penal code brought in by the right-wing ARENA government in 1997 banned abortion in all circumstances, and the following year the constitution was amended to include a commitment to protect human life from the moment of conception. In 2016, President Salvador Sánchez Cerén, a former guerrilla leader of the Farabundo Martí National Liberation Front (FMLN), proposed that Congress reform the country's abortion law to allow for some exceptions to the blanket prohibition. Yet there remain around 27 cases of women sentenced to jail terms of 6–35 years, according to the local Citizens' Group for the Decriminalization of Abortion, referred to as 'Las 17 y más' [The 17 and more]. María Teresa Rivera was one of them, until her release in May 2016. She had been sentenced to 40 years in prison after suffering a miscarriage, serving almost four before her conviction was overturned. Here she recalls her ordeal:

My name is María Teresa Rivera, I am 35 years old. I am Salvadorean by birth, but at the moment I'm living in Sweden. I had to leave my country because of everything I went through there.

I was born in the municipality of San Juan Opico in the department of La Libertad, El Salvador, in 1982. I'm the third of four siblings. We all have the same mother, but we don't share the same father. My father left us when I was three years old, and my mother disap-

María Teresa Rivera

peared during the civil war, when I was five. I ended up living with my aunts, who exploited my brother and me. They sent me out to work when I was just five. I went around selling fruit and vegetables door to door. If we didn't work they wouldn't feed us.

I had always wondered why only the boys went to school. My aunt used to tell me, 'Women are born to raise children and to look after the home.' I didn't think this was for me, so when I was eight years old, I started going to evening classes at a school close to where we lived. But coming back from school alone once, I was raped. Afterwards my aunts said it was all my fault. They said I was disobedient, that I shouldn't have tried to study.

I eventually ended up in one of the *aldeas infantiles* [set up by an NGO called SOS Children's Villages, for neglected, orphaned, or destitute children]. I left when I was 21. They looked after us very well and we had the opportunity to study. I got my diploma, but I was too old to stay there. The only thing I thought I could do to survive at that time was to find a man to look after me. I didn't want that; I wanted to continue studying, but I didn't have any family support. So I found a man and I had somewhere to live. I had my first child at 22, Oscar David. He's 12 now. It's been very difficult, because I also experienced domestic violence. In the end I left my partner.

When my son was five I had a 'blind pregnancy'; there were no symptoms. I was having periods and everything was normal. One morning in November 2011, I felt the urge to go to the toilet. I felt that something had happened, but it had been so quick. When I went to clean myself, I saw that I was bleeding heavily. I got dizzy, but I managed to make it back to the bedroom and I told my mother-in-law [with whom she had continued to live] to call the police [in El Salvador it's common for the police to be called rather than the ambulance in cases of medical emergency].

My mother-in-law told me that when the police arrived I was unconscious. I don't remember anything. When I regained consciousness, I was in hospital surrounded by police. They were accusing me of the aggravated homicide of my child. I told them I hadn't killed anyone. I asked for proof, I asked them to do tests on me. But they did nothing, and the doctors just backed up what the police were saying. There was no investigation. A female doctor who saw me said that I had had a miscarriage – and she later repeated this assessment at my trial – but they ignored her. I was in hospital for just a day. I had a fever and hypovolemic shock when I was discharged, though they gave me some medication. If I hadn't received treatment, I would have died.

Then I was sent to the *bartolinas* – this is a kind of preliminary prison, before the real thing – where I was treated very badly. They called me a bitch, a murderer. They wouldn't give me the food that my mother-in-law brought or any clothes, I had to wear the same clothes in which I entered. We slept on the floor, in shifts, because there were more than 26 women in the same small space. The other women there saw that I was in a bad way, and they would make space for me, ask the staff for medicine on my behalf, but the staff said that I had no rights and wouldn't give me even a single pill. I had been there for five days when I went to my first hearing. The judge asked me what I had used to cut the umbilical cord. I told him I hadn't touched anything, and again I asked for proof. They never produced any. They gave me a public lawyer, but she only arrived as the hearing was about to start and didn't ask me anything. She was just there to keep up appearances.

Then I was sent to a women's prison, which was hell. When you're accused of a crime like this, most of the other prisoners will judge you.

They'll call you a child killer, a child eater. They threaten you, say they'll kill you just like you killed your child. The women seemed very angry. I thought, 'If I don't get out of here, what will happen to my son?' I tried to stay positive, but when they sentenced me to 40 years in prison, I felt like I had lost everything. I thought about how old my son would be when I got out. But then I thought – and I don't know where it came from – 'No, I have great faith in God, I'm going to be out of here in four years.' The four and a half years I was in prison, without my son, is time that I'll never get back. They only let my son visit me twice while I was inside. It was the same for the other women. They robbed us of everything.

I first met the Citizens' Group for the Decriminalization of Abortion in 2012, six months after I was convicted. My mother-in-law took my case to a church that was very supportive in our community and it was passed on to the Citizens' Group. They came to visit me in prison that year with a list that had my name on it. I told them I didn't have any money. 'No,' they said, 'you don't have to pay. We just need to know if you want us to help you.' So I said, 'Of course I do!'

That was when I found out about the other 17 women who were in prison for the same reason. Thinking that I was the only one had made me feel much worse, so when I found out about the others I felt like I had a support network. I felt a connection with them very quickly. The communication that started between us then was beautiful. We gave each other strength and told each other, 'We're going to get out of here.' We made a promise to each other in prison. We said that the first one to get out would carry on fighting for the others on the outside. They are very strong women; I really admire them. Some of them had been in prison for nine or ten years. In the case of Maira Figueroa, she had been in prison for fifteen years, paying for a crime she didn't commit. It's so unfair. It made me wonder how long I would be in there myself.

The other women of Las 17 had similar stories. Maira was raped and kidnapped. She worked as a housekeeper, and the son or nephew of her employer's wife raped her. She was pregnant and couldn't leave the house until the nine months had passed. When she was in labour, they sent for a midwife. They said that the baby died. Maira doesn't know anything because the baby disappeared. She was sentenced to 30 years and she's been in prison for 15. There was some news in March and, finally, she was released [on 14 March 2018].

On 20 May 2016, I was freed unconditionally. It was a very difficult process. My hearing started on 11 May, but it was suspended because the pathologist didn't want to attend. I had a very fair judge, though, who said that the hearing couldn't go ahead unless the doctor was present. So they suspended my hearing until 20 May. The doctor presented photos and the judge asked if there had been signs of abuse. They had accused me of cutting the baby's throat and many other things. But when the judge asked the doctor if there had been any physical abuse of the foetus he said, 'No. There was liquid in the lungs', which means that the baby hadn't taken a breath. They had previously stated that the baby had been breathing, but it wasn't true. The pathologist said that it had been a stillbirth and it had happened naturally.

Half an hour after the end of the hearing, they said that I was free to go. In the letter authorizing my release, the judge said that the state of El Salvador should pay me damages for the four and a half years I had spent in prison. The day I was released I felt incredibly happy. I didn't have anything, but I had my freedom. I was fit and healthy, and I could get a job – I've never been afraid of work, I've always really enjoyed it. My son said, 'Mama, we're going to make it.' Those words, coming from a boy of only 11, gave me strength. But 10 days after I was set free the prosecutor's office appealed the decision. Instead of being compensated, I received only persecution.

On 12 October they were going to decide whether I should go back to prison or be released unconditionally. So, on 6 October 2016, I left the country, helped and supported by Individuell Människohjälp (IM), a Swedish women's organization. It's so hard to leave the little that you have and go to another country, where you don't know anybody and the language is different. But it's not impossible, and after everything I had lived through, it was nothing. I'd get through it.

The day I arrived was very difficult because we didn't know where we were at first. I was advised to go to the Swedish migration agency, where they treated me very well. I was really scared that they would send me back. Most people think that nothing is happening in El Salvador, but there is practically a civil war between gangs. They asked me if I had anywhere to live, and I told them that I didn't, that I didn't know anyone. They took me to a place for refugees and that's where my asylum application process started [it only took two months]. They granted me asylum primarily because of the human rights abuses that I'd suffered as a woman in El Salvador.

I honestly don't know what is happening with my case now. When they granted me asylum, they gave me a passport and told me that I could travel anywhere except to El Salvador, for my own protection. The prosecutor's office was still pursuing me because I wouldn't keep quiet about what had happened to me … When I was released [but still in El Salvador] I tried to get on with my life, one day at a time, but you meet people who insult you. They say things like, 'Here comes the child killer.' I suffered from discrimination in employment too. When I went out with my CV they would take one look at me and say, 'No, the position is already filled.' Even though the sign was still up! All of this helped me get asylum.

Abortion was legal in El Salvador until 1998, but unfortunately things changed because of religious prejudice and the mentality of the people in power. What makes me angry is that in their own families there might be more than one woman who has suffered a miscarriage, or who has been ill and had to have an abortion, but their daughters can go to private clinics. They have enough money to leave the country, have an abortion, come back, and nothing happens. Why is it only poor people who must obey the law? They think we can't defend ourselves. If you ask women with money, a lot of them will admit to having had an abortion.

What we want is to have a law passed, Article 133, giving women the chance to decide. It's not to force anyone. The Salvadorean State makes decisions about our bodies, but our bodies belong to no one but ourselves. They say, 'No, it's a sin.' They won't allow other women to have their lives saved. We are all at risk, so why do we judge and accuse each other? It's machismo, the same as with the men. First, people's mentality needs to change, and then this unjust law. Every woman is at risk of ending up in a similar situation to the one we have experienced. Nobody is immune. People think it's fine for you to die in childbirth. But who will look after your children? They don't think about that. There need to be workshops and programmes to empower women. We have no such programmes in schools in El Salvador – even talking about condoms is forbidden. These are things that children need to be taught from a young age.

Right now, there is an abortion bill going through the Legislative Assembly, though it has been stuck for over a year. It proposes four grounds for abortion: when the woman's life is at risk; when the baby won't survive due to a malformation – there have been cases where there is no brain, with both mother and baby dying in childbirth. Why risk the mother's life? They already know that the baby can't live, but they risk the mother's life too. Another is when the pregnancy is the result of the rape of a minor, and the last one, I think, is about human trafficking. But many in the Assembly don't want to pass it.

We have had some achievements. That the state recognizes the errors it has committed is a step forward. Sara García [of the Citizens' Group] said that [my case] was the first time asylum had been granted to a woman who had suffered a miscarriage. This opens the door for other women to be helped too. But for this to happen I've had to show my face publicly. Sometimes I get home and think I'm not going to give any more interviews, because of the effect it has. In El Salvador, I've been treated horribly by the media. But when I see other women's cases again and again I think, 'Why should I keep quiet?' I've been through the same thing, so I have to speak out and fight on for my *compañeras*.

* * *

The voices in this chapter illustrate just some of the diverse struggles women are involved in across Latin America. The strength and resilience of grassroots organizations have brought real change. Yet the odds stacked against them are inevitably high and often the work done by these groups serves to fill the gaps where the state has failed to protect women's rights and provide adequate support. Community leaders and campaigners, many of them women, are picking up the pieces of damaged infrastructure, weak public policy, and poorly funded women's initiatives.

Women have been recognized for bringing certain positive attributes to social struggles. They are seen to be persistent, to be protectors of the environment, to take a long-term view, and be more prone to rational discussion and mediation than arguing and aggression. For Patricia Gualinga, 'If there's a confrontation, men versus men, then there'll be violence for sure. What the women do is put themselves in the middle, to prevent violence and keep the peace.' However, whether working independently in women's organizations or within mixed-gender groups for various causes, women face constraints to achieving their goals, being given a platform to speak out, or gaining public respect. These stem from entrenched traditional views perpetuated by patriarchal and *machista* societies.

Women activists therefore often have to struggle twice as hard as their male counterparts to be elected to positions of power in organizations and in their dealings with usually male-dominated institutions or political groups. They also bear the extra burden of their traditional responsibilities in the home, as well as campaigning, which often demands long hours and travel away from their families. As Alicia Cawiya says, 'As representatives, we no longer have time to be with our families, because we have to travel to political events as well as watching over and administering our territories and consulting with our communities … It is not easy for us … Sometimes the women decide not to travel because of their husbands, who object to their travelling.' Better understanding and support for these double burdens is needed to enable more women to engage politically and take on social responsibilities outside the home.

Common factors throughout these interviews are a sheer determination to improve the position of women, a selfless drive to work towards this despite personal risk and hardship, and an impressive resilience in the face of continued setbacks, lack of funds, and harassment. This level of hard work, dedication, communal organizing, and optimism for the future must surely drive concrete changes to Latin America's social and institutional structure. However, governments need to do their part. They must rethink harsh anti-abortion legislation, properly enforce laws that protect women's rights, and impose punitive measures against perpetrators of violence. Impunity needs to be tackled before these campaigns and organizations can achieve real change, for, as Eva Sánchez notes, if the aggressors do not face justice, they are effectively given 'carte blanche to keep committing the crimes'. Improving access to education and family planning and enforcing payment of child support would also go some way towards relieving the abject situations many women continue to endure.

Furthermore, there needs to be a wider cultural recognition and condemnation of ingrained machismo – from both men and women – as this continues to be a major cause of much violence and hardship. The increasing visibility that women's rights organizations and leaders are gaining and the prevalence of pan-Latin American and global campaigns combating violence against women should help alter public perspectives, but it will likely be a slow transition. Nonetheless, women are continuing to step forward, shoulder the struggles of their communities, and defend their rights. The future of Latin America is set to be increasingly steered by women.

About the author

Louise Morris is a journalist, audio and TV producer. She specializes in women's rights and the intersection between art and politics. Louise works primarily in radio, producing and presenting documentaries for BBC R4 and producing for NPR. She previously worked producing a daily TV magazine programme. She has written for The Wire, Delayed, Gratification, and BBC News Online, among others.

Interviews

Alicia Cawiya (vice president of the Huaorani people): interviewed in Quito and Puyo, Ecuador, on 16 and 20 August 2016 by Linda Etchart and James Thackara. Translated by Linda Etchart.

Patricia Gualinga (Sarayaku Kichwa activist): interviewed in Puyo, Ecuador, on 24 August 2016 by Linda Etchart and James Thackara. Translated by Linda Etchart.

María Teresa Rivera (Salvadorean reproductive rights activist): interviewed via Facebook Messenger on 15 January 2018 by Louise Morris. Translated by Matthew Kingston.

Eva Sánchez (Las Hormigas): interviewed in Intibucá, Honduras, on 26 October 2016 by Louise Morris. Translated by Louise Morris.

References

NB: All web references were checked and still available in May/June 2018 unless otherwise stated. All references are listed, with web-links, on the page for this chapter on the Voices website www.vola.org.uk

BBC News (2017) 'Honduras on "red alert" over female murders, say activists', 6 July, <http://www.bbc.co.uk/news/world-latin-america-40518212>

Belli, G. (2016) 'Why has "macho" Latin America elected more female leaders than the US?', *The Guardian*, 7 November, <https://www.theguardian.com/global-development-professionals-network/2016/nov/07/macho-latin-america-elected-more-female-leaders-than-us>

Bott, S., Guedes, A., Goodwin, M. and Mendoza, J.A. (2012) *Violence Against Women in Latin America and the Caribbean: A Comparative Analysis of*

Population-Based Data from 12 Countries, Pan American Health Organization, Washington DC, <https://www.paho.org/hq/index.php?option=com_content&view=article&id=8175:violence-against-women-in-latin-america-and-the-caribbean&Itemid=1519&lang=en>

Clavel, T. (2018) 'Why Latin America dominates global homicide rankings', *InSight Crime*, 12 March, <https://www.insightcrime.org/news/analysis/why-latin-america-dominates-global-homicide-rankings>

Driver, A. (2017) 'What women's lives are like when abortion is a crime', CNN, 5 October, <http://edition.cnn.com/2017/10/05/opinions/united-states-el-salvador-abortion-prison-driver-opinion/index.html>

Goudreau, J. (2011) 'The Ten Worst Stereotypes About Powerful Women', *Forbes*, 24 October, <https://www.forbes.com/sites/jennagoudreau/2011/10/24/worst-stereotypes-powerful-women-christine-lagarde-hillary-clinton/#77c15f5561ca>

Lakhani, N. (2017) 'El Salvador teen rape victim sentenced to 30 years in prison after stillbirth', *The Guardian*, 6 July, <https://www.theguardian.com/global-development/2017/jul/06/el-salvador-teen-rape-victim-sentenced-30-years-prison-stillbirth>

Phillips, T. (2018) '"Breathtaking homicidal violence": Latin America in grip of murder crisis', *The Guardian*, 26 April, <https://www.theguardian.com/world/2018/apr/26/latin-america-murder-crisis-violence-homicide-report>

Sherwell, P. (2015) 'El Salvador's Las 17: the women jailed for 30 years for losing their babies by miscarriage', *The Telegraph*, 16 February, <http://www.telegraph.co.uk/news/worldnews/centralamericaandthecaribbean/elsalvador/11412928/El-Salvadors-Las-17-the-women-jailed-for-30-years-for-losing-their-babies-by-miscarriage.html>

Tello Rozas, P. and Floru, C. (2017) 'Women's political participation in Latin America: some progress and many challenges', Institute for Democracy and Electoral Assistance (IDEA), 7 March, <https://www.idea.int/news-media/news/women's-political-participation-latin-america-some-progress-and-many-challenges>

VOA (2017) 'OAS chief: violence against Latin America's women a "never-ending story"', 7 November, <https://www.voanews.com/a/violence-women-latin-america/4105894.html>

Waiselfisz, J.J. (2015) *Mapa da violência 2015: homicídio de mulheres no Brasil*, FLACSO, Brasília, <http://www.mapadaviolencia.org.br/pdf2015/MapaViolencia_2015_mulheres.pdf>

WHO (2012) 'Understanding and addressing violence against women', World Health Organization, <http://apps.who.int/iris/bitstream/10665/77432/1/WHO_RHR_12.36_eng.pdf>

Yagoub, M. (2017) 'How violence against women fuels more crime', *InSight Crime*, 8 March, <https://www.insightcrime.org/news/brief/how-violence-against-women-fuels-more-crime>

CHAPTER 3
LGBT rights: the rainbow tide
Ali Rocha

Abstract

Latin American countries have passed some of the world's most advanced pro-LGBT laws. However, rates of discrimination, violence, and murder affecting gay and trans people are extremely high, especially in Brazil and Central America. LGBT people are campaigning for same-sex marriage, laws against homophobia and pathologization, and the right to change gender identity by simple administrative procedures, though the churches, both Catholic and Evangelical, present a formidable barrier.

Despite its reputation as a bastion of machismo, religion, and conservative social values, in recent years Latin America has enthusiastically embraced LGBT rights. Some of the world's most advanced pro-LGBT legislation is found in Latin American countries, particularly Argentina and Uruguay. São Paulo hosts the biggest gay pride celebration on the planet and is often rated as one of the most gay-friendly cities in the world, as are Rio de Janeiro, Buenos Aires, and Montevideo.

In *Out in the Periphery: Latin America's Gay Rights Revolution*, Omar Encarnación argues that economic and political modernization, constitutional and judicial reforms, and the rise of socially liberal governments have all contributed to recent improvements in gay rights. However, none of this would have been possible without the tireless work of activists and grassroots organizations across the region, who have adapted the LGBT struggle to their own contexts, put pressure on governments, and created highly effective awareness campaigns. Inspired by external events and trends, but firmly grounded in local politics and realities, these campaigns have not only changed the law but transformed the wider society and culture.

But this progress is a relatively recent phenomenon. Homosexual activity was illegal in Venezuela until 1997, Chile until 1999, and Nicaragua and Panama until 2008. Belize lifted its ban only in 2016, when its Supreme Court declared colonial-era sodomy laws unconstitutional. And there is enormous regional variation. LGBT travellers in Latin America may find locals far more accommodating in Argentina, Uruguay, or Brazil, say, than in Paraguay or the Central American Northern Triangle (Honduras, El Salvador, and Guatemala) – countries which are both significantly poorer and far more

http://dx.doi.org/10.3362/9781909014213.003

Rainbow flag on Avenida Paulista in São Paulo at LGBT Pride 2014

socially conservative. There is also considerable variation within countries, with enormous cultural differences between the larger cities and rural areas.

Governments of the so-called 'pink tide' that came to power across much of the region in the early 2000s were, in general, receptive to the demands of the LGBT movement. When the UN passed resolutions on sexual orientation and gender identity in 2011, 2014, and 2016, all Latin American states that were on the 47-member Human Rights Council at the time voted in favour. Likewise, seven Latin American countries – Argentina, Brazil, Chile, Colombia, Costa Rica, Mexico, and Uruguay – together with the United States and Canada, are part of the LGBTI Core Group of the Organization of American States (OAS), founded to promote the rights of LGBTI (Lesbian, Gay, Bisexual, Transgender/ Transsexual and Intersex) persons.

In countries without LGBT legislation, activists, members of the LGBT community, and victims of LGBT-related violence have resorted to the Inter-American Court of Human Rights, part of the OAS system of human rights protection. Government leaders have also sought advice from the Court. In May 2016, the then president of Costa Rica, Luis Guillermo Solís, asked the Court for an advisory opinion on the interpretation of the American Convention on Human Rights (ACHR) regarding a change of name and gender marker for transgender individuals in official documents, and patrimonial rights for same-sex couples.

On 9 January 2018, the Court ruled that signatories to the ACHR have an obligation to permit transgender individuals to change their name, gender, and photo on identity documents without invasive and pathologizing requirements, such as medical or psychiatric evaluation, or divorce. It also called for full recognition of same-sex marriage, arguing that civil unions – even if guaranteeing the same rights as marriage – are insufficient, as the existence of two separate legal frameworks is a mark of inequality, an acknowledgement that the state values one type of relationship over another. It ruled that signatories must ensure that people in same-sex relationships enjoy all family rights without discrimination.

This ruling is poised to bring about a wave of change in Latin America, especially on trans rights, which remain very limited in most of the countries that have signed up to the ACHR. However, there is much opposition. A delegation of politicians from several countries has already protested, arguing that such decisions are the exclusive responsibility of member states. Conservatives maintain that an advisory opinion of the Court issued to one country does not directly oblige other countries to comply. However, the ruling left no doubt that the ACHR does indeed guarantee these rights to LGBT people, with member states required to take the Court's opinion into consideration when making law and policy. Activists are already preparing to put the ruling to the test. In Paraguay, two same-sex couples announced that they intend to register their marriages at the Civil Registry. If they fail, they plan to proceed to national courts and, as a last resort, the Inter-American Commission, which can refer cases to the Inter-American Court (Ghoshal, 2018).

The three main demands of the LGBT community in Latin America, and worldwide, are anti-discrimination laws, same-sex marriage, and gender identity laws. Anti-discrimination laws protect LGBT individuals from discrimination or persecution in employment, education, and public services, while imposing tougher penalties for homophobic and transphobic violence. Same-sex marriage laws recognize homosexual couples and guarantee them the same legal rights as heterosexuals, such as rights to pensions, inheritance, social security and common household, as well as the right to adopt children as a couple. Finally, gender identity laws grant transgender people the right to be recognized in a gender different to the one they were assigned at birth, by changing their name and gender in public records and legal documents. In this chapter we hear the voices of activists in Latin America who are involved in all three struggles.

Anti-discrimination

Prejudice and discrimination are a daily reality for many LGBT individuals in Latin America. Because of his frequent appearances on TV Globo, Jean Wyllys is Brazil's best-known gay activist. Born in 1974 in Alagoinhas, a small town in the north-eastern state of Bahia, Wyllys was one of seven children from a poor family. His mother took in washing, and when he was 10 he was selling candyfloss to boost the family income.

In his flat in Rio de Janeiro, Jean has a picture of Ogun, the Yoruba god of war, politics, and fire. And he has needed fire in his belly to become one of Brazil's most effective human rights activists, a federal deputy for the left-wing Socialism and Liberty Party (PSOL), and the country's only openly gay member of Congress. He has become a hate figure for the more extreme elements of the religious right. One accused him of waging a 'personal war' against religion and a 'campaign against Christianity'.

Jean recalls his early experiences of homophobia:

Jean Wyllys

© Pedro França/Câmara dos Deputados 2011

> The issue first arose in my life in a negative way when I was six years old and heard an anti-gay insult for the first time, the word *veado* [derogatory term in Brazil for a gay man]. I didn't know what it meant, but I understood at six years old that I shouldn't be a *veado*, because the word was being used pejoratively, to humiliate me, a six-year-old child. I didn't know what sexual orientation was, but I was already suffering a symbolic attack because in some way I was breaking gender boundaries. Sexism – heterosexism – works in this way; homophobia is driven by heterosexism, heterosexuality. The division of sexual roles. The woman should do this, the man should do that. It appears very early in our lives and above all in the form of insults. All the institutions which educate us and make us into citizens – the family, language, school, the Church, the factory – are based on this assumption about the roles of men and women, which is the driving force of homophobia.
>
> So, as a child perhaps I flirted with gender boundaries, perhaps I was crossing them. I certainly liked girls' things, or things society considered girls' things. I played with dolls, I spent time with girls, I wasn't into football. This was the first time that homophobia and LGBT issues appeared in my life. It was very early, as it nearly always is.
>
> And when I started to develop feelings of desire, around 13 years old, I noticed that I liked boys, that I looked at boys in a different way. This is the age everyone starts to discover their own desires, both heterosexuals and homosexuals. The difference is that in a heteronormative society, it's no problem for a boy to come home and say he likes a girl in his class – quite the opposite. The parents will encourage it. But if a 13-year-old boy says he likes a boy, then automatically it's a problem. He'll be taken to a psychologist, a psychiatrist; he'll be beaten by his parents and thrown out the house.

In neighbouring Argentina, gay rights activist Edgardo Fernández has used his success as a teacher of 'queer tango' to promote social and political causes. He has been a vocal campaigner against the persecution suffered by LGBT people in many parts of the world. Like Wyllys, he discovered at an early age that he was gay and suffered prejudice as a consequence. We spoke to him at his book-filled flat in Buenos Aires, his bicycle propped on the balcony outside:

> I was born in a small town in the south of the province of Tucumán, in the north of Argentina. I'm from a very large, conservative, Catholic

family. It's a very traditional town. At 18, I decided to go and live in Buenos Aires simply because my homosexuality was a problem in the town. I began to study law and stayed here with the idea of living in anonymity, to try and change, just as many others were doing. At 24, I met my first [male] partner. I took him to Tucumán to meet my family and everyone else. Before that, I used to have girlfriends. My activism in LGBT organizations had started before that trip.

Edgardo Fernández

© Kevin Footer 2016

I was an activist in secret groups between 1983 and 1985, and we would have meetings in different neighbourhoods. These groups then came together to form an organization called the Comunidad Homosexual Argentina, which still exists today. All our activism at that time was aimed at stopping the police and the state from arresting people from the gay community. It was all about preventing state repression. Afterwards, we began to campaign against other forms of discrimination.

I was in a good socioeconomic position, I wasn't effeminate, so I wasn't really that scared, unlike many others. Every day they would arrest someone you knew. That happened throughout the eighties and into the early nineties.

Across the Andes in Chile, Michel Riquelme, a trans activist, met us in the meeting room of Organizando Trans Diversidades (OTD), a national association for transgender people in Chile, which provides a meeting space for the trans community. OTD is based in Bellavista, the traditional home of Santiago's artist community, where the poet Pablo Neruda had a house. Michel also experienced problems within his family:

I knew my father, but when I was 15 we lost touch and I've not heard from him since. And I'm not interested in getting in contact, because he's very conservative and misogynistic. I have an aunt and uncle as well – mum's brother and sister – but our relationship is quite distant. That's my choice, because I spend so much time in

Michel Riquelme

© Armando Escoffier 2017

trans environments that when I spend time in hetero environments, I think, 'How can you say that?' People say things which are sexist and homophobic, and as an activist it's very hard for me to be there. I just end up fighting with everyone.

Violence and killings

Discrimination against LGBT people can take many forms, from bullying in schools to harassment in the street to restricted access to public services. Its most extreme manifestation is physical violence, of which Latin America has the highest rates worldwide. Whereas in Europe there were 123 killings of trans people between 2008 and 2017, the same period saw 2,048 killed in Central and South America. Of the 325 people killed worldwide in the year from October 2016, 171 were killed in Brazil alone, while 56 were killed in Mexico. Honduras, though much smaller, has over twice Brazil's rate of killings (Transgender Europe, 2016). Violence against trans women is particularly widespread and it is not unheard of for police to deliberately ignore violence, or even to refuse to help victims whilst they are being attacked.

Brazil has long topped the list for homophobic and transphobic murders worldwide (Strobl, 2017) and hit an all-time high in 2017 (Cowie, 2018). Unlike some other countries, Brazil does not have federal laws which impose stiffer penalties for violent crime motivated by the victim's sexual orientation. However, about 78 per cent of the population live in regions where local laws provide such protection (Carroll and Mendos, 2017). Some states have enacted local laws that impose penalties such as fines for acts of violence and/ or other acts of discrimination based on sexual orientation.

The LGBT movement has always pressed for the criminalization of homophobia, but Jean Wyllys is not sure that this is the right priority:

> We have been campaigning for this for years. 'Criminalize Homophobia Now.' Not least because of the deaths, homophobic and transphobic murders. We publicize the statistics, the number of bodies. This is very important work because Brazil has shocking rates of homophobic murders – nearly one LGBT person is killed every day. These are shocking numbers and this needs to be dealt with.
>
> But I think those of us who are human rights activists need to remember that this agenda is complex. We need to understand that in criminalizing all expressions of homophobia, we are empowering the penal and punitive state. This state has attacked us in the past and can do so again at any time. Homosexuality used to be a crime in many countries, and it remains so in 37 [in fact it is 74 – Ed.], in some cases punishable by death. We shouldn't be strengthening the penal or punitive state. We need to have a critical view of this agenda. This became my attitude, and this set me on a collision course with part of the LGBT movement, which doesn't understand or want to understand the complexity of my argument.
>
> Criminalize Homophobia Now? Yes. But what kind of criminalization do we want? I would argue that the penal code should recognize homophobia as a motive in the case of life-threatening crimes: murder, attempted murder, assault, torture, crimes already classified in the

penal code. In which case, the sentences should be more severe where these motives are present. This way, we criminalize the worst violence against LGBT people. But homophobic insults, calumny, and defamation shouldn't be punished with a prison sentence. There should be alternative socioeducational punishments, aimed at reforming the person. Because nobody is born LGBT-phobic, society makes them that way. This applies not just to heterosexuals, it can be anyone. LGBT people can be homophobic, transphobic, or lesbophobic. It's better to think of alternative punishments, including fines, aimed at reforming the person. Our prisons are medieval dungeons, they don't re-educate or reintegrate anyone. They are a system for managing poverty, where poor, illiterate, and black people are incarcerated. Why would I want to increase the number of people sent to prison? No. That's my position.

Violence is increasing in Brazil, though this may also be an indication that LGBT individuals are more likely to report it than in the past. Nonetheless, many cases continue to go unreported. Victims may be reluctant to come forward, either out of fear of reprisals or of abuse from police officers who are often homophobic or transphobic themselves, and frequently blame and belittle the victims. The Brazilian media routinely misgenders transgender victims, using their birth names, which often means they get omitted from transphobia statistics. And even when cases are reported, authorities do not always recognize the motivation, with the result that the crimes are not correctly registered. Recording the violence often falls to civil society organizations who may have little more to go on than media reports. The oldest of these is Grupo Gay de Bahia, the oldest, largest, and most active gay rights organization in Brazil. Founded in 1980, they provide statistics to the International Lesbian, Gay, Bisexual, Trans, and Intersex Association (ILGA). But the lack of comprehensive and reliable statistical data contributes to a culture of impunity for perpetrators, with the most consistent violence occurring where there is least government documentation and least civil society presence.

Pathologization

Pathologization is the claim that LGBT people are suffering from a bodily disease or mental illness. The World Health Organization (WHO) removed homosexuality from its list of mental disorders on 17 May 1990, the International Day Against Homophobia, Transphobia, and Biphobia. In May 2016 a group of United Nations and international human rights experts called for an urgent end to this practice. 'Branding them as ill based on their sexual orientation, gender identity or gender expression has historically been, and continues to be, one of the root causes behind the human rights violations they face', they concluded. 'It is also an obstacle to overcoming negative attitudes, stereotypes, and the multiple barriers for the realization of LGBT people's fundamental rights' (UN OHCHR, 2016). However, conservative religious groups still treat homosexuality as an illness, and conversion therapies are available throughout the region.

In Brazil, the Federal Council of Psychologists banned the practice of offering treatment that claims to change people's sexuality or gender identity in 1999. Licensed psychologists, it said, must refrain from coercive or unsolicited treatment of homosexuals and cannot participate in events or services offering a 'gay cure'. However, this progressive ruling has become increasingly under attack in recent years. In 2013, the Commission for Human Rights of Brazil's lower house of Congress, at the time presided over by an openly homophobic Evangelical pastor, approved a bill proposed by a conservative deputy allowing psychiatrists in the country to treat homosexuality as a disease. The bill provoked nationwide protests and was subsequently withdrawn. But in 2017, a ruling by a federal judge made it legally possible for psychologists to offer sexual orientation reversal therapy, though the decision was met with protests from within the profession. 'There is no way to cure what is not a disease,' said Rogério Giannini, head of the Federal Council of Psychology. 'It is not a serious, academic debate, it is a debate connected to religious or conservative positions' (Phillips, 2017).

In Ecuador, while conversion therapies are banned, campaigners say the country still has dozens of illicit 'gay cure' clinics. Primarily targeting lesbians, these centres use methods ranging from electrocution and submersion in ice-cold water to forcing their 'patients' to wear make-up and high heels (Moloney, 2018). The country's former health minister Carina Vance Mafla

© Photo: Mídia NINJA 2017

Protest against pathologization of LGBT people in São Paulo

also said she had received reports of women suffering corrective rape at such centres. The government promised to shut them down in 2012, but according to Tatiana Cordeiro of the women's rights campaign group Urgent Action Fund, very little has changed. Clinics are still being allowed to operate and some are even owned by government officials (Jenkin, 2016).

Pathologization is also a major issue for the trans community. OTD's Michel Riquelme and his mother Jimena Norambuena say that the pathologization issue has brought them into conflict with other sections of the LGBT movement, who argue that being classified as ill by society is part of the process of gaining a separate identity. Michel explains:

> There's the struggle against the pathologization of transgender people. We even have it with leaders in the gay rights movement. They say, 'If you don't let them pathologize you, you won't be recognized.' So setting this as a priority has been difficult even with people who supposedly support us, like gays, lesbians, and feminists.
>
> We did the first festival for the de-pathologization of trans people, which was called Transfest. There were more than 50 people working on this festival, and throughout the day between 800 and 1,000 people turned up. It was great, a total success. It was the biggest event that a transgender group had ever staged in Chile. There are the pride marches, but they're not just a trans thing, it's LGBT ...
>
> At the pride marches the trans women are depoliticized because they just invite them there to dance. To make up the numbers. The Transfest was a more political event and we had the participation of human rights groups – Amnesty, and so on – and with a big emphasis on preventing the pathologization of transgender people. October this year was International Transgender Month, and on the 22nd there was a de-pathologization day, with demonstrations in various places across the world under the banner of 'Stop Trans Pathologization'.

Same-sex marriage

In 2009, Mexico City became the first capital in Latin America to allow same-sex marriages, followed by 12 Mexican states. In 2010, Argentina became the first country in the region to legalize same-sex marriage nationwide, giving same-sex couples equal rights, including the right to adopt children. Uruguay and Brazil (through a court ruling rather than legislation) both legalized same-sex marriage in 2013, and Colombia in 2016. Chile and Ecuador allow same-sex civil partnerships.

In Chile, the then president Michelle Bachelet signed a marriage equality bill in August 2017, at a ceremony at the presidential palace La Moneda. 'It cannot be that old prejudices are stronger than love,' she said. 'It's neither ethical nor just to impose artificial limits on love' (AlJazeera, 2017). However, with the Chilean right back in power under Sebastián Piñera, the fate of the bill is uncertain. According to the BBC, Piñera said, 'There should not be discrimination, but at the same time the essence of an institution such as marriage should be respected, which has always been about conserving the human race' (BBC, 2017). He has also repeatedly stated that he believes marriage can only be between a man and a woman.

Following the ruling by the Inter-American Court of Human Rights that the right to same-sex marriage should be recognized, the issue also dominated the 2018 Costa Rican presidential election campaign, which provided a microcosm of Latin America's current acrimonious culture wars. The winning candidate, Carlos Alvarado Quesada – a novelist, journalist, and alumnus of the University of Sussex – ran on a progressive platform and promised to implement the Court ruling. His conservative opponent, Fabricio Alvarado Muñoz – an Evangelical preacher and singer – railed against 'gender ideology' (see box) and the secular state, promising to pull Costa Rica out of both the Inter-American Court and the OAS.

For some activists, like the Brazilian Jean Wyllys, winning the right to same-sex marriage should be the number one priority:

> Same-sex marriage is a positive agenda. It doesn't restrict anyone's rights, but broadens them. Marriage also guarantees LGBT couples their material rights and benefits such as healthcare plans, child support, and inheritance rights. On top of this, gaining the right to same-sex marriage addresses legal discrimination as practised by the state itself. As long as it divides people into first- and second-class citizens, the state reinforces homophobia. Without same-sex marriage, heterosexual people are first-class citizens in that they have all their rights, whereas LGBT people are second-class because they don't. They don't have the right to marry, which means they are also denied a whole range of rights that go along with that. We needed to fight this legal injustice, because in the end this legal discrimination props up the whole homophobic culture. The idea that we are second-class citizens means that it's much easier to kill us.
>
> The marriage agenda, then, isn't about forcing anyone to get married. It's not forcing conservatism onto the LGBT community. It doesn't mean that from tomorrow, people who like to have different partners and relationships must suddenly get married and be monogamous. No, it's about ensuring you have the right to get married if you want and it's about sending the message to society that you are a citizen, equal to any other. The day you want to get married, the state can't deny you that right.
>
> It also provides a positive image, a connection with family … Religious leaders always portray us in their speeches as if we are a threat to family, to children, a danger in schools. The demand for same-sex marriage challenges this, because it encompasses the idea of family, promotes the idea of a loving homosexual family. This has been a lovely

movement and we emerged victorious. We won through the judiciary –
Brazil's Supreme Court has recognized same-sex civil marriage.
Wyllys considers the legalization of same-sex marriage one of the great
achievements of his mandate, arguing that it makes progress on the other
two main demands of the LGBT community – criminalization of homophobia
and recognition of gender identity – more likely. However, it is currently permitted only because the Supreme Court authorized it, and this decision could
be overturned by a later ruling. Once same-sex marriage has been approved
by Congress and enshrined in legislation, it becomes binding. The same-sex
marriage bill is pending approval in Congress. Wyllys comments:

> The law is still being processed. Today, gay couples have the right to
> marry, but let's suppose that the make-up of the Supreme Court changes.
> There could be an appeal and the Court might decide to interpret things
> differently, with the result that homosexuals would no longer have the
> right to marry. To prevent that from happening, we have to get the leg-
> islation approved in the Chamber of Deputies. That's where the fight
> is now.

A vote was set for November 2017, but it was taken off the agenda. With
Brazil's current Congress the most conservative since the military dictatorship
(1964–85), no one expects a vote soon. One senator, Magno Malta, told a
newspaper that most congressional deputies are against the project because
'marriage is a union between a man and a woman' and the project should be
'chucked in the bin, which is where it belongs' (Lindner, 2017). Wyllys is not
optimistic of progress under present circumstances:

> There's no chance at all [of the bill being approved] with the current
> Congress and political climate in Brazil. There's very little chance of get-
> ting any pro-LGBT legislation approved, not only same-sex marriage but
> also criminalization [of homophobia] in the terms I've described. As a
> result, we've changed our strategy – we have taken action in society,
> made it a cultural issue. As I said, the law is not enough, there has to
> be change in the culture – so we involved artists, people from TV, musi-
> cians, people from the cinema, in a campaign in favour of LGBT love.
> The discourse of love is powerful, it creates empathy. We applied pres-
> sure and persuaded the Supreme Court to guarantee that things won't
> change, for now. Could they change in the future? It's possible.

We will return later to the importance of changing the culture. Approval of
same-sex marriage tends to be accompanied or followed by legislation on
same-sex adoption. Argentina, Uruguay, Brazil, and Colombia all allow joint
adoption of children by same-sex couples, while in Mexico – though there is
no federal law on the issue – 11 states, alongside Mexico City, have legislated
for joint adoption by same-sex couples.

Gender ideology

'Gender ideology' – which has never existed as either an academic school of thought or a political movement – is a dog-whistle, a catch-all term used by conservatives and religious groups to designate whatever they feel threatens the traditional family and Judaeo-Christian civilization, principally LGBT rights, feminism, and reproductive rights. It is not unique to Latin America; it originated in the Vatican in the 1990s and similar campaigns have emerged in several European countries. However, Latin America is where it is currently most prominent, and it is being used to dangerous effect, as the following incidents illustrate.

In November 2017 the American philosopher and gender theorist, Judith Butler, spoke at an event in São Paulo entitled 'The End of Democracy'. Butler has actively supported lesbian and gay rights movements and has spoken out on many contemporary political issues. The event was targeted by a small but highly vociferous group of ultra-conservative protesters, who burned an effigy of Butler outside the venue, whilst chanting 'Burn the witch!' On Facebook, one of the groups behind the protest, Ativistas Independentes, accused Butler of being the 'proponent of hatred against Israel and the advocate of GENDER IDEOLOGY around the world' (Ativistas Independentes, 2017).

The term appears frequently in debates about education. In Peru, a row over a new school curriculum in 2017 led to nationwide protests under the banner of 'Con Mis Hijos No Te Metas' ('Don't Mess With My Kids'). Organizers accused the Peruvian government and particularly the minister of education, Marilú Martens, of imposing 'gender ideology' in schools, though Martens insisted that the offending paragraphs referred to gender equality between men and women rather than sexuality or gender identity (Stewart, 2017). Similarly, a new programme of sex education in Costa Rican schools sparked a demonstration on the streets of San José attended by 7 of the 13 presidential candidates. Again, protesters railed against what they called 'gender ideology'.

In Colombia, education minister Gina Parody ordered schools to revise their policies on sexual and gender identity, following the suicide in 2014 of a gay 16-year-old who had suffered bullying and harassment from teachers and directors at his school. This unleashed a vicious campaign against the minister by the opposition, led by the former president, Álvaro Uribe. Ángela Hernández, a deputy for Uribe's party, claimed that Parody – who is openly gay – wanted to enforce 'homosexual colonization' in schools. On 10 August 2016, big marches took place in several Colombian cities against 'gender ideology', with the support of Uribe, Hernández, the pre-candidate in the 2018 elections Alejandro Ordóñez, and conservative and religious groups. Moreover, the Colombian opposition managed to associate the term successfully with the peace agreement between the government and the FARC guerrillas, contributing to its rejection by voters in the October 2016 referendum. Objecting to its use of the term 'gender equity', campaigners claimed that the agreement would establish 'gender ideology' as official state policy (Giraldo, 2017). Following the referendum, Parody, who had been a leading figure in the 'Yes' campaign, resigned.

Gender-identity law and practice

For Jean Wyllys, the gender identity demands of the trans community – particularly the right to change name and gender marker on official documents – are particularly urgent:

> This is the third point in the agenda, which relates to the demands of the 'T community' – transvestite, transsexual, and transgender. This part

of the LGBT melting pot is the most vulnerable, because gender identity can't be hidden like sexual orientation. I could have spent my whole life in the closet, pretending I was straight. Leading a divided life. And I understand people who do this, because it's not easy in a world as homophobic as ours. But I always say that living in fear is like being only half alive. It's better to live a whole life, to be upfront with the world about who you are. But gender identity can't be hidden away. The trans identity is impressed on that person, it's a stigma, like skin colour. So this group needs to be given priority. When they wear a skirt, jewellery, and make-up, they automatically put their identity on show, and are often insulted and attacked.

Many trans people face problems in daily life because the legal gender on their ID does not match their gender identity. Picking up a parcel at the post office, applying for a job, boarding a plane, or reporting a crime can all be occasions for harassment, unfounded suspicion, and even violence. Jean provides another example:

> Let's say someone is at the health centre and the nurse calls for a Leandro, when in fact she is dealing with Bruna. The trans woman has to correct her. Often trans people don't have the courage to get up in this situation, when they are called by their former name. If Bruna gets up when they call for Leandro, people will say, 'Oh, she's a tranny', and the bullying begins. So she keeps quiet and just leaves, meaning her right to healthcare is affected ...
>
> There is an institutional violence which works in a similar way to denying homosexual couples the right to marry. When trans people are denied the right to a name you are denying them their existence as a citizen. Imagine, if I identify as Lorrana, if that's the name my friends use, if my identity is feminine, yet my papers don't acknowledge that, then I'm an invisible citizen. I don't exist, legally. The citizen on paper doesn't exist. The true citizen doesn't have the state's backing. What a mess! So we need to correct this.
>
> That's why we created the law for gender identity, which ensures new official papers for transsexual, transvestite, and transgender people, according to their gender identity: all documents, from civil registration to educational diplomas, everything. When someone changes their gender identity, the state must change everything, without leaving any trace of the former identity, because it's the individual's decision whether to disclose that or not.

However, in most Latin American countries, transgender individuals cannot change their gender marker in public records and legal documents. Where countries do make provision for it, there are usually restrictions. Transgender Bolivians must attend an interview with a psychologist before new documents can be issued, while in Peru they are required to appear before a judge. Even in

Uruguay, which has some of the region's most progressive LGBT legislation, individuals who wish to change their gender in public documents must live in their 'acquired gender' for at least two years, and their application is subject to review by a 'multidisciplinary panel specializing in gender identity'. In Ecuador, the change is permitted, but the authorities leave a permanent record on the individual's documents (Chiam et al., 2017), which can be even more stigmatizing.

Only Argentina, Colombia, Mexico City, and – since 1 March 2018 – Brazil, allow name and gender reaffirmation in a fast, easy, and inexpensive manner. Argentina's Gender Identity Law of 2012 is considered the most advanced in the world. It ensures transgender equality and grants adults sex reassignment surgery and hormone therapy as a part of their public or private healthcare plans. The law also allows for changes to gender, image, or birth name on civil registries without the approval of a doctor or a judge.

In Chile, OTD has been campaigning for a new gender identity law. The project had some support from Michelle Bachelet's administration, but lawmakers wanted to maintain a requirement that transgender people would have to appear before a judge in order to change their name. Michel Riquelme objected to this:

> The Chilean government didn't want to listen to us. They were rigid on this point. So we held a protest against the governing Socialist Party. We met Senator [Isabel] Allende, who is president of the party and daughter of Salvador Allende, and we told her this had to change, that it shouldn't be up to a judge. It's as if we're in the 1960s! We were so insistent on that point that eventually the government gave in. It's going to be an administrative procedure for people of 18 years of age and above. We were the ones who pushed hardest for this change.

Jimena Norambuena explains the difference between a judicial and administrative procedure:

> Now you have to go to a lawyer, then the lawyer goes to the judge. And the judge is the one who decides. The idea behind turning it into an administrative procedure is that you go to a registry office to recognize your identity and it's done, that's it. It's like when a baby is born, you just take the paperwork from the doctor and go and register the name with the authorities. The law is a means of protecting the right to identity.

'The idea is that you should be in control of defining your identity,' emphasizes Michel. 'Not a judge, not a psychiatrist, not anyone else who tells you who you are or gives you permission.' At the time of writing, the details of the bill were under discussion at a parliamentary commission. Though the bill was tabled by his predecessor, President Sebastián Piñera has indicated that he will not block it, despite opposition from within his coalition.

Chilean trans rights activists at a Ni Una Menos march

The bill Jean Wyllys co-authored in 2013 goes beyond the issue of documentation to address the right to sex- and gender-changing procedures in the public health system:

> The [bill] also addresses the process of transsexualization [changing sex] or transgenerity [changing gender] in the health system. Hormone therapy, mastectomy for trans men, sexual reassignment surgery. Our project covers all of this and guarantees it for those who want it. There's no obligation; transgender and transsexual people only go through reassignment if they want to. And if they make this decision, they will have access to it through the healthcare system. We want to have these rights guaranteed by law. In the meantime, we have some initiatives with hospitals who offer this service – not all do. I think there are maybe three in Brazil.

In fact, sex reassignment procedures have been available in Brazil's public health system (SUS) since 2008. There are currently nine medical centres in the national health system offering free hormone therapy and psychological support for trans people before and after surgery, and five health centres offering sex reassignment procedures such as mastectomy (Rossi and Novaes, 2015).

As with the gay marriage bill, there has not been sufficient support in Congress to pass the bill into law. Religious fundamentalists in Congress immediately opposed it, claiming it would allow homosexual parents who adopted children to force them to change gender. However, on 1 March 2018, Brazil's

Supreme Court unanimously approved name and gender change directly in the notary's office, with no need for a judicial decision, sex reassignment surgery, hormone therapy, or medical reports. This is a historic victory for Brazil's transgender community.

Changing the culture

The fight against prejudice is not just legal or political: it is cultural. As Jean Wyllys says, 'We have a huge and complex task ahead of us, because homophobia and transphobia are cultural and institutional. And they can't be challenged by the law alone; laws are important but there are other ways of challenging them which laws don't cover. Sometimes the law is just worthless paper.'

Wyllys's own rise to prominence in Brazil was itself part of an attempt to counter cultural homophobia:

> After becoming a university professor, still in Bahia, I went to Rio in 2004/05 to take part in the TV programme *Big Brother*, which has a phenomenal following in Brazil. *Big Brother Brasil* (BBB) became my PhD subject; I intended to study it. I have a degree in communication and journalism and did a master's in language and linguistics. I wanted to study this programme, make a kind of ethnography of it. So I applied, and to my surprise I was selected. I moved to Rio de Janeiro and the programme made me famous.
>
> There was a whole agenda of issues to present – criminalizing homophobia, gender identities – which had never been addressed. But I managed to do it, because on *Big Brother* I came across as a charismatic, charming figure in the cultural world. I was an openly gay man, and my presence on the programme generated a lot of debate amongst the families who watched it – it was a huge audience. I posed people a question they had never had to consider before, of what it meant to have a gay man in the house, on the TV, people following his life. And at the same time, I was a university lecturer, with a cultural background, and I came from Bahia. I had a multifaceted identity, which was very important for the LGBT movement. When the programme finished, I was seen as a man who gave impetus to the movement in Brazil, supported it. The LGBT groups at the time were united in support of me. It was a mutual relationship, in that my presence strengthened the movement outside, and the movement mobilized to keep me on the programme.

His participation was an enormous success. Not only did he win the competition, he was subsequently offered further work on Rede Globo, Brazil's largest and most popular TV network. Eventually he went into politics and remains an influential public figure:

> The preferred profile for these programmes is never black, gay, or a woman. Until I won I think only one woman had ever won. She didn't

win because of her gender but because of her class: she was poor. In general, men win. Then, in the fifth contest, the winner was a gay man, an activist, with completely different characteristics. I didn't expect to win, but I was conscious of where I was. I was a lecturer in communications theory, so I understood that it was an unparalleled opportunity to influence the Brazilian public's mentality, to interfere with their imagination. I was aware of this. And so my behaviour on *Big Brother* was completely honest and truthful, but at the same time political and conscious of what I wanted to achieve. This was why it was so important, and, modesty aside, it was a turning point for the LGBT movement in Brazil. I don't mean that to sound arrogant at all, that's just what happened.

I signed a contract with Globo and stayed on working with them. I took a step back from grassroots activism for a while, but I remained engaged with LGBT issues because I was invited to write a column in *G Magazine*, which was the only LGBT magazine in Brazil. In 1995, the magazine *Sui-Generis* was launched, which was a milestone for my generation. It was a magazine aimed at the LGBT community. There was no nudity, but it was a magazine with an obvious gay identity. Very little trans or lesbian identity, the face of the movement was still macho, of the male gender. Men were still at the fore, even within the movement.

Then, after a while working at Globo, I started to miss the more grassroots activism. I resigned from the channel and went back to university, that being a place where I was able to act politically in a clearer, less restricted way, where I could be connected to the movement, and express political opinions which wouldn't cause me any trouble at work.

I felt the need to be involved in something more collective, more organized. I had never belonged to any group, but I decided then to join a political party. Three different people had invited me to stand as a candidate – ACM Neto [from the right-wing party PFL, now called DEM] in 2006, then Aloizio Mercadante [from the left-of-centre Workers' Party, PT] in 2008, and Heloisa Helena [from the socialist party PSOL] at the end of that year. I thought, well, there's a message there. Perhaps this would be the way to make use of the popularity the programme gave me, which I couldn't actually get away from. Even as the years went by, people didn't forget me, I was still getting recognized in the street. I am not an actor, a model, or a singer. How could I make the most of this opportunity, just doing what I had always done? And so I decided to join PSOL and became a candidate in 2010. That's when I became a political representative in parliament.

In Argentina, it occurred to Edgardo Fernández that he could use tango – as a national cultural symbol – to promote social and cultural change:

> Why did I choose tango? I've been an activist in gay rights organizations for 33 years, since the end of the last dictatorship here. I saw an opportunity to use tango to do something different. I saw that nobody was using

dance to try and effect social and political change anywhere, and I had the idea of using dance to try and send messages. That was the reason for my interest in starting to give classes in different places and especially in spaces of activism.

Nobody involved in tango wanted to get mixed up in social and political activism. When I started giving classes, I saw the possibility of using them as spaces where students could mingle and get interested in activism, as well as learn to dance. I wanted to interest them in the idea of social change. And then people began to come forward and get involved.

Edgardo dances what is known as queer tango, as he explains:

Queer tango is a different way of teaching, learning, dancing, and behaving in the realm of tango. This style started up in Buenos Aires in around 1997. In those days, tango was completely misogynistic. Women were in a situation of total inferiority in all areas of tango and the teaching of it was completely sectionalized. Everyone had their role and their place. The same roles that men and women had in society were the roles they had in the *milongas* [tango dance salons] and tango classes. What happened then was that tango started appearing in places frequented by the gay community, as gays and lesbians wanted to dance tango but couldn't fulfil the traditional roles because they were two men or two women. So, without ever explicitly setting out to do so, they began to change the rules of tango in these small places, and this had a knock-on effect on the wider tango culture. Currently, you can dance queer tango in about 35 countries. There are large and small queer *milongas* in Buenos Aires, attended by gay and straight alike. Now it's mixed. There are also 'free' *milongas* which are not queer tango as such, but follow the same rules. But the very conservative, traditional *milongas* are still there.

The most fundamental change concerns the role of the woman. For example, at a traditional *milonga* – let's say a big one with 300 people – if there are 200 women, a woman might sit waiting for six to eight hours – all night, basically – for a man to ask her to dance. Perhaps nobody wants to dance with her and she goes home without dancing at all. She has no power of decision; she can't ask anyone herself. That's why a lot of the foreign women pay a taxi dancer to dance with them at traditional *milongas*, so they don't risk spending the whole night waiting. But at the queer *milongas*, she never waits. She can just pull a guy out to dance, and the men do the same with the women. Everyone dances and nobody spends the night waiting.

When we teach tango, we never talk about men or women. We talk about the 'Lead' and the 'Follow'. We never say that the roles are fixed, but that they can change. We also never say that anyone should obey what the other person does, but that both should make suggestions.

While presence on TV and in a popular art such as tango is important, LGBT campaigners emphasize the importance of education. Educated people tend to be more tolerant of difference and Latin America is no exception to this (Seligson and Moreno Morales, 2010). There is an urgent need for better programmes of sex education, even in the region's more developed countries. According to the United Nations Population Fund, comprehensive sex education 'enables young people to protect their health, wellbeing and dignity' as well as advancing 'gender equality and the rights and empowerment of young people' (UNFPA, n.d.). But religion, particularly Catholicism, continues to influence sex education programmes, meaning that often the approach is either simply biological, or explicitly religious, looking at sexuality only within the context of marriage (Frayssinet, 2014).

In such a climate, it is scarcely surprising that it is taboo to discuss LGBT issues at school. Attempts to do so have met with angry protests, as we have seen in the cases of Peru, Colombia, and Costa Rica. In Brazil the PT government launched Brasil sem Homofobia in 2004. As part of this, in 2011 the government of Dilma Rousseff developed a programme called Escola sem Homofobia (School without Homophobia), in partnership with the Brazilian Association of Lesbians, Gays, Bisexuals, and Transsexuals (ABLGBT), which consisted of educational videos and materials to be distributed to schoolteachers and staff, and other education professionals. The material was produced with the participation of teaching professionals and civil society groups, and received backing from UNESCO.

The project was attacked by the religious caucus in Congress, which branded it the 'Gay Primer' or 'Gay Kit' and claimed that it encouraged homosexuality, promiscuity, and even paedophilia. Faced with this uproar, the Rousseff administration shamefully caved in and cancelled the programme. The protesters went on to attack the Ministry of Health's harm reduction programme, which was aimed at getting drug users to consume safely and practise safe sex, involving the distribution of syringes and condoms. Former army captain and far-right congressman Jair Bolsonaro was one of the architects of this campaign, as Jean Wyllys recalls:

> President Dilma initiated a project through André Lázaro, the executive secretary of the human rights ministry. It was called Escola sem Homofobia, and it aimed to target homophobic bullying in schools, using educational material to be distributed amongst teachers and staff, to deal with issues related to gender and sexuality in schools. These were government materials, nothing to do with parliament.
>
> The project was drawn up by the Executive of the PT administration. But that crook [Bolsonaro], he spreads lies on social media, saying I was behind the project. I had nothing to do with it. I am not a member of the PT. And so it began. I get so angry talking about it because there are so many stupid, hateful people who reproduced the lie, spreading it further and putting forward the idea of pamphlets which would turn people

gay. This is what happened in Brazil, a mass wave of hysteria, based on a lie. He took the materials from the harm reduction programme of the Ministry of Health and claimed they were in the schools project. People believed it and this mass hysteria started. I am so angry about this. I hope that one day the damage can be fixed.

The Catholic Church has historically been anti-LGBT and consistently opposes legislation promoting LGBT rights. Jean Wyllys describes his own experience as a young boy becoming aware of his sexuality, looking to the Church as a potential sanctuary from oppression at home and in the community:

> When I started to have feelings of desire, I was in the Catholic Church, working against oppression, becoming an activist, reflecting on the choices and social injustices of which I was also a victim. I was born into poverty: my parents were poor, and we lived in a poor neighbourhood. But I started to ask myself why the Church didn't deal with these issues, the oppression of people like me. There were several others like me in the Church; it was full of boys who went there to escape from violent homophobia at home. It was also to conceal their homosexuality, because there was a perception you couldn't be gay and be in the Church.
>
> At 14, when I was preparing to sit the entrance exam for a boarding school called Fundação José Carvalho, I asked the bishop, Dom Jaime, why the Church didn't concern itself with gay people, with LGBT people, though that term didn't exist then. He told me that was a question that could only be made by someone who was losing their faith. Wow, I thought, maybe that's it, then. I can't question the Church, which says it is against oppression and for love; it's God's representative on earth, God's goodness, God's justice. I was condemned to being what I was, what I felt I was. Homophobia in the Church is cloaked, silenced. No one tackles it. We were Church boys, we weren't gay. When we got called gay elsewhere, someone would say, 'No, they're not gay, they're in the Church.' This is how homophobia worked in the Church. But when he said that to me I realized it was time to leave the Catholic Church.

There has been a significant change in tone from the Vatican under Pope Francis in recent years, to the point where the pontiff allegedly told Juan Carlos Cruz, a survivor of abuse by a priest in Chile, 'It doesn't matter that you're gay. God made you that way and that is the way he wants you to be, and I don't mind ... you have to be happy with who you are.'

However, this has not translated into substantive change in the behaviour of Catholic clergy towards the LGBT community in Latin America. The Church continues to put pressure on governments not to pass pro-LGBT legislation and mobilizes believers to demonstrate when it feels its values are under threat. This opposition is at least equalled, if not surpassed, by the region's Evangelical churches, which are growing rapidly, particularly in Brazil, where

Catholics are expected to be a religious minority by 2030 (Pulliam Bailey, 2017). These Evangelical churches are in general extremely vociferous in their rejection of sexual diversity, and surveys by the Pew Research Center suggest that Latin American Protestants are even more conservative on social issues than practising Catholics.

Prospects

What are the prospects for the future?

Some people we spoke to were pessimistic, at least in the short term. With conservative governments coming back into power across the region, there is concern not only that many of the legislative gains the LGBT community has fought so hard for in recent years will be reversed, but also that, with an increase in aggressive homophobic and transphobic rhetoric, violence against the LGBT community will increase further. These concerns are particularly acute in Brazil, where the Temer administration scrapped all funding for public policies against homophobia in 2017. At the time of writing, Jair Bolsonaro is one of the front runners for the 2018 presidential elections. Bolsonaro is a man who has, in a June 2011 interview in *Playboy*, declared that he would rather have his son die in a road accident 'than show up with a man, because then he would have died for me anyway', and that parents of gay children are responsible for their sexuality because they 'didn't beat them enough'. Jean Wyllys thinks people should prepare to resist:

> I hope things improve, because I'm a hopeful person, but more than that I'm an activist. I fight for better days. The mood in Latin America is not good. What's happened in Argentina, Venezuela, what's going on in Bolivia and Brazil, is a move to the right, with a growth in power of the far right, who want to curb not only the rights of workers and the welfare state – the fragile welfare states we have in Latin America – but also our freedoms. I always hope for the best, but we also have to be ready for the worst. Brazil has suffered a coup, a coup against Brazilian democracy. We're governed by a criminal organization which defends the interests of the market, which is why its members haven't been arrested yet. They defend the interests of the wealthiest people in our society: millionaires, the elites, large commercial corporations. They all want to control wealth and practically enslave workers and the poor, through a pension reform and economic policies which will pass on to us the cost of the economic crisis which they have created, so they suffer no losses. We're going through a very difficult moment in Brazil, and our rights are being affected. I hope for the best, but I'm prepared for the worst. Because the worst may well come, and people must know that.
>
> What we must hope for in the future is resistance. That's down to us in the LGBT community, other marginalized groups, black people, women, people on the left, people who want an inclusive world, a plural world,

a diverse world, with social justice. We must resist, because fascists are growing in strength the world over. Fascists don't want diversity. Fascists are stupid; their thinking is simple, they oppose the complexities of life.

Even on the left, understanding of LGBT concerns can never be taken for granted. While the 'pink tide' administrations of the Kirchners in Argentina (2003–15), the Frente Amplio in Uruguay (2004–present), and the Workers' Party in Brazil (2003–16) were broadly sympathetic, elsewhere things have been less clear, despite legislative advances. In 2010, Bolivian president Evo Morales infamously linked homosexuality to the consumption of chicken raised with growth hormones. Little or no progress was made on LGBT rights in Venezuela under Hugo Chávez, while his successor Nicolás Maduro has a history of homophobic comments, including insinuations about the sexuality of Henrique Capriles, his opponent in the 2013 elections. In Ecuador, Rafael Correa repeatedly voiced opposition to same-sex marriage and suggested that gender identity laws were a ruse to allow homosexuals to marry.

Machismo is not the exclusive preserve of the right, and nor is the right uniformly anti-LGBT. When the Argentine judge Gabriela Seijas permitted a gay couple in Buenos Aires to marry in 2009 – a move which paved the way for proper legislation the following year – Mauricio Macri (now the country's president, then mayor of Buenos Aires) opted not to appeal the ruling. 'The world is going in this direction,' he said in a video he posted online (La Nación, 2009). 'We have to coexist and accept this reality. I hope they'll be happy.' Macri has not always been consistent on this issue, and in 2017 he was rebuked by Amnesty International for tabling a controversial bill on religious freedom. The bill will establish the right to conscientious objection to judicial rulings on religious and/or moral grounds, including for civil servants. Critics argue that such a law would put same-sex marriage in jeopardy (El Destape, 2017). Nonetheless, Edgardo Fernández is confident that the changes in Argentina are irreversible:

> Our biggest achievements have happened over the last few years, under the governments of Néstor and Cristina Kirchner. However, there were also very important achievements before that, though they were smaller. I think, in the current social and political context, there's no going back. There's been a big political shift with the change of government, but on these sorts of issues the new administration is on the same page as the last one. Particularly in Buenos Aires, it's been the same politics for years.

Despite the present rise of conservative administrations and ideologies, it is hard to imagine that there will be serious long-term reversals on LGBT issues, even if there are some short-term setbacks. There has been a global revolution in LGBT rights over the last three or four decades and Latin America has been very much a part of this. This trend is likely to continue, with research showing that younger generations in the region are generally (with the exception of the Central

American countries) more tolerant of sexual diversity. Assuming that education continues to expand in the region, tolerance towards sexual minorities should increase over time (Seligson and Moreno Morales, 2010). Though there may be dangerous currents to navigate, the rainbow tide seems set to move forward.

About the author

Ali Rocha is a news and documentary producer who has contributed to the BBC, Channel Four, ITN, Al Jazeera English, and SBS (Australia) on their Brazil coverage since 2003. She is a human rights activist and researches police violence in Brazil. She now runs social media group Brazil Matters, aimed at drawing international attention to social, environmental, and human rights issues in Brazil.

Interviews

Edgardo Fernández (tango teacher and LGBT activist): interviewed in Buenos Aires on 7 November 2016 by Nina Meghji. Translated by Dominic Power.

Michel Riquelme and **Jimena Norambuena** (OTD Chile): interviewed in Santiago de Chile on 24 November 2016 by Nina Meghji. Transcribed by Nina Meghji.

Jean Wyllys (PSOL deputy for Rio de Janeiro): interviewed in Rio de Janeiro on 8 December 2016 by Ali Rocha. Translated by Jennifer Alexander and Hugo Moss.

References

NB: All web references were checked and still available in May/June 2018 unless otherwise stated. All references are listed, with web-links, on the page for this chapter on the Voices website www.vola.org.uk

Al Jazeera (2017) 'Chile's Bachelet sends gay marriage bill to congress', 28 August, <https://www.aljazeera.com/news/2017/08/chile-bachelet-sends-gay-marriage-bill-congress-170828174326501.html>

Ativistas Independentes (2017) 'Judith Butler, a propagadora de odio', 10 November, <https://www.facebook.com/AtivistasIndependentes/videos/299008317261240/>

BBC (2017) 'Chile leader sends gay marriage bill to congress', 29 August, <https://www.bbc.co.uk/news/world-latin-america-41081246>

Carroll, A. and Mendos, L. R. (2017) *State Sponsored Homophobia 2017: A World Survey of Sexual Orientation Laws 2017: Criminalisation, Protection and Recognition*, International Lesbian, Gay, Bisexual, Trans and Intersex Association (ILGA), Geneva, May, <https://ilga.org/downloads/2017/ILGA_State_Sponsored_Homophobia_2017_WEB.pdf>

Chiam, Z., Duffy, S. and González Gil, M. (2017) *Trans Legal Mapping Report 2017: Recognition before the Law*, ILGA, Geneva, November, <https://ilga.org/downloads/ILGA_Trans_Legal_Mapping_Report_2017_ENG.pdf>

Cowie, S. (2018) 'Violent deaths of LGBT people in Brazil hit all-time high', *The Guardian*, 22 January, <https://www.theguardian.com/world/2018/jan/22/brazil-lgbt-violence-deaths-all-time-high-new-research>

El Destape (2017) 'El controvertido proyecto de Macri que pone en peligro al matrimonio igualitario', <https://www.eldestapeweb.com/el-controvertido-proyecto-macri-que-pone-peligro-al-matrimonio-igualitario-n30376>

Frayssinet, F. (2014) 'Comprehensive sex education: a pending task in Latin America', Inter Press Service, <http://www.ipsnews.net/2014/09/comprehensive-sex-education-a-pending-task-in-latin-america>

Ghoshal, N. (2018) 'For LGBT rights, 2018 will be the year of the courts', Human Rights Watch, <https://www.hrw.org/news/2018/01/24/lgbt-rights-2018-will-be-year-courts>

Giraldo, I. (2017) 'The "gender ideology" menace and the rejection of the peace agreement in Colombia', Discover Society, <https://discoversociety.org/2017/12/06/the-gender-ideology-menace-and-the-rejection-of-the-peace-agreement-in-colombia>

Jenkin, M. (2016) 'Electric shocks, rape and submersion: "gay cures" and the fight to end them', *The Guardian*, 9 February, <https://www.theguardian.com/global-development-professionals-network/2016/feb/09/electrocution-and-submersion-gay-cures-and-the-fight-to-end-them>

La Nación (2009) video fragment of interview with Mauricio Macri <https://www.youtube.com/watch?v=xzsT2ZEm5lg>

Lindner, J. (2017) 'CCJ aprova reconhecimento de união estável e casamento entre pessoas do mesmo sexo', *Estadão*, 3 May, <http://brasil.estadao.com.br/noticias/geral,ccj-aprova-projeto-que-reconhece-uniao-estavel-entre-pessoas-do-mesmo-sexo,70001761799>

Moloney, A. (2018) 'FEATURE – Gays in Ecuador raped and beaten in rehab clinics to "cure" them', Reuters, 8 February, <https://www.reuters.com/article/ecuador-lgbt-rights/feature-gays-in-ecuador-raped-and-beaten-in-rehab-clinics-to-cure-them-idUSL8N1P03QO>

Phillips, D. (2017) 'Brazilian judge approves "gay conversion therapy", sparking national outrage', *The Guardian*, 19 September, <https://www.theguardian.com/world/2017/sep/19/brazilian-judge-approves-gay-conversion-therapy>

Pulliam Bailey, S. (2017) 'How the prosperity gospel is sparking a major change in predominantly Catholic Brazil', *Washington Post*, 29 October, <https://www.washingtonpost.com/local/social-issues/forget-the-germans-this-is-where-the-protestant-reformation-debates-are-happening-now/2017/10/29/7723af30-b807-11e7-be94-fabb0f1e9ffb_story.html?utm_term=.9f16dfaae568>

Rossi, M. and Novaes, M. (2015) 'Os direitos básicos aos quais transexuais e travestis não têm acesso', *El País Brasil*, 28 August, <https://brasil.elpais.com/brasil/2015/08/28/politica/1440778259_469516.html>

Seligson, M. and Moreno Morales, D. (2010) 'Gay in the Americas', *Americas Quarterly*, <http://www.americasquarterly.org/node/1301>

Stewart, K. (2017) 'School books with section on gender equality cause uproar in Peru', VICE News, <https://news.vice.com/en_us/article/4349dd/school-books-with-section-on-gender-equality-cause-uproar-in-peru>

Strobl, T. (2017) 'Brazil as world LGBT murder capital and Rio's place in the data', RioOnWatch, <http://www.rioonwatch.org/?p=37249>

Transgender Europe (2016) 'Transgender Day of Visibility 2016 – Trans Murder Monitoring update', <https://tgeu.org/transgender-day-of-visibility-2016-trans-murder-monitoring-update>

UN OHCHR (UN Office of the High Commissioner for Human Rights) (2016) '"Pathologization – Being lesbian, gay, bisexual and/or trans is not an illness", for International Day against Homophobia, Transphobia and Biphobia', 17 May, <http://www.ohchr.org/EN/NewsEvents/Pages/DisplayNews.aspx?NewsID=19956&LangID=E>

UNFPA (United Nations Population Fund) (n.d.) 'Comprehensive sexuality education', <https://www.unfpa.org/comprehensive-sexuality-education>

CHAPTER 4
The student revolution

Emily Gregg

Abstract

Latin American students have organized some of the largest mass mobilizations in the region's recent history, calling for a free, universal system of high-quality education, from primary school to university. The students see this as key to ending the reproduction of inequality that continues to plague their societies. The Chilean movement has been particularly strong and has influenced others in Brazil and elsewhere. Meanwhile, a new popular university in Honduras aims to equip students with the skills traditional education in the country fails to provide.

> **'To be young and not a revolutionary is a biological contradiction.'**
> **– Salvador Allende**

Student movements have played a vital role in the social, cultural, and political history of Latin America. In his influential work *Ariel*, published in 1900, the Uruguayan essayist José Enrique Rodó called on Latin American youth to create a unique regional culture, free from outside interference, while the early 20th-century Argentine intellectual José Ingenieros wrote that 'the university ought to be a school of social and political action'. As early as 1918, students were demanding democratic universities open to all, and they went on to take a prominent role in denouncing 'dollar diplomacy' and the United States' repeated interventions in Latin American affairs (Pensado, 2012). As in North America and Europe, student movements were particularly effervescent during the 1960s, resulting in sometimes violent confrontations with state security forces. This unrest came to a head in tragic circumstances in Mexico City in 1968, when around 300 students and their supporters were killed by the military and police at the Plaza de las Tres Culturas de Tlatelolco. Just 10 days before the opening of the Olympic Games, the massacre was an attempt to crush the student-led resistance to the authoritarian regime of the Institutional Revolutionary Party (PRI).

In the same year came the murder by Brazilian police of the secondary school student Edson Luís de Lima Souto during a protest led to the March of the One Hundred Thousand in Rio de Janeiro, until then the biggest demonstration against the country's long military dictatorship (1964–85). In the following months, the military arrested thousands of students and at the end

http://dx.doi.org/10.3362/9781909014213.004

of the year passed the infamous Institutional Act No. 5, which shut down Congress, censored the press and ramped up the repression, students being one of the main targets. In Chile, less than a month after the coup d'état in 1973, the junta embarked upon an extensive purge of the universities, appointing serving military officers as rectors. Thousands of professors and students were expelled and those who remained were encouraged to inform on anyone they suspected of leftist sympathies. Entire academic disciplines – such as sociology and political science – were abolished and replaced with technical courses. Ultimately, around 15 per cent of all those detained by the Chilean military dictatorship (1973–90) were students (Comisión Nacional sobre Prisión Política y Tortura, 2005). In neighbouring Argentina, nearly 60 per cent of the estimated 30,000 who disappeared during the 1976–83 dictatorship were young people aged from 21 to 30, and 21 per cent of that total were students (Cultura Argentina, 2015). One of the regime's most notorious crimes was the 1976 abduction, detention, and torture of 10 secondary school students aged from 16 to 18 in what became known as the Night of the Pencils. Six of them were never seen again. They belonged to the secondary school students' union and had campaigned for a discounted bus pass the previous year.

All over Latin America, school and university students, teachers, professors, and other education professionals have been systematically and repeatedly targeted by authoritarian and military regimes. Even today, although the generals are no longer in power, the relationship between Latin American elites and the education sector remains an uneasy one. With some justification, the Latin American ruling classes perceive educational institutions as hotbeds for ideas that threaten their entrenched wealth and power, and they continue to resist the introduction of a comprehensive, high-quality system of education available to all regardless of their socioeconomic background. As a result, vast discrepancies in quality and access persist in education systems throughout the region.

In recent years, Latin American students have mobilized repeatedly, leading some of the largest mass demonstrations the region has seen since the end of the dictatorship period. The movements vary according to local context, but underpinning them is the demand for free, universal, and high-quality systems of education. While the students have obtained some significant concessions, this principal demand remains unsatisfied. Nonetheless, they have inspired a generation, contributed to the re-politicization of societies still traumatized by dictatorships, and put the issue of education firmly on the political agenda.

Secondary school movements in Chile and Brazil

Chile's current model of education is very much a legacy of the military dictatorship. Pinochet's regime brought an end to free, universal public education, replacing it with a model of 'voucher schools' based on proposals by the radical laissez-faire economist Milton Friedman. Under this system, students and their families receive vouchers from the government, which they can use either to access education at a state school or contribute to the fees charged by a private school. Private schools retained control over enrolment and could charge whatever they liked, whereas state schools could not charge at all and were required to admit anyone who applied. The basic principles of this system remained in place until 2007, when the Chilean government increased the value of the vouchers for children from low-income families. Most students attend these voucher schools (*colegios subvencionados*); fewer than half study in state schools (*colegios públicos*); and a small minority attend elite private schools (*colegios privados*), which are outside the voucher system and paid for entirely by students' families.

Proponents of the voucher system argue it has been a success. According to the Organisation for Economic Co-operation and Development (OECD), Chile leads Latin America in terms of educational attainment. Access to university has expanded in recent years, with 29 per cent having completed a university degree, not far short of the average of 32 per cent for OECD countries (Arsht and Sanchez Zinny, 2014). However, this does not tell the whole story. While Chile's economy grew by 4 per cent from 2001 to 2011, over a quarter of Chileans believed that education had deteriorated in that time and almost half believed that it had stagnated (Long, 2011). OECD research also shows that out of 65 countries, Chile's education system is the second most segregated by social class, behind only Peru. Critics argue that students from wealthy families receive the best education in the region, while those from poorer families attend underfunded and decrepit schools from which they have little chance of being admitted to university.

In 2006, Chilean secondary school students mobilized in what became known as the Penguin Revolution, or the *pingüinazo*, so called for the students' black-and-white uniforms. The movement began in Santiago but spread throughout the country, with the size of the demonstrations taking not only the authorities but the students themselves by surprise. At its height, the movement managed to shut down more than 400 schools and brought hundreds of thousands of students – of an average age of just 16 – to the streets. Their main short-term demands were the abolition of fees for university admission tests and a year-round bus pass. But beyond that, the movement was the first mass expression of serious discontent with the Chilean model of education. Students pointed to the acute inequality between schools in different areas and between the state, voucher, and fully private schools, arguing that the model had effectively created a two-tier system. Elite private schools and voucher schools in wealthy areas delivered high-quality education, while voucher schools in poorer areas and particularly the state schools provided not only a far inferior quality of education, but sometimes very precarious conditions for students and teachers. At the time of the *pingüinazo*, 50 per cent of the country's students routinely failed the university entrance exam – though the failure rate was less than 10 per cent in the private schools (Franklin, 2006).

At the time of our interview, Marcelo Correa was the president of the National Coordination of Secondary School Students (CONES). He explains how and why he became involved in the student movement:

> When it comes to schools, the first thing you have to understand is that there is a lot of competition between them for student enrolment. Our system has a model of financing by attendance. This means that the higher the student attendance, the more money the school receives. More students, more money. And there's been no regulation of those who sponsor the public-private and the fully private schools ... We wanted to change the way the state finances these schools. Currently, it provides the resources to local government, where money gets lost.
>
> In the areas with elite schools, it's clear that the students will end up going to university, while in schools in poorer communities on the outskirts of the cities, it's clear they won't, because they don't have the financial means. This means that the ones who go to university are always the children of businesspeople, for example, whereas poor students, or those from poorer areas, are not even taught practical skills. They're supposedly taught the same thing as students in richer areas, but in practice they're not really taught anything at all. There is a phrase – 'nini' – which refers to young people who neither work nor study. There are 500,000 of them in Chile, mostly from the working class and the lower middle class. So our biggest problem is inequality.
>
> We've got a proposal going through the Chilean Congress now, which would bring an end to the municipal model of education. In other words, control of schools would no longer be the responsibility of the local municipality but there would be an independent body, the National Education Service, to oversee the schools and distribute resources. This is something that students have been fighting for over the last 16 years in Chile, and this year we've made a public demand in Congress.
>
> Currently, the way it works is this: the local authorities in Providencia [a district in Santiago] control the state schools in Providencia, in terms of both organization and funding. We want there to be a National Education Service, with smaller, local education services beneath it. These local education services would administer many districts and distribute the money according to the needs of each, thus reducing the inequality between schools in, for example, Las Condes, which is Santiago's richest area, and Renca, which is the poorest.

Chilean students have also complained about a lack of arts and humanities on school curricula and a silencing of debate. According to Marcelo, this is a legacy of the dictatorship:

> My school is a traditional, conservative school. It's famous because it was the school for the children of the soldiers who fought in the War of

the Pacific. For that reason, the Chilean State gave the school a gift – the Iglesia de la Gratitud Nacional [Church of National Gratitude]. Five days after the military coup in 1973, there was a ceremony at the church, recognizing the contribution of the Catholic Church to the country. Effectively, it recognized the Catholic Church as the state religion, although the Chilean State is supposedly secular. The school is now one of the public-private schools and belongs to the Salesian order of the Catholic Church. The mentality is very narrow-minded. Throughout its history it has denied the possibility of opening up spaces for political discussion; everything's very strict, very traditional, and you really feel that pressure on both the students and teachers.

In general, in Chile, when you see someone talking about politics, you assume they're corrupt. This attitude was something that helped the dictatorship, at the time. People couldn't be politically active, people couldn't think differently from the regime. This has continued, generation after generation, and persists today. The schools still follow the same doctrine. They don't want students to think or criticize. The students don't have much freedom. At my school it's worse, because it has this religious element. You can't talk about politics or openly express an opinion without them hauling you in to say, 'You shouldn't be doing this. We don't want to see this.' Especially the school directors. They believe that if lots of students were to think like this, then it would change their whole model of indoctrination.

Marcelo joined the Communist Party, which has a considerable following among students and young people in Chile and played a significant role in the student protests:

I became involved with the Communist Party because it was the only political party that was active among young people. It gave genuine political training and education to all those who joined. That was the main reason. They taught us political theory, Marxist analysis, what it means to involve yourself politically, about other parties, ideology, economics. In the Latin American context, I think the Chilean Communist Party provides some of the best training and education. There was also a kind of a mystique about becoming involved in politics which appealed to me – I felt like I had to get involved.

In Brazil, students have protested against similar suppression of social and political discussion. Since 2015, a number of laws have been proposed to reflect the demands of the Escola Sem Partido (Schools Without Politics) movement. Miguel Nagib, one of the architects of Escola Sem Partido, states that the aim is to prevent 'political and ideological indoctrination in the classroom' on the one hand, while, on the other, upholding 'parents' rights over the moral and religious education of their children' (Santana, 2016). Again, this insistence on keeping politics out of education is an echo of the dictatorship period.

Critics of the movement argue that what it proposes are 'gag laws' restricting students' freedom of thought and expression, while the United Nations has labelled them censorship.

Camila Lanes was president of the Brazilian Union of Secondary School Students (UBES) from 2015 to 2017. She became involved in the student movement after becoming her class representative on her school's student council. Here she describes her opposition to the gag law:

Camila Lanes

© Yuri Salvador/UBES 2015

The gag law is the law of the Escola Sem Partido movement. We call it the gag law because I see no problem with students understanding how the political system works and how political parties work. Their attempts to deny us this just show exactly what their plans are for young people – in other words we, as state secondary school students, have no right to understand how the constitution should work, how the political system inside Congress works. Why? Why should only one group of people have the right to know these things? It aims to put an end to the 'indoctrination' going on in classrooms, even though nowadays schools can barely provide school meals, the classrooms are massively overcrowded ... so this law really isn't focusing on what needs to be addressed, is it?

In 2015–16 the Brazilian government consulted the public on the creation of a new National Curriculum (BNCC). However, since the impeachment of Dilma Rousseff in 2016, government education policy has been increasingly centralized, as Camila describes:

The BNCC is a programme to which more than 12 million Brazilians contributed, both via an online platform and in mass public meetings that were almost like open-air conferences for whole towns. People could make suggestions about all aspects of education, not just students and teachers, but other employees and whoever else wanted to contribute to the school community. This was all thrown out as soon as [Michel] Temer came to power.

In Dilma's government, there was the National Education Plan, which was put together through meetings and wide-ranging discussions and debates with the sectors of society it affected. The current reforms [since 2016] were dreamt up by people who don't know anything about the problems and needs of students. They go against the previous programme completely and are just being imposed on us. The National Education Plan was approved by CONAE, the National Conference on Education. I was there as a delegate, representing the state of Paraná.

It was an enormous conference, with four days of voting, four days of studying all the issues, amendments, and contributions. It was an epic moment for the education movement in this country. The Plan set several targets, so the Brazilian education system can reach the standards we are demanding. Brazil is an immense country, and we're not going to be able to change the reality of 50 million secondary school students overnight with just an interim measure. There are schools in Brazil that are made of tin, schools that are just mud huts, schools raised on stilts above water, schools that don't have toilets. And here I'm just touching upon structural issues, never mind the whole host of other problems schools have.

To the surprise of some, one of the sectors of Brazilian society that has been most active in opposition to the Temer administration has been secondary school students. In the Primavera Secundarista (Secondary School Students' Spring) of 2016, students all over Brazil held demonstrations and occupied schools and universities, to protest school closures and gag laws, as well as PEC 241, a controversial constitutional amendment that has frozen spending in key areas – including education – for 20 years, adjusting only for inflation. The movement's origins go back to 2015 and the decision of São Paulo state governor Geraldo Alckmin to reorganize schools in the state, pointing to a lack of funding, chronic truancy, and empty classrooms. The reorganization would have resulted in the closure of 190 schools. Camila describes what happened:

> They said that the classrooms were empty, so it was better to close down those schools and reallocate the students to others, rather than investing money in the schools so that students came back to study there. So the students started to occupy the schools that were going to be closed down. That was how the whole school occupation movement began. Last year [2015] 220 schools were occupied in São Paulo. The students showed the whole of Brazil that the struggle was worth it. School reorganizations happen all over Brazil every year, but people outside the schools don't realize it's going on. What happened in São Paulo led students in various other states to start doing the same thing. There were occupations in Goiás, Minas Gerais, Rio de Janeiro, Rio Grande do Sul, Pernambuco, and Ceará. Each of the occupations had its own motivation. In Goiás it was against the militarization of schools; in Rio Grande do Sul it was against closures; in Ceará and Rio de Janeiro it was to protest the gag law.
>
> An occupation isn't just about sleeping at school, closing down the building, and stopping the classes. As students, we're supposed to go to school 200 days of the year and everything should be ready for us – the desks already set out in rows; the food – when we actually have it – already prepared; the lessons planned. Despite all the problems, everything is set up and ready for us. What all this means is that the student – who is the school's most important figure – doesn't participate

Students occupy the legislative assembly in São Paulo to protest embezzlement of funding for school meals.

at all in this process. But when we occupy schools, this isn't the case. We clean, we do repairs, we paint, we give classes, we look after the building, we take care of security. Most parents don't know their children's schools well. Unfortunately, this is a tradition in this country, but one that we tried, and managed, to change. More than 1,174 schools were occupied. The occupations were criminalized and attacked, and there were some political parties who came out against them, but there was great resistance on our part.

In both Chile and Brazil, the secondary school movements faced tough repression from the police – something which only galvanized the movements further and won the students widespread popular sympathy. As Camila says:

In every single demonstration the police targeted us. There was barely a single occasion in São Paulo where students went out onto the streets to protest and weren't attacked by the police. It was very rare. I've witnessed fights between parents and children in the street – a father who is a policeman and his son a student taking part in the protest. I've seen a lot of policemen get arrested for disobeying orders – this happened twice during the occupations, and there were similar situations during the marches. It's really hard to try and occupy without resisting. Our motto is 'Occupy and Resist'.

We held a demonstration that attracted 100,000 people – approximately 30,000 of whom were students who had arrived en masse from other parts of the country – outside the National Congress in Brasília. And even after all the occupations that had taken place in universities and schools, even after all the protests on social media and on the streets, some still weren't paying attention to what was going on outside the ivory tower that is the National Congress. The repression was severe: we were badly beaten up. The clashes lasted for four hours. Four hours of stun grenades, tear gas, and police horses; four hours of people being threatened. I saw women practically having heart attacks because of the chaos surrounding them and the suffocating tear gas, people running around, lost children – it was like a war scene. No, not a war – in a war it's one side versus another – but a massacre, an attempt by the government to expel us from the area. But it only galvanized us further, and that's why after that demonstration there were others across several states, and there will be more, because we know we can't give up the fight.

In December 2015, Alckmin suspended the reorganization of São Paulo's secondary schools and the state education secretary, Herman Voorwald, stepped down. However, a subsequent study suggested that a 'hidden' reorganization is happening, with the gradual closure of classes in schools across the state (Palhares and Toledo, 2016).

This resembles the tactics adopted by the Chilean authorities after 2006, when some smart negotiation by the administration of Michelle Bachelet succeeded in largely demobilizing the student movement. Bachelet offered to meet most of the students' main demands, permitting use of the school bus pass 24/7 during the school year, pledging grants to cover the cost of the university admissions exam for 155,000 of the poorest students, and earmarking more funds to improve infrastructure in schools. A new General Education Law came into force in 2009, which ended the practice of selecting primary school students based on their family income and performance record, as well as introducing a system to measure student performance. However, while Bachelet's reforms did improve conditions for some of Chile's poorest students, they did little to change the basic structure of the country's education system.

It was this feeling of unfinished business amongst the former *pingüinos* and their supporters that led to the emergence of an even bigger student movement in 2011 that shook Chile to the core.

The higher education movement and the Chilean Winter

The movement that became known as the Chilean Winter began in May 2011, with a march of 15,000 people in Santiago demanding greater funding for the public education system, increased access to higher education for young people from low-income families, and the improvement of internal democracy within higher education institutions. By 16 June there were 100,000 students on the streets of Santiago and schools and universities were occupied all over the country, with another huge march at the end of that month and several others throughout the winter. The students also called for fairer admissions mechanisms for universities, with the abolition of the University Selection Test (PSU); an end to profit-making in the education sector; and the end of the municipalized system of education in schools.

The strength of the movement took the government by surprise and their negotiating strategy only antagonized the students further. Part of the problem was President Sebastián Piñera's choice for minister of education, Joaquín Lavín. Lavín was a descendant of the Chicago Boys, a group of Chilean economists who had studied under Milton Friedman at the University of Chicago between 1956 and 1961, and who would later provide the ideological foundations for Pinochet's dictatorship. Lavín, who obtained a master's degree at Chicago in 1979, worked at the Ministry of Finance during the dictatorship and in 1987 published *La Revolución Silenciosa*, a book praising Pinochet's economic model. He campaigned for 'Yes' in the 1988 referendum on whether to extend Pinochet's stay in power for another eight years and visited the former dictator in London following his arrest in 1998. He was also a co-founder of the Universidad de Desarrollo (UDD), one of Chile's leading private universities, and while he was education minister he owned shares in companies with links to the UDD. In short, he was toxic, a perfect symbol of the Chile that the students wanted to overcome.

The Confederation of Chilean Students (CONFECH) incorporated the student demands into a political strategy, extended its network to include teachers and workers, and led the negotiations with government ministers. The most visible faces of the movement were Giorgio Jackson, then president of the Student Federation at the Universidad Católica, and Camila Vallejo, his counterpart at the Universidad de Chile, both of whom were spokespeople for CONFECH. Valérie Abad was another student involved in CONFECH and the wider 2011 university protests. She describes how she became involved:

> In my first year of university I got involved in the students' centre for my department. In a Chilean university each department has its own students' centre, which is like a board of student representatives that helps the students to organize and holds meetings to discuss internal political issues within the university itself, as well as external issues affecting the country more widely. Essentially, what happened in 2011 was that all the departments from all the universities across Chile came together and started to get organized. The departments that didn't have a students' centre established one so that they too could get involved in the movement, under the banner of CONFECH. CONFECH plays a key role in the student movement in Chile in that it regularly brings together student unions from every university. In 2011, CONFECH was holding meetings

Valérie Abad.

basically every week to discuss issues and plan the path that we wanted the student movement to take.

I was at the Universidad Alberto Hurtado for a year in 2012, then the Universidad Católica for four years. Just by being in that environment, it was hard not to get involved in the student movement, because there was – and still is – a very high level of organization among students in Chile, especially since 2011. Chile had gone through a long process of de-politicization – the dictatorship had a de-politicizing effect on the country and it made people afraid to talk about politics because they were afraid of the persecution, torture, and massacres that people had suffered. Recently, however, thanks to the emergence of social movements like the movement for education, people have started to get organized, as they did before the dictatorship, to demand change and try to influence government policy.

In my first year at the Universidad Católica in 2013, I became the president of my department's students' centre. I found that the more people I represented, the more interesting it became. Another thing I noticed was that after the student movement erupted in 2011, people started to get organized and become active not just within their departments, but in the movement as a whole. Getting involved in the wider activist movement allowed them to create a space for discussion about things like strategy, tactics, and ideology. People were working together to build and improve the movement, not only making demands but

coming up with solutions and proposals too. We wanted to take ownership of the issues we faced and come up with proposals to show the government how change could be achieved. That's what was happening in
education. At the start of the academic year, CONFECH would bring students together to assess government policy, discuss it, and work together
trying to come up with proposals for how things could be improved. We
went on holding weekly assemblies to keep strengthening our message
and building on our demands, proposals, and amendments.

The level of organization was impressive. For me personally, having studied in Canada and China, I had experienced student environments in different parts of the world, but I had never seen anything
like what was going on in Chile. Sure, in those other countries there
were student movements, but what I saw in Chile really made an
impression on me, and it was what led to me putting down roots here.
Since the student movement erupted, we have emerged as a force
that has exerted an influence on public policy and political discourse.
Everything that we are currently seeing on a nationwide political level
owes a lot to the issues raised by the student movement and its actions
since 2011.

The protesters adopted various methods. Students and their families occupied
universities and secondary schools for up to six months, despite warnings that
they would have to repeat the year. One school in the district of Providencia,
Santiago, expelled the pupils who occupied the school and prohibited
them from re-registering the following year. The movement also employed
cacerolazos (pot-banging protests), a popular form of protest during the dictatorship, when street demonstrations were prohibited. However, the most
common and effective strategy was mass public demonstrations.

Although the students enjoyed widespread popular support, the demonstrations were criticized by politicians and the media and were violently repressed
by the police, who often resorted to the use of tear gas, batons, and water
cannons, drawing criticism from the Inter-American Commission on Human
Rights. The media tended to blame the demonstrators for the violence, which
somewhat undermined the legitimacy of the movement in the eyes of wider
society, as Valérie comments below:

> Demonstrations in Chile are severely repressed by the security forces.
> Naturally, these actions tend to provoke a reaction from the protesters
> and demonstrations can often turn violent. This, of course, is what the
> media focuses on, which means that unfortunately, outside the student
> bubble, the public start to lose faith in the movement. These demon-
> strations don't become violent because of the students, but because the
> authorities suppress them in such a way that it provokes a reaction.
> A recurring feature of this reaction has been the *encapuchados* – secret
> groups of protesters who cover their faces – who throw stones at the

police, light fires, invade churches, and that sort of thing. Lots of the marches have deteriorated into riots, delegitimizing the student movement in the eyes of wider society, and we really need to learn from this. One of the dictatorship's legacies is a fear of violence that has never gone away.

The student movement has started to be criminalized a bit by the government and students have been accused in the press of things they haven't done. Both the last Piñera and Bachelet administrations were involved in this. In 2015, for example, the repression and force used against the student protests was so excessive. One of my classmates from Universidad Católica was shot with a water cannon at point-blank range. It knocked him to the ground, he hit his head and was in a coma for weeks. This caused such uproar that for the rest of the year students marched demanding an end to such repression and violence against them. This violence is generated by certain interest groups in society who know that these marches and our demands will hit their pockets, because at the end of the day those who dominate power in Chile are the businessmen.

In an attempt to calm the protests, President Piñera appeared on national television in July 2011 to unveil the Great National Education Agreement (GANE), which was immediately rejected by the students. 'It's more of the same, just with a few extra pesos thrown in,' said Camila Vallejo (Alvarez Parra, 2011). They also complained that the 'agreement' was unilateral: they had not been consulted. The same month, Lavín was moved to the Ministry of Social Planning. However, the reshuffle was not accompanied by any substantial change in policy. Just two weeks after unveiling GANE, Piñera declared that 'education is a consumer good', while Harald Beyer, who was appointed minister of education at the end of the year, stated in 2012, 'We are going to convince public opinion and the Congress that free education is not an appropriate policy' (Stromquist and Sanyal, 2013: 169). Both men argued that free education is a regressive policy, which would mainly benefit the middle and upper classes, though the students were arguing that the wealthy should fund the education of the poor. To increase pressure on the government, the movement organized a national referendum on education in October 2011. Massive majorities came out in support of all the students' demands. However, the referendum was a symbolic act and the results were not legally binding.

This is not to say that the movement was unsuccessful. The demonstrations caused Piñera enormous political damage, from which his first administration never entirely recovered. Education also featured heavily in the 2013 election campaign, with Michelle Bachelet meeting with student leaders and pledging to legislate for their key demands. She promised to extend free education to 70 per cent of students by the end of her administration in 2018 and for Chile to achieve universal free education by 2020.

Here, Giorgio Jackson assesses the success of the 2011 movement:

I think that in quantitative terms we didn't achieve the transformations we wanted, that's plain to see. Making these changes is very difficult, especially with a right-wing government. The system of political representation we have today also makes things very tough. The institutional framework slams the door shut and

© Alborada Films 2014

Giorgio Jackson

there's a minority veto. But some things that were unthinkable were achieved. We blocked the government agenda and made more progress than they wanted us to, though not as much as the strength of the movement deserved. Expectations are never met.

On the other hand, looking on the bright side, in qualitative terms we changed the perception of what is possible. We stopped thinking about how to negotiate and win minor concessions, and in the end we got them anyway as a result of popular pressure. The taboos and fears attached to thinking about a different model were forgotten and it was broached in a really honest way, meaning that the message got through clearly and people were sympathetic because it wasn't false, it was a real message. Reproduction of inequality and privilege in Chile are real, but now there's a generation saying 'enough'. The neoliberal model, in which education is treated as a consumer good, has had free rein for 30 years. And it hasn't delivered the benefits it promised. So it's time for us Chileans to start changing it.

The legacy of the Chilean student movement

In April 2017, there was another wave of student protests in Chile ahead of debates over reforms. The students argued that Bachelet had not sufficiently improved the quality of higher education and access to it, nor had the students been consulted in the drafting of new legislation. Bachelet's educational reforms decentralized the administration of 6,500 schools and kindergartens to new-ly-created Local Public Education Services, but the 2015 Inclusive Education Act, which intended to make access to quality education more equitable, was criticized for covering only 14 per cent of tuition costs. It failed to provide free universal education for all students, nor did it end profit-driven higher education. Of the Chilean public, 70 per cent opposed the reform (Benedikter and Zlosilo, 2017). With Piñera returning to power in 2018, the stakes are now even higher. Valérie describes the student response to the reforms:

In the student movement we are extremely critical of how the Nueva Mayoría [Michelle Bachelet's coalition] appropriated our demands and discourse, because for us they are a centre-left coalition which just tries to give neoliberalism a pretty face. The bill they put before parliament didn't understand the concept of free, high-quality education, which is what we, the student movement, stand for above all else. We want a high-quality education system that is free for students, and not run as a profit-making enterprise but is accessible to all Chileans as a social right. It must also not be sexist in its approach and practice. None of these issues – free education, putting an end to profiteering in education, high standards, and feminist demands – were reflected in the reforms proposed by the Nueva Mayoría government. What Michelle Bachelet's administration did achieve was to increase the percentage of students entering university whose tuition fees were completely covered by bursaries and grants, but this wasn't the universal access to free education that the student movement was looking for. We see universal access to free education as having the potential to transform society and lead to wider social, cultural, and political change, which needs to happen in order to reclaim what was taken away from us during the dictatorship.

Michelle Bachelet's government forced through these reforms, but now with the right coming back into power there is a fear among the student movement and people generally that things will go backwards. Even though Bachelet's reforms were severely criticized by social movements, they at least represented some sort of progress. They were baby steps forward, but they were at least in the right direction. Now, with a right-wing government coming in, we expect that over the next few years they will chip away at what the student movement has achieved. And I'm not just talking about material setbacks, but less tangible ones too, in terms of raising awareness and politicizing people in Chile.

Some of the student leaders of the 2011 movement went into politics. Camila Vallejo and Karol Cariola became deputies for the Communist Party, joining Bachelet's Nueva Mayoría coalition, while Giorgio Jackson and Gabriel Boric were elected as independents. This was controversial, and many in the movement were concerned they would end up compromising on their principles. Vallejo especially received some fierce criticism. However, their continued prominence has helped to legitimize the student movement further and counter negative media portrayals. As Valérie comments:

There were tensions within the student movement when they went into politics. For example, Camila Vallejo was a really important and strong leader who won international recognition in 2011, so when she became a deputy for the Communist Party and entered Bachelet's government as part of the Nueva Mayoría, this caused a small degree of division among the student movement, with a split emerging between those who backed Camila and everyone else. The impact of this was quite negative because having Camila Vallejo on the side of those who were in power, on the side of a government that was centre-left and not

properly left-wing – which is how the student movement in Chile iden-
tifies itself – complicated the matter a lot. However, with Gabriel Boric
and Giorgio Jackson acting as independents, they have been spokesmen
for the student movement in Congress, which has given us an extra level
of influence and responsibility. Having those two in Congress makes us
more visible, allowing us to get our message across to society at large and
reach sectors of the population we wouldn't otherwise be able to.

[Their presence in Congress] makes us more mature as a movement.
They are also taking responsibility for representing other social movements and struggles taking place across Chilean society. They have provided a channel for talking about other issues like feminism, abortion,
and our completely privatized pension system. The No Más AFP movement, currently a very strong movement here campaigning for pension
reform, owes its success in part to the exposure the students achieved.

This division within the student movement regarding support for Bachelet
and the Nueva Mayoría is reflected in a wider sense amongst the Chilean left.
This led to the emergence of a new political movement in 2017 called the
Frente Amplio (Broad Front). Valérie describes the link between the student
movement and the Frente Amplio:

Having Gabriel and Giorgio in Congress really has been fundamental and was one of the things that led to the foundation of the Frente
Amplio coalition at the start of 2017, which brought together all the
left-wing organizations and movements involved in mobilizing and supporting the student movement. This coalition resembles the Uruguayan
political movement of the same name – the one that the former president, José 'Pepe' Mujica, belonged to – in that it's similar in its com-
position and left-wing ideological position. Gabriel and Giorgio are in
the Frente Amplio and both of them have huge democratic mandates
– in the recent elections, Giorgio Jackson received the most votes of any
congressional candidate in the country, more than 100,000 votes from
people in his constituency. They've got enormous legitimacy and their
participation in the Frente Amplio means we can think of ourselves not
just as representatives of one sector of society – the student movement
– but as something much broader, more all-encompassing. We can now
think of ourselves as a truly left-wing political option for Chile which is
born from the social movements.

Since the return to democracy in Chile there has been a duopoly on
political power, whereby only the centre-left Concertación (now Nueva
Mayoría), or the right-wing coalitions dominated by the Independent
Democratic Union (UDI), have held power. We are breaking up this
duopoly: the centre-left coalition is starting to fragment and we are
emerging as a third political force. In the recent elections our presidential candidate lost the first round of voting by just 2 per cent, which is

nothing, so we were really, really close to getting through the first round of voting and going into the run-off against Piñera.

The Frente Amplio was born from the student movement. And this is a critical part of the Frente Amplio's identity, our identity: it is a product of the student movement and other social movements coming together, and it's now consolidating itself as a real political force in the country.

Finally, Valérie reflects on the wider significance of the student movement:

I think the student movement managed to give fresh hope to all those people across Chile who despaired that the country could ever change for the better, especially the older generations who had lived through the dictatorship and had been oppressed for so many years. We have made the chance of regaining our social rights a real possibility, so people are filled with hope once again and I think this is a huge achievement. We have also managed to shake up and renew the political system in Chile – we have gone from having two deputies in Congress to having twenty, all of whom are young, and this has brought about an important and much needed political renewal.

Our most recent intervention was last year when we made a new demand for debt relief for students. Material demands such as these are important, and this one figured prominently in the campaign speeches of the presidential candidates. I think for such a recent demand of the student movement to gain such traction and be appropriated by presidential candidates is a sign that the movement has legitimacy and should keep on fighting, making demands, and trying to influence the political agenda. Furthermore, given that the Frente Amplio is a coalition that, to a large extent, was born from the student movement, when you consider the number of votes it received in the last elections and its consolidation as a political force, then yes, I believe the student movement is seen as legitimate by society at large, in spite of everything it has gone through.

Popular education in Honduras

According to Brazilian educator Paulo Freire, with whom the concept is most closely associated, 'Popular education is an educational approach that collectively and critically examines everyday experiences and raises consciousness for organizing and movement building, acting on injustices with a political vision in the interests of the most marginalized' (Llanos del Corral, n.d.). Its approach is horizontal and participatory, whereby students learn as much from each other as they do from their teacher. It is based on the principle that all education is political and neutrality is impossible; therefore, any system of education that does not act in the interests of the most marginalized necessarily reinforces the structures of their oppression. Its history in Latin America goes back to the 1930s and it is closely aligned with liberation theology, a movement in Christian (principally Catholic) theology which emphasized that the church should work with the poor and working classes, and act as an agent of social change. Popular education has informed a wide array of different educational, social, and political endeavours, not only in Latin America but all over the world.

One recent example comes from Honduras, where the brothers Pavel and Lester Núñez have created the Universidad Clementina Suárez, a popular university. Pavel describes its inspiration and the process of setting it up:

> I left university in 2006 and my thesis was about liberation pedagogy, about the work of Paulo Freire and all the work that has been done in Latin America to create new systems of education adapted to our reality. I was a student leader too, with my brother, who is a philosopher and sociologist, as well as a liberation theology priest and follower of Óscar Arnulfo Romero [Salvadorean archbishop, assassinated in 1980], another crazy eccentric. And with him I theorized and critiqued the education system a lot. We criticized the pedagogic model above all. We spoke about very advanced pedagogical structures, pedagogical constructivism, but they were models which came from Europe, or from Mexico, from other realities. They teach you how to use computers, when in our schools there aren't even blackboards. There are schools where you have to sit on the floor with the students. There are schools which don't even have buildings; classes take place beneath a mango tree. That's how we educate our people.

© Pierre Fromentin 2016

Pavel Núñez.

We talked a lot about one day starting a university. Last year the conditions were right – I was out of work and had the time to dedicate to it. The first thing was to assemble a team, which was interesting, because if you're going to set up a popular university then you have to follow the rules of popular education, the first of which is that no money changes hands. Zero lempiras. How do you start a university without a single lempira? We set up the first course, which was theory of organization. We gathered 25 young people and we gave each one of them their role from the first day – public relations, teaching, setting up the library, film projects, etc. The aim of the first course of the university was the foundation of the university itself, which we called the Universidad Clementina Suárez [named after the Honduran poet]. The name and everything else was decided on that first course. It was an interesting curriculum. I took on the role of rector, knowing that later we had to get in more students, open it to the people. More and more people started coming, and we've had more than 100 people after only a year.

The Universidad Clementina Suárez isn't about me talking. We don't have buildings, it's a popular university so our philosophy is that we don't need four walls to educate, we can meet in cafés, other universities, houses, anywhere.

It is estimated that only 15 per cent of Hondurans have access to higher education, and even amongst those who do make it to university dropout rates are high, at around 63 per cent. A 2016 report on higher education in Honduras indicated that public universities fail to prepare their students for employment, especially compared to private universities which have sought to compete with their counterparts in the region (Duriez et al., 2016). For Pavel, Clementina Suárez is a response to an education system that has failed:

With Clementina Suárez we are confronting the education system, telling them to their face that the education they provide is useless. We have the proof: less than 10 per cent of Hondurans have a university degree and 70 per cent of those are unemployed. What's the logical conclusion? The Honduran education system doesn't work, and I won't hear otherwise.

Reflecting the demands of the Chilean and Brazilian activists, the Universidad Clementina Suárez places an emphasis on culture, humanities, and political science:

We also run a course called Sciences for Survival, because if the universities aren't fit for purpose it means that they aren't preparing our young people for survival. That's why there's poverty, that's why so many young people get into gangs, because there are no opportunities. That's why there's so much violence, so many murders. There needs to be a new type of science, not just a historiography, like in philosophy, which is just about a load of people who died 2,400 years ago. It isn't taught as a tool for thinking. There needs to be a science of survival in every field of education. At Clementina Suárez we don't only teach digital journalism in the digital diploma. We deliver a complete parallel education. There's a lot of art, talks about cinema, theatre workshops, live concerts. What will really help them get ahead is being cultured. When a person is cultured, learns to think, learns the tools of philosophy and thought, then they can get ahead. When a person only does maths and doesn't get given any other tools, then this person isn't ready to go out into real life, because if they don't find a job in their field they'll be left with nothing.

José Martí, the great Cuban independence leader, said that to be cultured is to be free. For Martí – and I share his ideas – the purpose of education is to free the mind. That's why it's called liberation pedagogy, it frees you from all your bonds, whether religious, political, or coming from the media. That's what freedom of thought means. Martí thought the only way of achieving this was to become cultured. That means teaching the whole wealth of knowledge that has been created by humanity, which is what the system denies people. Historically speaking, the capitalist division of labour makes people specialists in a single area, so they can only do one type of work. Making a certain product in a factory, teaching the same class every year. So culture plays a really important role.

The Latin American Cold War dictatorships were extremely hostile to popular education. The Brazilian military came down hard on the programmes that had spread throughout the country in the early 1960s, and Freire himself was jailed for 70 days, before going into exile in Bolivia and Chile. He interpreted this experience as proof of his conviction that education is inherently political. In Honduras, the government of the National Party – which came to power via a coup in 2009 and has remained there through a toxic mixture of state violence, rampant corruption, manipulation of the judiciary, and, most recently, elections widely criticized as fraudulent (see box in Chapter 2) – has the Universidad Clementina Suárez under surveillance. Pavel continues:

Most students came to do political science. Our universities don't run political science courses, at best it's a module on the sociology course. I don't think this happens elsewhere in Latin America, only in Honduras. Political science doesn't exist. I mean political science not in the sense of politics, as young people understand it here, but in the sense of history, sociology, and philosophy. It's not about dogma. I'm not interested in teaching Marxism, or teaching anything that ends in '-ism', to anyone. I'm interested, first of all, in getting close to people who have ideas. At the Universidad Clementina Suárez we say that we don't have teachers. They're all guests – intellectuals, artists, politicians. The class we ran on the coup, for example, was taught by people close to [deposed former president Manuel] Zelaya, including a former minister who had direct experience of it – in fact she had been beaten. Who is better qualified to speak about it than her?

The Universidad Nacional and the school of journalism are asking for us to be closed. We discovered just this week that there's a petition to the school of journalism to close us down. They say it's the university of Mel [Manuel] Zelaya, that he's behind everything we do here ... He's like the devil in this country, they blame him for everything. They say it's the Libre [Zelaya's party] university, despite us having students from every opposition party – we have students who support the Anti-Corruption Party (PAC) and the Liberal Party. I'm open about my politics; I have the right to an ideology and a political party, same as anyone else. But the social and political organizations don't have any kind of influence over us. Neither Mel, nor Xiomara [Zelaya's wife and 2013 presidential candidate], nor Libre, nor anyone else can tell me what to do with the Universidad Clementina Suárez. No one had any say in designing the curriculum. The curriculum and the whole philosophy of the university were written by my brother and I, no one else was involved.

The risk is big, very big. We're facing the National Party, who know that we're creating a project that will produce activists. I'm involved in it, so that's a risk too. And we're teaching political science. We've been through what you might expect: they've sent people to photograph the classes and we've found their mobile phones with our photos on them.

I tell all the parents that there is a risk, I'm not going to hide it. I'm well known as a Libre activist and I don't try to hide this either. However, I don't want to influence anybody. What we say in Honduras is that we learn to deal with risks through living them. We meet early, we change houses, we move in groups, we give people lifts in cars ... there's a whole system of security.

* * *

Education remains a key battleground in Latin American politics and society. The Universidad Clementina Suárez and other initiatives like it across the region continue with the practice of popular education, whilst advancing another related and long-standing Latin American tradition: that of taking matters into one's own hands, of working with others to provide services and infrastructure where the state has failed to deliver. In Brazil, the secondary school students have fought school closures and led resistance to the hardcore austerity agenda imposed by the government of Michel Temer. In Chile, secondary school and university students have fought for over a decade for a radical overhaul of the country's model of education. The movement has turned the domestic political agenda on its head and led to the emergence of the Frente Amplio, a major new political force. And beyond that, it has inspired students and young people across Latin America and the world, as Camila Lanes comments:

> There are similarities in our struggle and modes of resistance. In Chile students have also occupied schools – there's a really informative

documentary called *Penguin Rebellion*, which talks about the student protests and the resistance going on there. I think resistance and struggle are intrinsic to Latin America's history. It's not just in Brazil where there are nationwide demonstrations in which thousands and thousands of people take to the streets, like the ones we had in 2013 – things like this happen in other countries across the continent. And we've tried to integrate the different movements so that we can unite under this one issue: to demand a high-quality, emancipatory, and inclusive state education – one that isn't *machista*, sexist, or racist. Also, education isn't a business. The struggle against the commercialization of education is something else we're fighting, not just here in Brazil but all over the world.

In Latin America we have an organization called OCLAE [Latin American and Caribbean Students' Organization] that brings together all the national student movements from every country. I've had the opportunity to meet a few of them – students from Chile, Colombia, Peru, Paraguay, and Cuba. We've established a good dialogue … For a while now we've been putting forward a positive agenda for the student movement across the continent.

Marches of solidarity with the Chilean students, as called for by CONFECH, were held in November 2011 across Latin America. There were particularly close ties between the Chilean students and their Colombian counterparts, who in the same year successfully fought a proposed education reform, which they argued was an attempt to partly privatize the sector by encouraging private investment and the creation of for-profit universities. They went on strike for over a month, holding mass demonstrations in Bogotá and other cities, and ultimately the government withdrew the bill.

Elsewhere, in Mexico, students have led the demonstrations to demand justice for the 43 students who disappeared near Ayotzinapa in the state of Guerrero in 2014 (see Chapter 8). The missing students had themselves attended a protest in Iguala to object to discriminatory hiring practices for teachers, and were planning a trip to Mexico City to mark the anniversary of the Tlatelolco massacre. The students came from a college with a history of left-wing activism and their disappearance – probably contrived by the police or military, with the possible involvement of criminal organizations – is one more tragic example in Latin America's long history of state persecution of students and young people involved in activism for progressive causes.

Student movements of various types continue to proliferate throughout the region, and the violence with which they are repressed is a sign of just how contentious the issue of education remains. The ruling classes across Latin America remain committed to the idea that high-quality education is a consumer good, which prepares young people for insertion into the labour market. The student movements, on the other hand, insist that it is a human right. They see it as a means of eliminating the reproduction of inequality in what remains the world's most unequal region, and ultimately of building societies which are fairer, kinder, and less discriminatory. This conflict persists, and in response the student movements will continue to struggle. As Camila Lanes says:

> I've learnt that Brazil is a really beautiful country with a phenomenally diverse culture. I've had the opportunity to travel from the northern states, through the north-east, right down to the south. I've experienced countless different realities and passed through such a range of landscapes – the roads, the *sertão* [semi-arid scrubland], the coast, the countryside – and this is what gives me strength every day and reinforces my conviction that a country as beautiful and rich as ours deserves to progress, improve, and be the best it can. And the people deserve it too, for they are so courageous and determined. I know for sure that in order to build a resistance, in order to win victories and achieve your goals, unity and, above all, mutual respect between everyone involved are vital, and this is exactly what I stand for. It's a really sad time for our democracy, a sort of collective depression. The global economic crisis is linked to an economic model and system of governance that go completely against people's needs – so what we need at the moment is a lot of joyful resistance. I want to contribute to this in the same way I have done since the start: by talking to and building relationships with people on the ground, at grassroots level, people who live these realities, as they do in schools, which are our main agent for change. I think that by changing the education system we can change the world, and that's why I've been protesting all these years.

About the author

Emily Gregg has written blogs for LAB on the Colombian Peace Process and the legacy of El Salvador's 1992 peace accords. She is now studying for an MSc in the history of international relations at the London School of Economics with a focus on human rights and Latin America.

Interviews

Valérie Abad (Universidad Católica): interviewed via Google Hangouts on 27 January 2018 by Tom Gatehouse. Translated by Matty Rose.

Marcelo Correa (CONES): interviewed in Santiago de Chile on 22 November 2016 by Nina Meghji. Transcribed by Nina Meghji.

Giorgio Jackson (former student leader, now congressional deputy and leader of Revolución Democrática party): interviewed in Santiago de Chile on 6 December 2011 by Roberto Navarrete (http://www.alboradafilms.net/). Translated by Rowan Ritchie.

Camila Lanes (UBES): interviewed in São Paulo on 13 December 2016 by Ali Rocha. Translated by Matty Rose.

Pavel Núñez (Universidad Clementina Suárez): interviewed in Tegucigalpa on 24 October and 2 November 2016 by Louise Morris. Translated by Louise Morris.

References

NB: All web references were checked and still available in May/June 2018 unless otherwise stated. All references are listed, with web-links, on the page for this chapter on the Voices website www.vola.org.uk

Alvarez Parra, N. (2011) 'Camila Vallejo: "Es más de lo mismo pero con unos pesos más"', La Tercera, 5 July, <http://www2.latercera.com/noticia/camila-vallejo-es-mas-de-lo-mismo-pero-con-unos-pesos-mas>

Arsht, A. and Sanchez Zinny, G. (2014) 'Chile's education system is the best in Latin America–so why is it being overhauled?', Atlantic Council, <http://www.atlanticcouncil.org/?view=article&id=18431:chile-best-education-system>

Benedikter, R. and Zlosilo, M. (2017) 'Chile's 2017 presidential election: evaluating the second Bachelet government', LSE Latin America and Caribbean Centre, <http://blogs.lse.ac.uk/latamcaribbean/2017/11/18/chiles-2017-presidential-election-evaluating-the-second-bachelet-government>

Comisión Nacional sobre Prisión Política y Tortura (2005) *Informe de la Comisión Nacional sobre Prisión Política y Tortura*, Ministerio del Interior, Chile, <http://bibliotecadigital.indh.cl/handle/123456789/455>

Cultura Argentina (2015) *El Nunca más y los crímenes de la dictadura*, Ministerio de Cultura, Argentina, <https://librosycasas.cultura.gob.ar/wp-content/uploads/2015/11/LC_NuncaMas_Digital1.pdf>

Duriez, M., López, V. and Moncada, G. (2016) *Informe Nacional: Honduras, Educación Superior en Iberoamérica*, CINDA, <http://www.cinda.cl/wp-content/uploads/2016/11/HONDURAS-Informe-Final.pdf>

Franklin, J. (2006) 'Protests paralyse Chile's education system', *The Guardian*, 7 June, <https://www.theguardian.com/world/2006/jun/07/chile.schoolsworldwide>

Llanos del Corral, M. (no date) 'Ways of Doing Development Differently: Methodologies for Adaptive & Systemic Development' Plymouth University, <https://www.academia.edu/32860154/Ways_of_Doing_Development_Differently_Methodologies_for_Adaptive_and_Systemic_Development?auto=download>

Long, G. (2011) 'Chile student protests point to deep discontent', BBC News, <http://www.bbc.co.uk/news/world-latin-america-14487555>

Palhares, I. and Toledo, L.F. (2016) 'Estudo aponta 'reorganização velada' no Estado de São Paulo', *O Estado de S. Paulo*, 28 June, <https://educacao.estadao.com.br/noticias/geral,estudo-aponta-reorganizacao-velada-em-sp,10000059571>

Pensado, J. (2012) 'Student activism', *ReVista: Harvard Review of Latin America*, <https://revista.drclas.harvard.edu/book/student-activism>

Santana, A. (2016) 'Escola sem Partido: entenda o que é movimento que divide opiniões na Educação', EBC, <http://www.ebc.com.br/educacao/2016/07/o-que-e-o-escola-sem-partido>

Stromquist, N.P. and Sanyal, A. (2013) 'Student resistance to neoliberalism in Chile', *International Studies in Sociology of Education* 23(2): 152–78, <http://www.tandfonline.com/doi/abs/10.1080/09620214.2013.790662>

CHAPTER 5
Indigenous peoples and the rights of nature
Linda Etchart

Abstract

In recent decades, indigenous people have displayed a new confidence and pride in their identity, using changes in the law at national and international level in order to defend themselves, their territory, and their culture, particularly against the extractive industries. They have been engaging with aspects of mainstream Western culture such as higher education and communications technology, reaching beyond the borders of their country in a struggle that is becoming increasingly global.

In his seminal work *Open Veins of Latin America*, Eduardo Galeano wrote that 500 years ago Renaissance Europeans ventured across the oceans and 'sank their teeth' into the throats of the Indian civilizations of 'Abya Yala' – the American continent (Galeano, 1971). Five centuries later, the plunder of gold and silver, rubber, wood, and now oil, from countries in Latin America continues to supply profits to the owners and shareholders of the extractive industries, state and private, as well as devastating the environment (see Chapter 7). Indigenous communities, meanwhile, continue to suffer from deeply ingrained discrimination. Eva Sánchez, an indigenous Lenca women's activist from the department of Intibucá, in the west of Honduras, says:

> The Lenca have always been undervalued and discriminated against. Though we're the native people, they've made us think we have no rights, that those who have more rights and more value are whites and people who come from elsewhere. Discrimination passes through our whole identity as Lenca – our ways of production, our culture, it surrounds everything.

While such marginalization of indigenous people is common throughout Latin America, a paradigm shift has taken place in recent decades. Indigenous peoples have emerged as global leaders in the struggle to protect their rights to land and the rights of nature. Defining moments for the indigenous peoples of Latin America were the International Labour Organization (ILO) Convention on Indigenous and Tribal Peoples, 1989 (No. 169), which came into force in 1991, and the Organization of American States' (OAS) American Declaration on the Rights of Indigenous Peoples of 1997, which was approved in 2016. Both these mechanisms established territorial rights to ancestral lands. Another key moment was the United Nations Conference on Environment

http://dx.doi.org/10.3362/9781909014213.005

and Development – the Rio de Janeiro Earth Summit of 1992 – which was a turning point in the history of global environmental governance. It brought together world leaders to address human rights and the environment, strengthening the position of indigenous peoples, whose voices had hitherto gone largely unheard in international forums.

In the 21st century, the collective voices of the world's most marginalized communities have been raised anew, in Latin America and across continents, challenging governments, private corporations, and international institutions, demanding and achieving changes to national and international law. Indigenous peoples have gained a new confidence, a new pride in their identity, travelling to international conferences to put forward their case and call for decision-making power at a global level.

In recent years, both Bolivia and Ecuador have incorporated the rights of indigenous peoples and the rights of nature into their national constitutions, a move that has radically changed the way states envision their responsibility to the environment within their borders. In Ecuador, president of the Constituent Assembly Alberto Acosta incorporated the indigenous Kichwa concept of *buen vivir* (*sumak kawsay*) and the rights of nature into the new constitution of 2008, creating a model for the world to follow. Bolivia followed suit, incorporating its own version, *vivir bien,* into its constitution in 2009 under the country's first indigenous president, Evo Morales. These concepts translate as 'good living' or 'living well', though they should not be confused with Western notions of wellbeing or welfare, which tend to focus on the individual in isolation. *Buen vivir*, on the other hand, denotes a way of living in which individuals are in harmony with both their social and their environmental surroundings (Balch, 2013).

The rise to power of figures such as former Ecuadorian president Rafael Correa (who has mestizo roots) and Morales (an indigenous Aymara) has been enormously significant for the indigenous people of their respective countries and of Latin America. However, the administrations of both men – as was the case for all governments of the 'pink tide' era to a certain extent – used profits from resource extraction to fund programmes of reform and progressive social policy. This involved the participation of foreign interests in violation of national laws and caused frequent conflict between private companies – backed up by national and local governments – and indigenous communities (see Chapter 7).

Recent institutional and legislative progress on indigenous rights, land ownership, and the rights of nature has been compromised by weak governance and a repeated failure to investigate human rights abuses against indigenous peoples and land defenders. Latin America is the most dangerous region in the world for activists working on issues of land ownership, human rights, and the environment. According to Michel Forst, UN Special Rapporteur on the situation of human rights defenders: 'The most common form of attack is criminalization, followed by killings, intimidation and threats. More than 52 per cent of the documented attacks [in 2016] took place in Latin America:

Guatemala (10 per cent), Colombia (10 per cent), Mexico (9 per cent), Brazil (9 per cent), Peru (8 per cent) and Honduras (6 per cent)' (Forst, 2017).

Many of these attacks are related to indigenous peoples' resistance to damage to their environment and livelihoods caused by the activities of the extractive industries, loggers, and agribusiness (the expansion of soya and palm oil plantations and cattle ranching). Of the 197 environmental defenders killed in the world in 2017, 116 were from Latin America.

Even as countries ratify the United Nations Declaration on the Rights of Indigenous Peoples (UNDRIP) of 2007 and the principle of Free Prior and Informed Consent (FPIC) contained within the Declaration, the historical processes of conquest, occupation, colonization, and expropriation, graphically described by Galeano in the 1970s, have continued into the 21st century, as demonstrated by the testimonies that follow.

Land rights and dispossession

Land is of fundamental importance to indigenous people and in the indigenous worldview. Alicia Cawiya – real name Weya – is the vice president of the Huaorani people of Ecuador. A spear-bearing tribe, they are known as the fiercest of the indigenous peoples of the Amazon. Formerly known as *aucas*, a pejorative Quechua term meaning 'savage', the Huaorani live in dispersed groups on the Napo River within the Yasuní National Park, a UNESCO biosphere reserve. Not only is this one of the most biodiverse areas on the planet, it is also home to the Tagaeri and Taromenane peoples, two of the last of the so-called 'uncontacted' tribes in the Americas, who continue to live in voluntary isolation, avoiding contact with outsiders. The oil drilling in the Ishpingo-Tambococha-Tiputini (ITT) oilfield in Yasuní represents an existential threat to all three groups. Here Alicia discusses the importance of territory:

> My name is Alicia Cawiya. I am vice president of the Huaorani Nation of Ecuador (NAWE). Our territory used to be immense, bordered by the Napo and Curaray rivers. The Huaorani and Taromenane lived freely in the Yasuní. We were so happy. But when the government opened the Auca Road for the oil companies [along the Napo River in the 1970s], the colonization, invasions, and logging began, reducing the size of our territory and that of the Taromenane people. Their territory is small now, and it's getting smaller all the time. When the missionaries came [in the 1950s] it was our first contact with the world, and the missionaries took the Huaorani away into Pastaza [a province to the south of Yasuní]. Our territory was left empty, and the oil companies took advantage of that. Every time the Huaorani had contact with the missionaries, they had problems and left their land. When they returned, their territory had been colonized and there was no way of recovering it. More colonizers entered our territory, and we were left with half our ancestral territory.

> Territory is important for the peoples who live in Yasuní, some of whom, like the Taromenane, want no contact whatsoever with the world outside. We, as Huaorani, respect their decision. They have a whole forest to themselves in Yasuní. They gather fruit, fish, and hunt freely. The forest provides them with everything they want; they don't need anything else. We want those territories respected, to ensure there will be future generations of Taromenane. We don't want anyone to go there and kill them, not the oil companies, not the loggers, nor the Huaorani people. I have always looked after their interests. We accept that the Taromenane and their relatives are the owners of the Yasuní.

Encroachment on indigenous land has intensified since the 19th century and continues apace today. As Eva Sánchez comments:

> In the west of Honduras the Lenca are known as the example of resistance – from Lempira, the Indian who resisted the Spanish, to Berta Cáceres [environmental activist and Lenca indigenous leader who was assassinated in 2016], who also led a strong campaign in defence of our territories. And there have been many others. We're known as a people who've been very resistant and belligerent, but we've also suffered, ever since colonization. When the Spanish arrived, we were expelled from the best land. They sent us to the mountains. Now, as the authorities realize that many of the riches are in the mountains – the forest, water, minerals – now they want to expel us from this land, too. They're always trying to dispossess us, whether through laws such as the agrarian reform law, or by means of force, through the militarization of these territories and criminalization or murder of those who resist.

Fany Kuiru is a Colombian lawyer, and at the time of writing is standing as a candidate for the national Senate. The historical displacement and dispossession of indigenous people in Colombia has been particularly violent, as she describes:

> My name is Fany Kuiru Castro. I am an indigenous woman of the Witoto people. My traditional name is Jitoma Monaya or Dawn Sun, which was given to me by my father in a traditional name-giving ceremony. I am from La Chorrera in the department of Amazonas, home to Casa Arana, where many atrocities took place during the rubber boom at the beginning of the last century. Many indigenous people were killed, tortured, and enslaved; they raped many women.
>
> La Chorrera is an indigenous territory in Predio Putumayo [Colombia's largest indigenous reserve]. La Chorrera is one sector of

Fany Kuiru.

© Maria Eugenia Caicedo 2017

the reserve, occupied exclusively by indigenous peoples. There are 22 communities. We have traditional indigenous authorities which arrange the ceremonies, rituals, and spiritual aspects of the communities. We have been gradually rebuilding on what little was left after the rubber boom [that involved] the Peruvian Amazon Company. It was a Peruvian company, but then it became a joint Anglo-Peruvian venture registered in London and funded by English capital. The workers living in La Chorrera, in the middle of the jungle, were British subjects from Barbados, brought over to tap rubber in the Amazon. Our people were treated horrifically. They were tortured and there were massacres. As a girl I grew up with this history. My older relatives would tell me stories of what happened at the Casa Arana. We were children of fear; we grew up with fear. When the sound of motors came from the river the children would run into the forest without giving a thought to the danger. Snakes, dangerous animals, and plants that could bite or sting us, we didn't care. We would run away, saying, 'Here come the Peruvians to get us again!'

This was because when rubber exploitation in the Amazon ended, the Peruvian boats came to take our people away to Peru. We have family in Peru, in the indigenous Witoto and Bora communities, so we lived with this fear. My childhood and youth were tainted by these inherited stories of violence against our people. From a very young age I felt that something had to be done, but our grandparents wouldn't talk about it because of the shame they felt for having allowed so many atrocities to take place. They were stories of fear, terror, slavery, rape, and murder. Children beaten against trees and the ground, women escaping into the night to save their children, women being raped in front of their families.

In 1910 the British consul, Roger Casement, arrived in La Chorrera to inspect the situation of the British subjects working for the company. When, to his surprise, he found out about these atrocities committed against the indigenous people, he wrote a report, also recording all the terrible things that he saw and heard about on a daily basis in his personal diary. We have just commemorated his death. The information about Roger has only come to light recently. The stories were directly related to my family. For example, my paternal grandfather was saved from the Colombia–Peru War because during the conflict they picked people up and took them in boats along the river to Peru, leaving La Chorrera unpopulated. I received the stories directly and I always wondered why nobody had fought against this repression and violence.

The reserve is a legally constituted area, but indigenous territory goes much further than its borders. Indigenous people have always lived in these territories and we maintain this relationship with the land, based on harmony and mutual protection. Human beings both protect the environment and benefit from its protection. It gives us our food; it's our life source. This is why we call it Mother Earth; it's not just a name. From the earth comes life. It provides us with abundance and wellbeing. She is like a mother who encompasses everything and looks after her children.

When the indigenous people presided over the territory the environmental management was very strict and sustainable. Unfortunately, things have changed. The rubber boom changed everything. For example, sustainable management of natural resources is based on the fact that you cannot consume them indiscriminately, whether they be trees, plants, vegetables, even water. Use must be proportionate and in accordance with the ecological calendar. This means thinking about which resources you can use during summer or the rainy season. It also applies to the crops: when you should water or harvest them and when to make *chagras*, which are small parcels of land for different seed types. Every year you should rotate so that there is never deforestation and the earth is always being repopulated with new trees and plants. This care is important not just for humanity but also for nature.

Our ancestors say that when there is discord between nature, the land, and the people, rituals must be performed to re-harmonize things. Animals, especially big ones like anacondas or jaguars, have their seasons too and they have energy conflicts with the humans. When there is discord, illness and conflict start to appear and living together becomes chaotic. This is when the wise elders of the community conduct a ritual ceremony to re-harmonize the territory. Everything is interrelated, humanity and nature. We also have to care for the cosmos. I come from the Jitómagaro clan, which means People of the Sun – the stars, in other words. When there is too much rain or sun or drought, we have to enter into dialogue with the stars to avoid problems. Our ancestors had this knowledge, but much of it has been lost, as only a few elders remain.

As in Colombia during the rubber boom, traditional farming methods in Honduras have been affected by the exigencies of modern extractive capitalism, as Eva Sánchez describes:

It's also difficult because they want to repress our culture in general. They came and told us that our ancestral farming methods were no good. We had to use other technical ways of farming: different seeds, chemical fertilizers, insecticides. These had a big impact and now our land is contaminated. There's a strong movement in this community to rescue our ancestral culture and restore harmony with Mother Earth, respecting the water, so that it isn't privatized. This contravenes what the state wants to do, which is to install big transnational companies in our lands and implement these projects.

One problem that indigenous peoples often face is that of land titles, as many of them are unable to produce land titles proving that they are the legal owners of their territory, though they may have inhabited it for millennia. The complexities surrounding land ownership, and the dangers inherent in the push towards privatization and away from collective ownership – a policy promoted by international organizations as well as national governments – are illustrated by the excerpt below from an interview with Froyla Tzalam of the Mayan community of Belize. Froyla is director of the Sarstoon-Temash Institute for Indigenous Management (SATIIM), an indigenous NGO created to empower Q'eqchi Maya and Garifuna communities through environmental conservation of their lands. Originally created when they discovered that the government had designated a national park on their lands, the organization soon had to step up to defend the new park against oil concessions granted by the government to US Capital Energy:

The government is campaigning for individual land titles as opposed to communal titles. Our job at SATIIM is not to tell communities which one they should pick, but rather to show what they have first, so they can make an informed decision. All the families in our communities have access to land. The issue is not whether we have access and are able to farm. The question is how we continue protecting our land to ensure everyone continues to have equal access to those resources.

Froyla Tzalam.

To accept a land title, to take on the responsibility of owning a piece of land, and to retain it, is not without cost, as Juan Ch'oc, a leader of the Q'eqchi Maya village Crique Sarco, points out:

If you lease land from the government, you need to pay, you need to pay your lease, your land tax, every year. The people here in the village, when they hear about leases, say, 'It's good! We want a lease.' But I tell them I think a lease is good when they have a little bit of income, so that every year you can pay your tax. If you make hardly any money and you need to buy food or you need to buy your clothing and whatnot, if you don't have enough money to do that, what about land tax? You don't have enough to do that.

The emphasis on individual land titles results not only in loss of access to common resources, but also the breakup of communities, as individual families sell up to private interests – including the extractive industries – and move to towns and cities. In order to preserve territorial integrity and indigenous culture, the emphasis is now on the retention of collective land rights, a central theme of the 2018 annual conference of the United Nations Permanent Forum on Indigenous Issues (UNPFII). Collective rights involve the demarcation of territories, which requires community involvement and mapping. SATIIM has been doing work with communities on replicable and participatory mapping, and has developed a Maya Land Registry, in response to a ruling by the Caribbean Court of Justice that the government of Belize must establish Maya communal land titles.

The battle over extraction

The Belizean government and US Capital Energy have employed a number of strategies in order to achieve their objectives. For example, to counter the designation of land as indigenous territory, the government has requisitioned it as national parks or 'ecological areas of sustainable development', thereby removing indigenous control. Indigenous communities may be expelled, or their hunting and fishing activities curtailed. It is not unusual for indigenous communities to find that this arrangement precedes the government's granting of concessions to extractive industries who then despoil that same land. As Froyla says:

> If you tell the communities they shouldn't be hunting or doing any kind of extractive activity, then how can you legitimize oil exploration in the same area? They didn't make the connection. Is it a protected area or not? Are you telling us that we might spend decades protecting an area which can be turned into an extractive zone overnight? So that's why this discussion about the oil issue was not just kept within the communities, it went beyond that. Because if the National Park as a protected area was under threat, that meant any protected area in any part of the country was open for oil drilling. So what is a protected area, then? That really made a lot of people question what the government of Belize was doing, what kind of development policy was being promoted. We are supposed to be into the environment; the Belize Tourism Board used to market us as 'Belize: Mother Nature's Best-Kept Secret.' The oil issue really brought out all these things. We tried to capture the public imagination by saying, 'It's us today, but it could be you tomorrow.' This had some success.
>
> In the case of SATIIM, what happened was that the government of Belize decided to create a protected area. The idea wasn't bad as such, but it was the way it was carried out in practice. The communities affected weren't consulted, and so, about two years after the park was established, the buffer communities realized that parts of their land were now included in a protected area. A steering committee [of indigenous representatives] was established, which sought to take back some control over how this protected area was managed. To a certain extent, this was something new, because protected areas were being promoted and established by the government; they were the ones who decided how they should be managed.

Initially, consultation over plans for oil exploration in the area was conducted as a rubber-stamping exercise, as Froyla comments:

> In 2006, SATIIM took US Capital Energy and the government to court on the grounds that they were not following the Environmental Impact Assessment (EIA). We won – the court agreed that the government wasn't following its own regulations. So we forced US Capital to produce

an effective EIA. We couldn't stop them from drilling, but that was a wake-up call for SATIIM.

We need to be given the information, so we can make informed decisions. The way they conducted the consultation was just a farce. I mean, they gave communities literally two weeks to digest a very dense report, in English. Our people aren't fluent in English. I am, but even so, I would still have difficulty analysing that very technical document in two weeks. The government said, 'OK, here is our report. Read it and tell us what you think.' They didn't make it easy at all for our communities to really understand what was being said in the document, for us to be able to make an informed decision as to whether or not we wanted the drilling to take place.

And when the consultation took place it was controlled by the government and US Capital. They prevented Greg [the interlocutor of the local community] from speaking on many occasions. We were given a minute to ask a question, and all of this was done in English. It clearly showed the government's true intent, which wasn't to inform the people. They had already given permission; as far as they were concerned, they were going through the process. Like it or not, this was going to take place. And so SATIIM coming in and demanding that we be a part of that process really threw a spanner in the works. They didn't like it.

Other strategies include promises of employment and the provision of essential services such as healthcare and education. Given that these communities tend to inhabit remote rural areas where such services are scant if not non-existent, such offers can end up being effective. Froyla continues:

When they did the work for seismic test lines it was just to clear the forest and there was no more work after that. With the drilling they promised jobs, but to keep people happy, US Capital had to rotate the work among I don't know how many people, so at least one family worked once a month. It was clear that the jobs that they promised were either short-lived or non-existent. People are beginning to realize that it's not going to be everything that US Capital promised. A Mexican company got the contract to do the drilling. The Mexicans came, houses were built for them, and they were given protective gear. It's different treatment for these foreign workers as opposed to the actual owners of the land. We said this is what was going to happen; people didn't believe us. But now they realize that SATIIM was right, that they're only going to get the dregs of whatever development there is.

Companies and governments also seek to divide communities, targeting individuals and families who are susceptible to the promise of gifts, cash, and all-expenses-paid trips to the capital city in exchange for granting permission for exploration. Such division has occurred amongst the Huaorani in Ecuador, where there is an acrimonious rift between Alicia Cawiya and Chief Moi Enomenga, the community leader. Alicia describes what happened:

> Moi has a travel agency, Wao Lodge. His idea was to develop ecotourism. But then he made an agreement with the government and the Chinese oil company Sinopec. He gave all his cabins to the oil company. The Huaorani complained they hadn't been consulted, but Moi signed more documents and contracts enabling the oil companies to come in. People were angry. Moi said, 'We will be given money, education, healthcare.' That is a lie. They spent the money they received. The communities were abandoned. There was nothing in the way of healthcare and education. We were deceived.
>
> We should be working together to progress. There shouldn't be any division in the leadership. That is why what Moi did was so bad. He says he is helping the government with plans for health and education. But nothing has been done for the communities. 'Why don't you recognize that you are on the side of the government?' I asked him. 'Your people are your people; the government is not your people. You should support the communities who elected you to represent them. Help them.' Since then, we haven't spoken. He only ever tries to pick a fight with me.

The consequences of operations by the extractive industries for indigenous peoples may be catastrophic. In Ecuador, consortia of oil companies have been drilling for oil in the Ecuadorian Amazon region since the 1930s. Texaco/Gulf Oil, bought out by Chevron in 2001, drilled 356 oil wells between 1964 and 1992, spilled 16.8 million gallons of crude oil, and left behind more than 18 billion gallons of toxic waste in the headwaters of the Amazon near Lago Agrio in the district of Aguarico, a disaster that has been labelled 'the Amazon's Chernobyl'. The dumping of oil waste in this way was abandoned in most US states in the 1940s and 1950s, and was outlawed by the federal government in 1979, yet in Ecuador, Texaco continued the practice in order to save on cost.

Nearly two and a half million acres of rainforest disappeared and at least two indigenous groups – the Tetetes and Sansahuaris – became extinct. Epidemiological studies in the affected area showed that the inhabitants faced significantly higher risks of cancer, while the risk of miscarriage was two and a half times greater for women living within three miles of an oil well. Thirty thousand people were affected by contamination caused by the oil waste in the Lago Agrio area (Miller, 2003). Those affected by the oil drilling in the headwaters of the Amazon, which included the Huaorani, Kichwa, Secoya, Siona, and Cofán indigenous peoples, mounted a class action case against Chevron – which bought Texaco in 2001 – beginning in 1993. In 2011, they won a US$18 billion ruling (later reduced to $9.5 billion) in their favour in the Ecuadorian courts (Etchart, 2018). Chevron – who famously vowed to 'fight until hell freezes over – and then we'll fight it out on the ice' (Barrett, 2013) – managed to have the judgement overturned by a US court in 2014, a decision reaffirmed by an appeals court in 2016.

Alicia Cawiya (front centre, with megaphone), Patricia Nenquihui, Patricia Gualinga (rear left, holding sign), and Katy Betancourt. International Women's Day March, Puyo, Ecuador, 8 March 2016.

Alicia describes some of the effects of the oil spills:

> We have no use for oil. It is killing us. For us life is a healthy river, a healthy tree, and good fruit. But this is no longer the future for us. Oil has contaminated us. We have new diseases. There is cancer in our communities, as there is for the Kichwa people, and we are worried.
>
> There are oil spills in the swamps and lakes which will cause illness among the people who live in the Yasuní. How will the lakes recover from the oil spills? The oil companies have done enough damage already. They cannot deceive us any more and cause us any more suffering.
>
> They [local government] say that they receive the income from oil to help the communities, but they're not helping our communities. We have nothing. There is no sanitation, no drinking water, nothing. We need a clean river, but now it is contaminated and is no use to us. You can see that the children are sick from the spots on their skin.

However, armed with mechanisms such as UNDRIP of 2007 and ILO Convention 169, indigenous communities have been mounting successful legal challenges, both to extractive companies that despoil indigenous land and to national governments that permit this to happen without obliging companies to obtain free, prior, and informed consent (FPIC). Though they have yet to be compensated for the havoc wreaked upon their territory by Texaco, the 2011 ruling in favour of Ecuadorian communities against Chevron was a landmark moment.

Similarly, the Sarayaku Kichwa – also of the Ecuadorian Amazon – took the Ecuadorian government to the Inter-American Commission on Human Rights (IACHR) in 2003, with the help of human rights lawyer Mario Melo. The case was referred to the Inter-American Court, which ruled in Sarayaku's favour in 2012, finding that they had not been consulted prior to oil exploration on their territory in the province of Pastaza. The government of Ecuador was forced to apologize to the Sarayaku people for violating their rights, their ancestral land, and their cultural identity. Compensation was awarded and oil exploration was halted. And in Belize, SATIIM has won several major legal victories in the Supreme Court, which has demanded proper EIAs and upheld the rights of indigenous communities to FPIC.

Such harnessing of legal and institutional frameworks by indigenous peoples in defence of their territories and cultures is a relatively recent development and is an example of the complex and ambiguous relationship between modernity and tradition in indigenous life today.

The clash of modernity and tradition

From a historical perspective, contact with Europeans has been disastrous for the indigenous peoples of Latin America. Infectious diseases introduced by Europeans – smallpox, measles, typhus, influenza, plague – killed an estimated 95 per cent of the pre-Columbian Native American population (Diamond, 2005). Many of those who did not die from disease were killed in battle or enslaved and forced to work on the land or in the mines. Today, modern capitalism continues to pose multiple threats to indigenous cultures in Latin America, whether from extractive industries such as mining and oil drilling, logging, agribusiness, and narcotrafficking, or from the influence of modern technology and contemporary consumer culture. In the case of Colombia, such threats have been exacerbated by the country's recent history of armed conflict, as Fany Kuiru describes:

> Indigenous youth today are so immersed in globalization that their own culture matters little to them. It is not just technology that has invaded, but the different cycles of violence that we have experienced. First it was the rubber plantations. Then came the drug trade. It arrived by river, like everything does, and it appropriated the sacred plant [coca] which our elders and ancestors use to *mambear* [chew] and thus to maintain balance and harmony in the territory. These businessmen, or narcotraffickers, arrived, and forced the communities to give them the plants that they had cultivated in their *chagras*. They said, 'In exchange for coca, I will give you engines, clothes, and enough beer and aguardiente for you to drink until you pass out.' These things were terrible for our culture. In two years everything changed. Families were separated, because money became more important than anything else. This was a terrible violence against the spirituality of La Chorrera and the surrounding area.

Once narcotrafficking disappeared, the guerrillas arrived. Both the FARC and the paramilitaries. In fact, the paramilitaries arrived first to do social cleansing in the areas along the Putumayo and Igara Paraná rivers. I think the infamous Castaño paramilitaries were in this area, though of course we didn't know who they were. Some cousins warned us about them and they were forced out of the community, though they stayed in the area. After the paramilitaries left, the guerrillas appeared and after that no one knew who we were dealing with, whether they were guerrillas, paramilitaries, or the army. We had three armed actors in our midst and they were fighting each other. They left live ammunition behind and a child almost died when a gun cartridge it had been playing with exploded. There were a lot of men in uniform around and you never knew who they were.

The introduction of alcohol – spirits in particular – to indigenous communities is a frequent source of trouble. Patricia Gualinga is director of external relations of the Sarayaku Kichwa community in the province of Pastaza in Ecuador. She is also a prominent activist working on issues relating to land, the environment, and indigenous rights and led a campaign within Sarayaku against the introduction of spirits from outside:

This isn't the same as the alcohol that we make in our own community. The [physical] impact of *chicha*, the alcohol that we make ourselves, is much less. *Chicha* is consumed in large quantities, but the effect is different from that of rum, which has penetrated all the indigenous groups. I personally know many communities caught in the alcohol trap. Some of us women don't drink alcohol, and we have taken a stand against it. Our struggle has been to outlaw alcohol [spirits] in the constitution of Sarayaku.

It'll take a long time. We have encountered resistance from a contingent of men who don't agree with what we have implemented within the structure of the Sarayaku community. We get angry, then measures have to be taken to impose the rules. There are leaders among those who resist; good, able, intellectual, powerful men. But when we come to discussing the issue of alcohol, they are unwilling to confront the problem or set an example, which I think is a big problem. As you will have seen when you arrived on Sunday, Marquitos [the Sarayakan artist and craftsman] had just died [of cirrhosis]. Candles were lit and the mourners drowned their grief, their sorrow, in alcohol. This is a way of avoiding the problem.

I have seen indigenous leaders, not just from Sarayaku, who have been under pressure and subjected to attempts to discredit them while defending our territory against the government or the oil companies. Sooner or later they break down under this pressure and seek solace in beer or spirits. This is a problem that we have to confront and also recognize as a health issue. Marquitos died of cirrhosis. But Hepatitis

B has also struck the indigenous peoples – the Huaorani, the Kichwa, and the Sápara. And when someone has Hepatitis B without knowing it and drinks alcohol, it destroys the liver, which is why there have been cases of cirrhosis. It's not just because they drink alcohol, but they have died because their defences are lower. It's the combination of Hepatitis B and alcohol which has caused the deaths of young people like Marquitos.

However, contact with the modern world is not negative per se. Indigenous communities have increasingly been appropriating the tools of modernity in order to defend themselves better against interests that threaten their existence. They travel outside their territories and sometimes their countries to put pressure on lawmakers and seek wider support, to make use of modern communications technologies, or to study at universities and obtain professional qualifications; in some cases they even go into politics themselves.

Eriberto Gualinga – real name Traya Muskuy – is communications director of the Sarayaku Kichwa and a documentary film-maker. His work includes the prizewinning documentary *The Children of the Jaguar* (2012), which portrays the struggle of the Sarayaku Kichwa to defend their culture and tells the story of the journey made by Sarayaku representatives to the Inter-American Court of Human Rights:

> I studied at the school here. My parents couldn't pay for university. I would have liked to study film – that was my dream, but there was no chance. I did have the opportunity to work on a two-hour radio programme in Spanish and Kichwa by Catholic missionaries, which helped me gain confidence. I went on to participate in cinema workshops in Quito. I studied radio and video in Chile, before going on to study video editing in the United States. So, while I don't have a formal qualification as a film-maker, I make documentary films from the perspective of the indigenous peoples to enable them to survive. If indigenous peoples aren't known about, they will disappear. That is my strategy, and it is working. Sarayaku is quite well known as a result of my work – my videos and my photographs – which provided first-hand evidence in the case we brought against the Ecuadorian State when it violated our rights by entering our territory without consultation.
>
> I have continued making short documentaries about things unknown to the modern world outside. If the world doesn't know about us, we'll be defenceless against the extractive industries. My idea is that people have to know about us if they're going to support us, the world has to realize the importance of the Amazon. This is what I do. I have worked since 1999, making my videos, living here in my house in Sarayaku with my family. Sometimes I have participated in film festivals, though that was never my intention.
>
> Even after I had finished my first film, when Sarayaku was trapped, and no one knew about us, the newspaper coverage was against us; entire

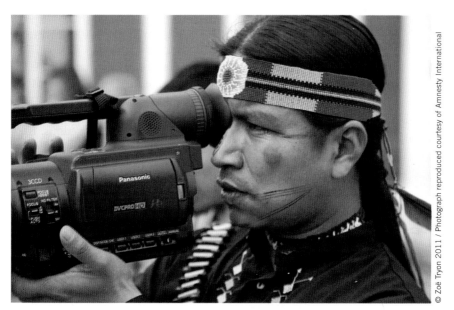

Eriberto Gualinga at the Inter-American Court of Human Rights, Costa Rica

pages in the newspapers were dedicated to labelling us as dangerous people. Airtime on the radio was allocated to discredit and demonize us. My first video showed that Sarayaku is a peaceful community with original ideas on how to save the rainforest. The video transformed the image of the Sarayaku people in the eyes of the universities and the journalists, and from that time on the reportage presented a different picture.

The video changed everything. It was first-hand evidence. All the sociology and anthropology master's students started coming to visit, to get to know the stories of the Sarayaku. Media studies students look at our case as an alternative way of presenting history. In some universities the Sarayaku have become a case study. You could say that we're now too well known. There has been constant media coverage of Sarayaku. Quite a few internationally well-known journalists have come here. We never imagined that our campaign would attract the attention of so many reporters.

The Sarayaku Kichwa are keen to reap the benefits that modernity can bring – for example, in healthcare and education – whilst also being aware that increased contact with mainstream Western knowledge may jeopardize their traditional knowledge and culture. Eriberto continues:

The Sarayaku leaders maintain that the Western model of education used in schools doesn't have to be the only one. The education that we provide our children with is also important. There has to be a balance. It is important that we preserve our culture, but at the same time, we mustn't stand still, without being able to speak Spanish and express what we feel. At the very least we must be able to speak and write in Spanish.

Migration to the cities is another problem. For the moment, we are fine. Our young people are aware of their identity and their territory. They are more committed to speaking Kichwa, without feeling ashamed, in the cities. We used to be ashamed of speaking Kichwa among people in the city, because they would see that we were indigenous. Now we want people to see us as indigenous. And what's interesting is that young people have started writing to each other in Kichwa on social media and WhatsApp. That's something the other communities still don't understand. They think that communication through computers and social media has to be in Spanish. Here we've overcome that. We write in Kichwa, a refined Kichwa. We make jokes. They come out well and people write with no fear of making mistakes.

Ayme Tanguila, a Kichwa from Tena, the capital of Napo province, left her home town to qualify as an architect in Quito. She echoes Eriberto's feelings:

First I am going to tell you why I studied architecture, because initially I wanted to study civil engineering. As you know, we didn't have a bridge where I lived – we had to cross the river by canoe. And on one of those nights when my mother had to be at the hospital to start her shift at 10 p.m., they had an accident because the river was high. It was then that I had the idea of building bridges and making other things, so that no children would become orphans, as I nearly did. That reinforced my resolve.

Ayme Tanguila.

© Ayme Tanguila 2018

After graduating as an architect, I returned to my home town of Tena to work on a government programme to provide homes for disabled people, because I wanted to give something back to my community. I realized that the public provision for disabled people is good, but there are conditions applied in order to qualify for a home, which most Kichwa can't meet as they don't have land titles. I had to look into this question further to understand the reasoning behind the government's decision-making. And I realized that architecture isn't just about building or making beautiful things, it goes beyond that. It demands that we understand space – how we share it and live together, as well as the positive and negative aspects of modernity. I felt compelled to continue studying in order to be a professional, because I felt I was something more than just a member of the Kichwa community. Studying in Quito changes your life: you are no longer just a Kichwa, you are a professional working at the service of society as a whole. You are transformed and see the world from another perspective, but the family back home is always there to remind you who you are by saying, 'You are a Kichwa woman, you have support, and you have to give something back to us, your people.' This motivates me.

Female protagonism and solidarity

In recent years, indigenous women have been growing in confidence and have been increasingly prominent in social movements, higher education, and politics. There is also growing solidarity between indigenous women of different areas, ethnic groups, and even countries. Ayme continues:

> What is this transformation? I asked myself. Western knowledge is consuming me, I thought, but then I understood that I am undergoing this change in order to promote women as symbols of struggle and resistance, so we can achieve our goals. We need to think about the transformation brought about by globalization, the reclaiming of our rights, and where we wish to be ...
>
> I believe that we women have always been oppressed culturally. We weren't seen as being able to speak, participate in important events, or express ourselves, because men have always spoken for us and decided what had to be done in our territories.
>
> Women are coming up with new ideas; we are strengthened by working together. I heard about Alicia Cawiya when she made a speech to the Ecuadorian National Assembly. They had brought her there to speak in support of the government, but she used the opportunity to tell the truth about the indigenous people in her territory. She is a Huaorani woman known for the value and significance of her defence of the Yasuní National Park, and she expressed her opposition to the state despite her limited Spanish. I also came to know Patricia Gualinga, a woman renowned for the case of the Sarayaku and for her Amazonian cosmovision. I've been impressed by her defence of the rights of nature and of indigenous territorial rights, including those of her own Sarayaku Kichwa.
>
> I see strong and brave women who have been recognized for the work they do in their territories. And I recognize their contribution in my own academic work in the city. I see the work Kichwa women do on the land, which is just as hard as that of any man. They work on the farm, take care of the children, sometimes fish in the river. With time, women have gained confidence by asserting the value of their work and of their voice.
>
> There is an interesting network of indigenous professional women. I'm not alone: I have a network of friends in the Amazon and here in the *sierra*. We support each other in every aspect of our lives. There are

ideological differences, but when we women meet in Quito, something magical happens. We're so powerful that when outsiders see us together, they find it very strange, this power of friendship. Even though we haven't known each other all our lives and we're not related to each other, we're linked by our attachment to our homeland.

Similar solidarity can also be seen in Colombia, where Fany Kuiru has created the organization Tejedoras de Memoria (Weavers of Memory), a refuge in Bogotá for indigenous Colombian women who have been displaced from their homes by the country's internal conflict:

Our women have been displaced by armed conflict. We saw how they were living in the city and saw how beaten down they were, how their spirit was gone, and how much they had to learn. But also, how they fight and endure, which was what motivated us. Initially we brought them here and found professional help for them – psychological help. We let them talk, but found that they left even more depressed than when they came in. They didn't seem relieved at all. We were trying to help them, in their pain, in their sorrow, but all we managed to do was to reopen old wounds and bring them into contact with urban professionals who didn't understand their culture and what they had been through. These professionals were trained for the city and their advice was for people from the city. We realized we were only damaging the women further.

Instead, we started little groups weaving and cooking. This allowed the women to begin talking amongst themselves. They were able to share their problems. This way – creating memories of what had happened to them and speaking about it in the context of another activity – they relieved their pain. What better psychosocial intervention than working together at the activities they liked to do? So that's what we decided to move forward with.

We started having a food fair once a month, in our kitchen here. The products we weave are also at the fair and we weave on Saturdays. Collective activity is what really helped these women. It allowed them to regain their health and start their lives afresh, in peace. The idea is to bring together women displaced by armed conflict and begin to weave the peace, through concrete activities that improve their lives materially. Our policy is that every woman is paid for the work she does here – we don't have funding; we haven't had any money apart from what we got from the International Organization for Migration (IOM) initially. The enterprise is sustained by the hard work of the women here; we sell what they produce. We also bring in products from the regions, maintaining links with women in those places. We buy the products, process them, and sell them, to benefit the women here.

We have various clients. Foreigners come here, university professors, employees of the academy, civil servants, and before you arrived, we had two women who work for a human rights organization. People like that, who are aware of the social issues involved in what we do. If it had been otherwise, this wouldn't have been possible. National and international leaders as well – we're very well known. TV and radio have helped raise our profile and make us visible all over the world.

Patricia Gualinga was part of a delegation of Ecuadorian Amazonian women who took their case against the government for arrest, violence, and intimidation to the Inter-American Commission on Human Rights in Washington DC in October 2015. She discusses the increasing female protagonism of recent years:

> The great indigenous mobilizations of 1990 and 1992 were led by men, but it all began to change in 2000, when the movements began to weaken. And there were direct challenges to the leadership. At least that was our experience. So, there was a moment when the women came together and said, 'We can't let this happen. We won't defend the men. There is a common objective, which is to defend our territory. This land must be inherited unpolluted by future generations. And if our men have been demoralized, have lost heart, very well: then the women will rise to the challenge, as wives, mothers, daughters, and sisters, and we will go to the front line.' And I believe that at least here, in the Amazon, this is what motivated us.
>
> We set off on the march to Quito from Puyo on 12 October 2013 at a time when marches were banned, to tell the government that we

Patricia Gualinga.

women did not give our consent [to oil and mineral extraction on our territory].

This was the beginning of the Amazonian women's movement, which many women have joined. Great female leaders have emerged, such as Alicia Cawiya, who has spoken to the National Assembly, and Gloria Ushigua [of the Sápara people]. Many women who can say, 'No, we don't want this, and we're going to say it ourselves. Not our president, not one of the male leaders, but me, I will speak.' Throwing ourselves into defending our territory has made us visible and given us status. We were there all along, but behind the scenes, getting everything ready. Now we're stepping forward, and some of us can be seen in the front line. But we have a long way to go, and there will be changes.

Besides being a leader in her own community, Patricia is also active on the world stage. She was part of a delegation to the Paris climate talks in December 2015, is a member of the Women's Earth and Climate Action Network, and participated in the IUCN World Conservation Congress in Hawaii in September 2016. Indigenous women all over the world have been increasingly finding common cause. Patricia continues:

Indigenous women appeared on the scene at the same time all over the Americas. In the north – in Canada and the US – they had the same idea, the same vision, of defending and protecting the rights of future generations. We knew nothing of each other, but gradually we've been meeting by chance in different parts of the world. I believe the world is created that way; things happen that we don't understand. We've met many women from all over. From the Inuit in Canada to those fighting tar sands, to those in North Dakota resisting the oil pipelines. There are the Mapuche in Chile. Women in different places, all committed to the struggle.

We signed the first agreement one year ago in New York in September 2015 at the time of the red moon. This wasn't by accident: we met again in Paris [at the COP21 climate talks in December 2015]. And some of those women joined us for the Women's March here in Ecuador on International Women's Day [2016]. It's a slow process, but we're doing it our way. We've just sent a message to the women of the north, some of whom are in Washington DC, others who are in Missouri opposing an oil pipeline. We keep in contact according to what's happening in each place.

We're also part of the world network against climate change, involving women in different parts of the world, like in India. We might be in different parts of the continent, of the world, but if we ask for support, we come together ... We can communicate with other groups of women who at a given moment can respond and display solidarity at the global level. I believe that we have to keep expanding these kinds of network.

We have a long way to go in forming an organizational structure, we're not quite there yet. It was spontaneous, unplanned. We just appeared, like plants. We're trying to get organized, seeing how it goes with new faces, new ideas. There are leaders who are well known in certain places. We don't speak the same language. Some speak English, but we manage to understand each other somehow. With some translation, with sign language, with our hearts and feelings. We can relate to each other, which is very positive in our quest to defend nature, Mother Earth, planet earth. If the earth is female, then her defence is in our hands.

* * *

The voices in this chapter are indicative of the radical transformation in the role of indigenous people in Latin America in recent years. They have attained a new pride and confidence in their identity and are active in the defence of their territories, resources, culture, and the planet itself. In order to achieve this they have been engaging with national political processes and institutions; attending school and university, both at undergraduate and postgraduate level; exploiting modern communications and audiovisual technology; and reaching beyond their territories and even national borders in order to find common cause and build solidarity. Indigenous women have been at the forefront of these changes, and the defence of their own territories and cultures has been increasingly intertwined with international environmentalism and the fight against climate change.

Of course, challenges persist. Extraction-based capitalism has expanded since the 1980s and large companies and landowners are often willing to use force where necessary to access land and resources. This is reflected in the proliferation of socioenvironmental conflicts involving indigenous communities, and the high murder rates for indigenous, environmental, and land-rights activists. National governments need to do more to ensure that those responsible for such crimes are brought to justice, and to protect indigenous peoples from those who seek to displace, dispossess, and murder them. This requires concerted political will and greater funding for law enforcement in remote rural areas. 'I would like the indigenous people to be able to return to their lands and go back to living according to their culture, despite globalization,' says Fany Kuiru. 'I'd like to see responsible public policy, as badly-made policies always affect indigenous communities worst of all. They damage and kill more people than bullets.'

Rather than being an obstacle to development, the indigenous people of Latin America are an inspiration for an alternative path. Their emphasis upon reverence for Pachamama (Mother Earth) and *buen vivir* or *vivir bien* – their desire to live in harmony with each other and with nature, sustainably managing the resources found in their territories – is of relevance for governments and citizens the world over, especially in the current context of rampant environmental destruction, mass extinction, and climate change. As Eriberto Gualinga says, 'The concept of *buen vivir* emerged from Sarayaku and then spread. What the government should do, but doesn't, is listen to the indigenous peoples of the rainforest.' Still, though there may be difficulties in obtaining the desired outcomes from government, it is clear that the voices of Abya Yala can no longer be silenced.

About the author

Linda Etchart is a lecturer in Human Geography at Kingston University, London. She has taught at Birkbeck College, University of London, and Anglia Ruskin University. She was an editor at Pluto Press, and a programme officer for the Commonwealth Secretariat. Her published work is in the area of conflict transformation and the role of indigenous peoples in global governance.

Interviews

Alicia Cawiya (vice president of the Huaorani people): interviewed in Quito and Puyo, Ecuador, on 16 and 20 August 2016 by Linda Etchart and James Thackara. Translated by Linda Etchart.

Juan Ch'oc (Crique Sarco village): interviewed in Crique Sarco, Belize, on 14 October 2016 by Rachel Simon. Transcribed by Rachel Simon.

Eriberto Gualinga (Sarayaku Kichwa communications director/film-maker): interviewed in Sarayaku, Ecuador, on 20 August 2016 by Linda Etchart and James Thackara. Translated by Linda Etchart.

Patricia Gualinga (Sarayaku Kichwa activist): interviewed in Puyo, Ecuador, on 24 August 2016 by Linda Etchart and James Thackara. Translated by Linda Etchart.

Fany Kuiru (Tejedoras de Memoria): interviewed in Bogotá on 12 August 2016 by Gwen Burnyeat. Translated by Olivia Plato and Hebe Powell.

Eva Sánchez (Las Hormigas): interviewed in Intibucá, Honduras, on 26 October 2016 by Louise Morris. Translated by Louise Morris.

Ayme Tanguila (Kichwa architect and urbanist): interviewed in Quito on 27 August 2016 by Linda Etchart. Translated by Linda Etchart.

Froyla Tzalam (SATIIM): interviewed in Punta Gorda, Belize, on 10 October 2016 by Rachel Simon. Transcribed by Rachel Simon.

References

NB: All web references were checked and still available in May/June 2018 unless otherwise stated. All references are listed, with web-links, on the page for this chapter on the Voices website www.vola.org.uk

Balch, O. (2013) 'Buen vivir: the social philosophy inspiring movements in South America', *The Guardian*, 4 February, <https://www.theguardian.com/sustainable-business/blog/buen-vivir-philosophy-south-america-eduardo-gudynas>

Barrett, P.M. (2013) 'Canada says 'No thanks' to Chevron pollution suit', *Bloomberg Businessweek*, 2 May, <https://www.bloomberg.com/news/articles/2013-05-02/canada-says-no-thanks-to-chevron-pollution-suit>

Diamond, J. (2005) *Guns, Germs, and Steel*, 2nd edn, Vintage, London.

Etchart, L. (2018) 'Ecuador, Chevron and the extractor's curse'', three-part article series, LAB, London, 17 September <https://lab.org.uk/chevron-ecuador-and-the-extractors-curse-1/>

Forst, M. (2017) cited in F. Martone, 'Defenders of the earth and the environment', *Other News*, 12 November, <http://www.other-news.info/2017/12/defenders-of-the-earth-and-the-environment>

Galeano, E. (1971) *Open Veins of Latin America*, translated from the Spanish by C. Belfrage (1997), Monthly Review Press, New York.

Miller, T. (2003) 'Ecuador: Texaco leaves trail of destruction', Corpwatch, <https://corpwatch.org/article/ecuador-texaco-leaves-trail-destruction>

CHAPTER 6

The hydroelectric threat to
the Amazon basin

Marilene Cardoso Ribeiro and Sue Branford

Abstract

For decades hydroelectric power was seen as the solution to Latin America's energy needs. However, serious questions have arisen over its long-term viability. Ecologists warn of the potentially catastrophic impact of dams on the Amazon basin, the most complex network of river channels in the world. Dams have also had hugely damaging impacts on indigenous and riverine communities. Moreover, major hydro projects have been plagued by massive corruption.

Fifty years ago, when the boom in dam-building began in Latin America, this new form of energy was greeted enthusiastically. Big dams became symbols of national pride and evidence of economic progress. The advocates argued that hydroelectricity would provide cheap, reliable energy for remote areas, would permit countries to develop their industries, and was renewable, allowing Latin America to promote itself as a progressive, environmentally friendly region. Today, no other region generates as much power from hydro as Latin America. It accounts for roughly 65 per cent of all electricity generated, while the world average is about 16 per cent.

Brazil is the region's leader, generating 74 per cent of all its electricity from hydropower. Over the last two decades Brazil (just like China) has been keen to generate even more energy from its rivers, announcing plans to dam all the major tributaries of the Amazon that lie to the east of the city of Manaus. Some of the world's most magnificent rivers – the Madeira, the Trombetas, the Tapajós, the Teles Pires, the Juruena, the Xingu – were all to be dammed and put to the task of generating energy. Brazil also sought to fund hydro projects in Peru, Bolivia, Ecuador, Guyana, Paraguay, and Venezuela. At one stage, it seemed that 288 dams would be built across the whole of the Amazon basin (Latrubesse et al., 2017).

However, for some time scientists and policymakers have been asking whether the environmental and social costs of the Amazon dams outweigh their benefits. In 2014, the anthropologist Paul Little published a report in which he said that there were plans for building dams on five of the six main rivers that drain into the Amazon from the Andes. The governments, he said, were carrying out a 'hydrological experiment of continental proportions' with

http://dx.doi.org/10.3362/9781909014213.006

'little knowledge of the ecological consequences of this policy'. He warned of the risk of 'provoking irreversible changes in rivers' (Little, 2014).

Many others shared his concerns. Last year, the University of Texas researcher Edgardo Latrubesse and 15 collaborators published an article in the journal *Nature*, in which they warned of the impact of hundreds of dams being built in and around the Amazon, which they called 'the largest and most complex network of river channels in the world' (Latrubesse et al., 2017). Rivers in the Amazon basin exchange sediments across continental distances to deliver nutrients to 'a mosaic of wetlands', argued Latrubesse and colleagues. This sustains wildlife, contributes to regional food supplies, and modulates river dynamics, resulting in high habitat and biotic diversity for both aquatic and non-aquatic organisms. Disrupting this network, which sustains the highest biodiversity on earth, could have a catastrophic impact, they warned.

Recent research also shows that hydropower is not the environmentally friendly form of energy that it was long believed to be. Indeed, damming rivers in the Amazon basin could compromise the region's efforts to combat global warming, as reservoirs located in tropical zones are known to produce significant amounts of greenhouse gases – sometimes, remarkably, generating much more of them than an ordinary coal-fed power plant (Fearnside, 2015). This would make it difficult for the countries to fulfil the commitments they made at the UN's 2015 Climate Change Conference in Paris.

Then there are the social costs. Kate Horner, director of International Rivers, a vociferous river protection group that is very active in Latin America, points to this problem. 'Rivers are seen by governments only as a resource, not as a source of livelihood,' she said. 'Vast money is involved in these mega-projects and seldom is anyone held responsible for the violence and intimidation that often accompanies dam-building.'

Researcher Ismael Vega, from the Amazonian Centre of Anthropology and Practical Application (CAAAP) in Peru, an institution that defends indigenous rights and the environment, says that governments have long ignored the damage done to nature and local communities by dams:

> The government of Alan García [former president of Peru] was very active in forging alliances with governments in South America, especially Brazil during the Lula administration. It signed an agreement, under which Peru would supply Brazil with energy produced at these hydro-electric plants. This would directly affect hundreds of native Amazonian communities located around these rivers, especially the Marañón, probably the most important river in the region after the Amazon. In the agreement between Peru and Brazil, as well as in legislation passed by Alan García, there are at least 20 dams planned, many of them on the Marañón. If that happens, the impact on the biodiversity and ecosystems of the river basin would be severe. In fact, it would affect the whole Amazon region.

To see the effects of big dams of this type, we will examine in some detail the fallout from the construction of the third-largest hydroelectric plant in the world: Belo Monte, located in the state of Pará, in the north of Brazil.

Living on the banks of the Xingu

Leonardo Batista, son of a non-indigenous *ribeirinho* father (as those living on riverbanks in the Brazilian Amazon are called) and an indigenous woman from the ethnic group Yudjá/Juruna, saw the Xingu river for the first time on the day he was born. He is also known as Aronor, the name given to him by his indigenous grandmother. For 58 years, the flow of the Xingu formed the backdrop of his life:

> I was born in 1959 on Araruna island in the last stretch of the Volta Grande do Xingu [Big Bend in the Xingu], almost downstream of it. In the 'winter' [the rainy season, when the river is in flood], I used to help my family collect Brazil nuts, tap rubber trees, and fish. That was how we made a living back then.
>
> I was about eight years old when my father moved to the region of Paratizão [upstream from the Volta Grande do Xingu] but life went on as before. The beach was our recreation. In June, we'd spend our holidays there: we'd sleep there, fish, cook what we caught, splash around in the rapids. It was so beautiful. There were lovely patches of shade on the island, where you could hang hammocks, watch the world go by, feel the breeze, hear the birds singing. It was beautiful.

Leonardo Batista, aka Aronor.

When I was older, I went to work as a cowboy on a ranch, and at weekends I used to go down to the river to fish. These were my two sources of income: the ranch, and fishing, which my wife helped me with. Some months we didn't need to touch the money I earned at the farm, because the income from the fishing was enough. We led a happy life, we were independent, we had food. We could afford everything we needed.

In 2011, the Brazilian government began work on Belo Monte. Norte Energia, the public-private company coordinating the project, started evicting people, about 40,000 in all. Most lived in or around Altamira, the main town in the region, through which the Xingu flows. Some 1,500 of them were *ribeirinhos*, including Aronor. Like most rural families, they had not registered their plots with the authorities and most were unaware that they still had rights, including the right to be resettled on comparable land. Until they began to organize and to demand more, Norte Energia either paid them an arbitrary (and usually derisory) amount of money in compensation or sent them to live in five concrete-and-asphalt housing estates specially built for them on the outskirts of Altamira.

Aronor and his family were resettled in one of these – the Jatobá Collective Urban Resettlement (RUC). It suffers from chronic water shortages and in late 2016, after having to cope for almost a week without water (in the scorching Amazonian weather), Aronor and other inhabitants from his estate went to the Norte Energia office to demand water. They got it back – for one day – and then the shortages began again.

Aronor joined the Movimento Xingu Vivo para Sempre, a grassroots movement that emerged in the early days of opposition to the Belo Monte project. He is also a member of the Ribeirinho Council, a collective created to campaign for the *ribeirinhos* to be resettled in places where they can carry on with their old way of life, as the law requires. Aronor describes what happened to them:

> People were scattered across the region. It was like when you have a rice field and a flock of chopi blackbirds starts pecking at your crop. If you fire a pistol, the birds fly off in every direction. That's how things happened here. We live almost four kilometres away from the river now. What happened to us was like leaving a turtle on a mountainside or throwing a tortoise into a lagoon. We're not from here; we're from the riverside, born and bred. How are we to live? How will we feed our families? What happened to our rights?
>
> After we'd left, they cleared the land. Sometimes they used chainsaws and piled up the timber on the shore. Then they loaded it onto ferries and transported it to land. I don't know where it went after that. Any wood they didn't want, they just burnt. That was something we never thought we'd see. There was no way of stopping them – for them it was the easiest thing in the world. But if we'd ever said we wanted to clear a patch of forest so we could plant manioc or beans, we were told we

The Belo Monte dam under construction, revealing the devastation of the river valley and surrounding forest.

needed a licence from IBAMA [the government environmental agency]. If we didn't get it, we were fined. Yet they were allowed to deforest the islands. We saw it happen, before our very eyes. Why did IBAMA let them do it? We don't understand.

When we saw those machines, clearing the forests, it felt as if they were removing a piece of us. They cut down all the trees on these islands; they're completely bare now. We thought that only the islands nearest the dam would be deforested. But they [Norte Energia] came here and deforested another nine … They'd put five, six, or seven diggers to work at the same time, on a single island. It all happened within a month. It was like a plague of machines. I told my children and my wife, 'There's a passage in the Bible, in the Apocalypse, which says that in the end grass-hoppers will come and destroy everything. The grasshoppers are these machines.' Bastards! They came here with their machines to destroy everything we had.

The environment is suffering just as much as we are, and we feel that. When we go into the forest, or down to the river, when we see those trees being cut down, we know they're suffering, just like us. If they had any respect for nature, they wouldn't have done that, right? How many beaches, where the turtles lay their eggs, were destroyed then? How many stone caves, where zebra plecos and other fish used to live, were filled in? It's all finished. They had no respect for anyone, not for the human population nor for nature. That's something I'm not afraid to say; I've never been afraid to speak the truth. They have no compassion! We care for things out of love; they destroy them for money.

I always say that, when we go back to the *beiradão* [riverbank] where we used to live, it feels like putting a photo of our mother or father on the wall: we can see them, but we know they're not alive any more. It's so sad!

I don't understand what kind of government would do this to us. I saw an interview with President Dilma [Rousseff], during her term of office, at the end of 2013. She was talking about Belo Monte, here in Altamira. On the *Jornal Nacional* [Globo TV's flagship news programme], she said that Belo Monte had come to Altamira to improve the town and to respect the rights of individuals, particularly those of indigenous people. But it wasn't true! What we are seeing is just violation of rights and lack of respect! This is very sad for us. We protested and tried to get the dam stopped. At times, a judge has ordered work to stop, but it never does.

Brazil promotes hydropower

Surprisingly perhaps, it was Brazil's first genuinely left-wing government following the country's re-democratization which was the staunchest defender of this big expansion of hydropower. Luiz Inácio Lula da Silva, from the Workers' Party (PT), elected president in 2002, did a great deal to lift very poor families out of poverty, but his government did not show much interest in the environment, biodiversity, or the thousands of traditional communities living in the Amazon basin.

Channelling vast amounts of highly subsidized credit to key private companies through the national development bank, BNDES, the government sought to create 'Brazilian champions', broadly similar to the Japanese *keiretsu* and the South Korean *chaebols*. The idea was to create corporations that could compete as equals with the biggest companies in the world. The main beneficiaries were the country's large engineering companies – Odebrecht, OAS, Camargo Corrêa, and Andrade Gutierrez. These companies began building dams around the region, not just in Brazil. Ecuador under President Rafael Correa agreed to eight dams and Peru to five (Aleixo and Condé, 2015).

Eventually Brazil's engineering companies would be sucked into Brazil's colossal *Lava Jato* (Car Wash) scandal, which landed Odebrecht's CEO, Marcelo Odebrecht, in prison for two and a half years. The scandal has extended into Peru, where several senior officials accused of receiving bribes from Odebrecht have been arrested. Ismael Vega says that this has created a problem for the Peruvian government:

This corruption scandal involving Odebrecht and the most recent governments in Peru has undoubtedly had a big impact on the construction and development of several mega-projects in various parts of the country ... There are big projects in the Amazon region, along with interoceanic roads in the north and south, that are complete, they were finished years ago. These projects are part of the Initiative for the Integration of the Regional Infrastructure of South America (IIRSA), a multi-billion-dollar project for integrating infrastructure in the region.

But the scandal has revealed cost overruns and illicit payments, and the fact that a lot of these projects were implemented without meeting certain standards. In a sense, it is logical to expect this because, if these projects were created in an atmosphere of corruption, in which Odebrecht and its associates received special favours, it's obvious that all the usual prerequisites, conditions, deadlines, and formalities, as required by law, will not have been met. If corruption has been present from the very beginning, it's obvious that everything else later on will be made easier for them.

I think all this is happening because in Brazil we are seeing a big increase in mining and oil extraction. This requires vast amounts of energy. Brazil has a big interest in getting energy from Peru because it is well known – and the Brazilians will know this for sure – that environmental standards and protections for indigenous peoples have been greatly relaxed in recent years. To give you a concrete example, whereas before an Environmental Impact Assessment (EIA) might take two years, it can now be done in six months – this is a big change. For certain projects, the state doesn't even require a detailed EIA, but instead something very preliminary and superficial. They're relaxing regulations even in cases where there may be relics or artefacts of archaeological or cultural value. The main priority of recent governments has been to attract private investment for mega development projects and extractive projects, and this is reflected in several important laws, norms, and decrees.

Meanwhile, the opposition to such projects has been growing and at times has been criminalized. For instance, Manuel Trujillo and Manuela Pacheco were charged with terrorism in 2016 for their opposition to the Hidrotambo dam in Ecuador's central province of Bolívar, though the courts eventually exonerated the pair. According to social movements, they were just two of over a hundred community leaders and activists whom the Correa administration criminalized for opposition to such projects.

In Brazil, too, there is growing resentment over the way the big construction companies act as a law unto themselves. Aronor explains:

Norte Energia and the Belo Monte Construction Consortium (CCBM) [which represents the big construction companies building the dam] do whatever they like. They don't obey IBAMA or the Federal Public Prosecutors [from the Federal Public Ministry, an independent branch of government], the DPU [the Public Defence of the Union, a judicial branch of government], or anyone else! No one seems able to control them. Why is there no authority, no tribunal that can issue an injunction stopping the Belo Monte project? And if we get together and claim our rights, we are treated as criminals and repressed by the police or by the National Public Security Force. No! We are claiming our rights, they cannot do this to us.

The obstinacy of the PT government in pushing ahead with hydropower may seem hard to comprehend. But, as the story of Belo Monte shows, there have long been powerful vested interests promoting the construction of dams in Brazil.

The story of Belo Monte

Belo Monte was first proposed by the military government in the late 1970s as one of several dams to be built on the Xingu river. At that time, it had a different name – Kararaô, or 'war cry' in the Kayapó indigenous language. The complex would have flooded almost 20,000 square kilometres of forest, affecting 12 indigenous territories, along with some groups of isolated Indians. But as the military came under increasing pressure to hand back power to civilians, the project was ditched.

In 1986, the civilian government that took over from the military made another attempt. But it was a time of growing international environmental awareness and Brazilian opponents of the dams found ready support abroad. The 'First Encounter of the Indigenous Nations of the Xingu', held in 1989, attracted environmentalists from all over the world.

The high point came when Tuíra, a woman warrior from the Kayapó people, interrupted a public hearing about the dam. She ran her blade across the cheeks of José Antônio Muniz Lopes, then president of the state-owned electric holding company, Eletrobras, saying in her own language, 'You are a liar, we don't need electricity. Electricity is not going to give us food. We need our rivers to flow freely, our future depends on it.' Shortly afterwards, the World Bank cancelled a US$500 million loan to Brazil and the plan to dam the Xingu was shelved.

But the authorities didn't give up. They put the project back on the table in 2005 for the third time (Pontes, 2011), showing much greater political nous. They scaled down the project from six independent plants to one complex, with a new design that meant that a smaller area would be flooded, 516 square kilometres.

Maria Eliete Felix Juruna is an indigenous teacher, and daughter of Manoel Juruna, the former chief of Paquiçamba village (located on the Paquiçamba Indigenous Reserve). She recalls the arrival of Belo Monte:

I first heard about this dam a long time ago. I was still a child when the protests began. My father took part. People said they were going to build a dam called Kararaô, that the land would be flooded. But then it seemed it wouldn't be built. About 30 years went by without a decision, then more people started arriving in the area around 2010. The National

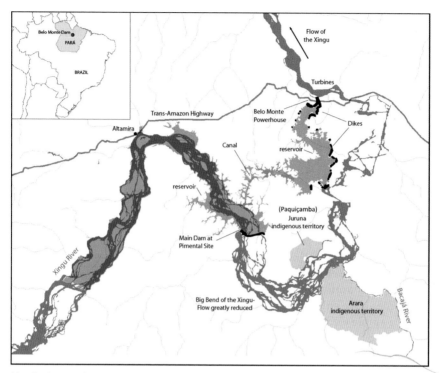

Map by International Rivers, adapted by Marilene Cardoso Ribeiro

Indian Foundation (FUNAI) came and told us it would be bringing in a team to conduct an assessment because the dam was going ahead. My father said to us, 'It won't happen. They've been saying it will go ahead for ages, but it never happens.' 'Really?' I replied. 'It looks to me like a lot of people are coming here … ' But he said, 'No. It won't happen.' Things continued like that, with people appearing from time to time to do assessments, study the animals and the fish. The next thing we knew, it was already happening.

The project remained highly controversial, largely because it became clear that the dam would fail miserably to generate the amount of energy promised. Walter Coronado Antunes, the former secretary of the environment of the state of São Paulo, called Belo Monte 'the worst engineering project in the history of hydroelectric dams in Brazil. Something that we engineers should truly feel ashamed of' (Instituto de Engenharia, 2010). He explained that the huge variations in flow between the rainy and dry seasons would spell technical and economic disaster for the dam. Engineers suggested that the dam would generate only about 4.5 GW of its maximum capacity of 11.233 GW. Brazil's engineering companies, apprehensive that the dam would operate with heavy losses, refused to invest their own money in the project, despite the BNDES offering what were 'among the best [terms] in the world' (Hurwitz et al., 2011). In the end, the companies agreed to carry out the construction work, with the state assuming most of the risk.

But the fiercest criticism came from researchers and environmentalists, fearful of the impact of the dam on the region's rich biodiversity (e.g. Sevá Filho, 2005; Santos and Hernández, 2009), and from NGOs and social movements, outraged at the way the authorities were excluding indigenous and riverine communities from the decision-making process. Once again, the government brushed off the criticisms, even dismissing concerns expressed by its own watchdog agencies, notably FUNAI and IBAMA. Among other highly publicized clashes, Abelardo Bayma Azevedo resigned as president of IBAMA in January 2011, after refusing to grant the project a licence, saying that Belo Monte was 'still full of environmental problems' (MediaLivre, 2011). Activists tried hard to stop the project again, but this time they failed.

Part of the explanation for successive governments' tenacity stems from the political power that engineering companies have held in Brazil since the building of Brasília in the late 1950s. Since then, political parties and these companies have enjoyed an ever cosier relationship, in which the companies provide ample electoral funding and, in return, are awarded big construction projects once the party comes to power. This scheme predated Lula's election, but the PT became particularly dependent on this money. It desperately needed Belo Monte to go ahead so it could pay back the engineering companies, particularly Odebrecht, for the huge sums it had taken (Branford, 2016).

Many people knew of this illegal scheme but were too frightened to denounce it publicly (Pontes, 2011). Felício Pontes Jr. a prosecutor at the Federal Public Ministry (MPF) for the state of Pará, an independent body of federal prosecutors, was one of the first to dare speak openly:

> The factor that explains the irrational option for hydroelectric stations in the Amazon is corruption. In other words, energy planning in Brazil is not treated as a strategic issue involving the future of the nation but, at least since the time of the military dictatorship, as a source of money for construction companies and politicians. I think that, until these questions are exposed and resolved, we will continue to have expensive and inefficient dams that have a serious social and environmental impact in Amazonia (Branford, 2018).

The impact of Belo Monte

Along with Aronor, other *ribeirinhos* had their lives turned upside down (Ribeiro, 2018). Maria Rosa Pessoa Piedade and her family, who for three generations lived in Palhau, beside the Xingu river, were also evicted. Her mother now lives in Paixão de Cristo, one of the new informal communities that have sprung up on the outskirts of Altamira since the Belo Monte project started. Her father died during the process of eviction. Maria Rosa now lives in Transunião, about two hours away by car and ferry, far from the river and from her mother:

We had to leave in 2013, but we still ache for it. It was where we grew up. We loved the place and they made us leave. We didn't want to go. We left because Norte Energia made us. If it were up to us, we'd still be there.

They said we couldn't plant or buy any more animals [cattle, chickens, etc.], but neither could we leave to work somewhere else. If we did, we'd be marked down as having abandoned our land. They said it would mean that we didn't need the land for our living and so we wouldn't get any compensation. So we had to stay, selling whatever we had so we could eat and survive.

At first, when Norte Energia started compensating people, they took the houses apart, separating the timber and everything else, and took it all away. They put it all in trucks and took it to our new homes. They helped the first people move, but not the rest of us. We had to pay people to dismantle our house and organize things. We had to pay for everything. It wasn't possible to take everything at once, because we had to arrange things at our new home and then go back. When we got back, Norte Energia had in the meantime dug a hole and buried everything we'd left behind! There was nothing left, it was all buried. We lost everything! They told us they were just obeying orders.

My mother lived peacefully in the rural area, raising her animals, bathing in the river, going anywhere she liked. Now she lives in a house with the doors locked, behind barred windows. She can't go out because crime has really been increasing in Altamira. Locked up, stifled, in a place like this!

There's no point in saying 'I've got money, I've got a car, I've got this, I've got that.' If you don't feel good, if you don't have the life you had before, it doesn't matter if you have a nice house. You might be stuck inside, with nowhere to go, because if you go out, then a criminal might kill you, or something might happen to you. If you have some money, you live with threats. These kids got into crime as soon as they came to the city, because most of them have had no education. They kill because they're ignorant, they didn't know what city life was like. Many older people who came here [to Altamira] have died as well. A lot, really. So I tell you there's no money that's worth the life we had before.

I'm still very bitter because of what happened to my father, who had a heart condition, amongst other health problems. Once he heard about the dam, he wouldn't stop talking about it. He didn't want to leave his home and abandon his things. He was very worried. His health deteriorated and eventually he died. It still shocks me. I used to spend the day with him, trying to take his mind off things, but he didn't stop talking about it. He didn't want people to destroy what he'd worked so hard to preserve. He had a great love for the rubber trees because tapping rubber was how he had supported his children, all 10 of them.

There were a few islands – Palhau, Inocêncio, Ilha Grande – which had rubber trees. My father took care of them all. But it wasn't just the rubber trees that were important for us, everything was. That was where we did all our fishing and relaxed. There were the [river] beaches and rapids, lots of them. It was all precious to us and now it's gone. When they were clearing the forest on the islands to be flooded, there was nowhere for the animals to go. They fled to the beach when the machines were clearing. If they went back, a machine ran them over. There was no way to avoid it. Many of them drowned.

We've seen the animals suffer a lot, including the fish, which lost their natural habitat. They lived in clean, flowing water. Now they're in stagnant water and many of them have died. Also, many people Norte Energia said wouldn't be affected were affected in the end, but they've ignored them, denying it's happened.

We feel a lot of anger and resentment. If we could change things … it's as my husband always says: if we knew who Norte Energia were, then we could go there and strangle them [laughs]. But we don't know who's who. When we go there [to Norte Energia's office in Altamira], the answer is always 'Oh, they're in Brasília.' We never find anyone in charge for us to speak to.

Antônia Melo is one of the leaders of the struggle against Belo Monte. Coordinator of Movimento Xingu Vivo para Sempre, she has often represented the movement in talks with the government. She recalls a meeting in Brasília which she, Dom Erwin Kräutler (the bishop of Xingu and another fighter in the struggle against Belo Monte), and other leaders had with Dilma Rousseff, at that time minister of mines and energy during Lula's first term. Dilma arrived late, says Antônia, and said just a single sentence, as she slammed her fist on the table: 'Belo Monte will happen!' She then stood up and left. Dilma was elected president in 2010, and Belo Monte, as she had declared, was built.

Antônia was part of another group which met Lula in 2009, at the end of his second term. The then president promised that Belo Monte 'wouldn't be forced down the throats' of the people. But as Aronor puts it, the government's intention was precisely to build Belo Monte at any cost: 'You know, Belo Monte came to our town and the Brazilian government said to Norte Energia: "Go there and do it! Come what may, whoever dies, just go there and do it."'

Years later, as she recalled those two meetings with the PT in Brasília, Antônia Melo wept at the betrayal (Brum, 2015). She had been one of the founders of the PT in Altamira and believed that the Lula government would put an end to the way the Amazon region had been treated as a colony by the rest of the country. But she has refused to surrender, despite being forced out of her home in Altamira in 2015:

Antônia Melo.

> Expelling me from here is another attempt to silence me. They won't succeed. They'll drag me away, destroy all this, but they'll never silence me. Even though they'll smile, feeling certain they defeated me, I still feel sorry for them. Because they're the ones who have lost out. They'll never again find the peace of mind I enjoy. The peace of mind of someone who wasn't a coward, who didn't surrender. I continue to hold my flag aloft. And hanging over the lot of them – the government, those companies – is the responsibility for a monstrous crime. I'll never forgive them. Nature will never forgive them. It is unforgivable. Lula and Dilma are criminals, traitors, cowards. I'm not afraid of saying so to their faces. I hope I meet them one day to do just that.
>
> Every time I look at what they're doing, destroying houses, destroying the river, destroying lives, the stronger my resolve to resist, the more courage and strength I find to say 'no' and continue the fight. For me, Belo Monte isn't a fait accompli … Belo Monte is a crime against humanity. I cannot give up. I can't, I must never, not for a second. Even if one day I'm the only one left, I'll still resist.
>
> Material things have least value. A chair, a bed, a shelf. To me their value is meaningless. What is meaningful is the value of these feelings, which will never end … What is meaningful is the certainty that I was happy here. Because I helped build all this. That's why it's difficult and painful for people to be torn from their homes on the banks of the Xingu. It's where they belong. It's painful, something they'll never forget for the rest of their days. That's what Belo Monte does: it tears out all forms of life, until even the memories are wiped out forever, until there are no longer any roots. The government is killing our memories.

For the Indians living on the reserves the situation was different, but no less harmful. There were no evictions, as no indigenous land needed to be flooded, but nonetheless FUNAI demanded that Norte Energia take emergency actions to prepare the Indians for the changes ahead. Under an Emergency Plan, Norte Energia agreed to provide every indigenous community with R$30,000 (around £7,500) on a monthly basis. This ran from 2010 to 2012, by which time it had achieved none of its goals (ISA, 2016; MPF, 2013). The consortium negotiated privately and directly with each of the indigenous leaders on how the monthly R$30,000 should be spent, asking for a 'list' of required items. These 'lists' ended up reflecting personal and random demands, including items like vehicles, boats, boat engines, fuel, soft drinks, biscuits, and TVs (MPF,

2015; ISA, 2016). Carolina Reis, a lawyer at the NGO Instituto Socioambiental, said that the authorities did not take into account the fact that the indigenous communities had little experience in dealing with the market economy and consumer society. 'This lack of familiarity led them to fritter away the rain of money suddenly coming from Norte Energia', she said (Sullivan, 2016).

As the Indians switched suddenly from a diet based on cassava flour, freshly caught fish, fruits, nuts, and game to one of processed food, they began to suffer from diet-related diseases such as hypertension, diabetes, and malnutrition. With their food needs supplied by monthly deliveries, people gave up farming. Crops vanished, and piles of litter accumulated on indigenous land. As well as this, local leaders were constantly travelling to Altamira to negotiate with the company. This undermined their autonomy and destroyed their cohesion as a group. In a retrospective analysis, the Federal Public Ministry was damning of the Emergency Plan. It said it was 'a massive policy of pacification and silencing, performed with the use of resources destined for ethno-development ... It quickly reached the most remote village of the middle Xingu, causing damage that has not yet been assessed but is clearly present' (MPF, 2014).

Maria Eliete soon realized that Norte Energia was attempting to undermine the cohesion of the indigenous groups:

> They [Norte Energia officials] said, 'We're going to listen to each leader in turn. This way, we both can each say what we need to say. At the moment, we're having trouble making you understand that the project really will be a good thing.'
>
> As far as I'm concerned, we were screwed from that point. Because it's different: having a meeting with the whole community is one thing but for the company to talk to just one or two leaders at a time undermines the group. Their people have been trained to talk to you, to make you think what they want you to think. And that's exactly what happened. They started to meet each group separately and then each leader in turn. That's how we ended up losing control. Our people used to live together in just one village. Now we have three, because people were upset they weren't being listened to. It used to just be Paquiçamba village. Now we have Mïratu, Paquiçamba, and Furo Seco.
>
> The caciques were always older people. They decided everything. My father was one of them. They couldn't read or write, they couldn't understand the technical terms that Norte Energia used. [My father] was involved at the start but then said, 'I can't do it.' He was very open with us. 'I don't understand it. There's so much we have to read, but I can't read. My daughter, it's no use.'
>
> So what happened? Norte Energia realized it was on to something and started to manipulate them. They persuaded them [the caciques] to sign documents they couldn't read. The leaders, including my father, told the community, 'This is going to benefit us', and the community

Maria Eliete Felix Juruna.

believed them: 'If the leaders say it's good, considering they've looked after us their whole lives, then it's going to be great!' It was people from outside, who were more aware of what was going on, who warned us about the harm the dam would do.

'What will happen?' we asked. 'Will the river run dry? What are we going to live on?' Norte Energia replied, 'You will plant cacao, we will help you set up the plantations on your land.' They reassured us. 'If the river runs dry, we'll build a road for you. You'll be able to come and go by car. Things will be much better.' People began to believe that everything really would improve. When the Norte Energia officials arrived, only one or two, maybe three, families had motorboats. So they started offering us boats and other things like that. They said that whatever we asked for they would give us. We'd never seen anything like it. People took the offers.

The same thing happened to other groups, like the Xikrin. Before, the villagers couldn't even ride a bicycle. Suddenly, they started driving cars, or boats with a 90 or 120 [horsepower] engine! At that time the water level was high enough to use the boats. But now, though we still have the boats, they're not much use because the water level is too low. In that first year, everybody was happy! But really the company just wanted to get on with the work and keep the indigenous peoples quiet.

I remember, I used to go to the meetings. Norte Energia said, 'What have these people ever given you?' Meaning the people from the indigenous movement, the Indigenous Missionary Council (CIMI) and I don't know who else. 'What have they ever done for you? Nothing! They only want to hold things up. Have they ever given you any boats? No? Didn't think so!' True, they didn't give us anything. But neither did they take anything from us.

Hydroelectric companies have adopted similar strategies in other countries. Ismael Vega describes the approach at the Lorena dam, being built by the Brazilian engineering company Andrade Gutierrez, on the Marañón in northern Peru:

> They establish direct relationships with members of a certain community or with a leader or chief. They take advantage of the lack of information and make initial agreements with individuals. Little by little they get their foot in the door and start paying people off or exploiting people's needs. They offer things. They always try to establish direct agreements with some of the members or leaders in the communities – especially in communities that will be directly affected by the project. This happens very frequently and the lack of oversight by the state gives the companies carte blanche to act in this way.

Belo Monte comes on stream

In May 2016 Belo Monte began operations. What have its impacts been so far? The most evident, clearly visible from the air, has been deforestation, with the felling of 15,000 hectares of rainforest for the project itself and a marked increase in illegal deforestation as demand for timber has grown. The river has also been seriously affected, with only a fifth of the earlier volume of water flowing through Volta Grande, the 100-kilometre bend, as most of the water has been diverted away from the main river to drive the turbines – another impact discernible from a plane.

Before Belo Monte, the amount of water flowing into the river from the forest varied hugely, from about 32,000 cubic metres of water per second at Altamira during the rainy season, to 450–500 cubic metres per second during the dry season. This means that the level of the river was generally about five metres lower in the summer than in the winter. Many species of fish depended on this seasonal variation to gain access to food in the forest canopy. But now the 'pulse' of the river has been disrupted and fish are going hungry and dying. As *American Scientist* put it, 'the new environmental flow regime is part of a grand experiment that no aquatic biologist would risk. The results could be catastrophic' (Pérez, 2015).

Aronor describes what it meant for him:

> Before the dam we could make our home on the *beiradão*. We knew that during the 'winter', it would be under water, after the river flooded. But we also knew that the beach would return in 'summer', and we would have our home back. Now the beach has gone for good, and that's tough.

Fishing is no longer possible. Even if I could live on the riverbank, it wouldn't be possible, because our fish have gone. Until 2015, I used to go fishing with my wife and son in the summer. We would catch about 50 kilos of fish and a hundred kilos or more of *acari*, a thick-skinned catfish. Because *acari* is really popular, sometimes we'd sell all the *acari* but not the other fish. But the *acari* was one of the first species to be affected by the changes. Nobody wants them any more. They're sick, dying. They're bottom feeders, they survive from the moss on the riverbed. They need fast-flowing currents, but our river is gone, it has become a lake.

Since the water is no longer flowing, the moss and the stones where the *acari* live are all covered in mud. The current used to wash the rocks, leaving behind only the moss, which was the fish's food. Now the islands have been deforested, there's a lot more mud around, and it gets stuck between the rocks. The *acaris* are eating the mud and it's making them ill. You can catch them with your bare hands, from dry land! Between one and two o'clock in the afternoon you can find them hiding under pieces of wood, because there aren't any rocks. They've been forced into the shallows now, and they're suffering from the heat of the sun as well.

Many aquatic species, like the zebra pleco [another kind of catfish], are all dying. They don't move. They stay and die. Just like the *acari*. What will happen to the other fish? No one knows. There's a fish that used to be only found here in our Xingu, which is the *pacu-de-seringa*, so called because it feeds on the flower and fruit of the rubber tree [*seringue-ira*] and on whelks, a kind of river slug. These were the first fish to disappear, because the whelks were buried by the mud and died, and the rubber trees were cut down when the islands were cleared.

Birds such as the guan and the hoatzin are also suffering. The hoatzin feeds on leaves, but there are no leaves left. They're so weak that they're falling into the water. Those that aren't rescued die. The iguanas are also dying. They haven't laid eggs this year. The beaches where they lay their eggs have disappeared. Not to mention the yellow-spotted river turtles; we have no idea where they went. We've lost what we used to help preserve. Hunting these turtles for food used to be forbidden. We understood that this was done to preserve them.

The Xingu river was a mother who embraced us. She provided us with everything we needed. I still dream about having our mother back, about looking out over our mighty river, seeing our relatives happy. I wish it were all true. I dreamt that the dams burst. We were yelling for joy, seeing our river, our beaches, everything just the way it used to be. Suddenly – because everything happens so fast in dreams – we were all together again, hugging each other and seeing our nature alive again, our river, beaches, fish, and everything else. Who knows whether we'll ever see this one day?

There are times when we get desperate, but we need to think positively. We must breathe and ask God for better days, for good things to come, given that we've only had trouble since 2011. Our situation is difficult. It'll get worse if we don't take action. I worry a lot, but the time will come when everyone is ready to fight. We must fight. We can't permit them to violate our rights like this. We don't want to fight, but we'll have no choice.

Maria Eliete describes what the changes have meant for the Juruna of Paquiçamba:

What happened after they built the road? More accidents. It became easier for people to come here. It became easier to bring drink in. Easier to bring anything in! Things like roads might seem attractive, but they can also come with a lot of problems. By the time the indigenous people woke up, it was too late.

The road also brought poachers. They wait for nightfall and then come to hunt. I bumped into one once. It used to be difficult for poachers to get close to the village. They would hunt further away. But the road has made their life easier. We also have a problem with fishermen who trespass on indigenous land. The game is moving further away and, if we have no way of controlling who comes to hunt, then over time, it will get worse. We depend on hunting and fishing for our food.

We used to have small plots, which provided enough food for us. It was great! The boys fished in the river and sold the fish. There was no need to chop any trees down. The plots were small but big enough

Maria Eliete's son walks on a stretch of the Xingu that would usually have been in flood in the season the photo was taken. Paquiçamba village, Paquiçamba Indigenous Reserve

© Marilene Cardoso Ribeiro 2016

to make sure we didn't have to do any shopping in town. Not now. Now we have a tractor in the community, for making new plots. But planting cacao is new to us. Nobody has any experience of working with it. Things have been going badly for four years because the cacao dies. We plant more and that dies as well. We don't know what to do. And, if we start to grow more cacao, we'll have to chop down more trees every year. What will happen then? There will soon be no animals to hunt and the forest will be destroyed. We've lost the river, now we're losing the forest. One thing leads to another.

I feel sad when I start thinking that my young son, who is three years old, will only be able to see what the landscape was once like by looking at photos, videos, and films. I feel hopeless and desperate when I think about it. I try not to, but it's impossible, because it's happening right in front of me every day. Every year, we go to the beach [on the riverbank]. I don't know what has happened to the yellow-spotted river turtles. This year [one year after the sluice gates were first shut] for the first time they didn't lay their eggs on the beach. My father is 76 and he says he's never seen so few eggs.

The fish we eat most here is the *pacu branco*. I think there will be none left in a few years because it only feeds on fruit. The guavas, *golosas*, camu camus, and all the other fruit fell on dry land this season. There were no floodwaters for the fish to swim into and get the fruit, and the last guava will also fall on dry land. This year the *pacu branco* have been very thin. We went to pick up the fruit that hadn't fallen into the river. We used to go in the boat to place nets, but this time we went on foot.

If I close my eyes and think back to how things were in the Xingu ... a lot of water, strong currents, at this time of year. It could be dangerous. I've seen the river really high. We had to be very careful when we went swimming. Not now. It's dried up. There's a big difference. Now we barely use the river to get into town [Altamira]. It takes too long now. We used to do it in four hours but now it takes nine or ten. The river is like a stranger to us now. One day the water level is low. The next day, the dam releases water and that changes everything.

I felt sad the other day. My father almost cried. He had gone fishing and brought in a big catch. He was happy, but then I spoke to him. 'Dad,' I said, 'you know you shouldn't be so happy, because you can't carry on fishing like that.' 'Why?' he asked. 'The fishing isn't as good as you think,' I said. 'It's only because the river is so low and the fish have accumulated there, in that pool. When you go back there, there will be fewer and fewer fish because the water level won't be high enough for them to reproduce.' He said, 'You mean I won't be able to fish again?' I said, 'Not like this. You'll have to stop.' He looked downcast, almost cried and said, 'What am I going to do for the rest of my life? I've fished all my life. I raised you by fishing and selling what I caught. Now you're telling me that next year I might not be able to catch so many fish?' I said, 'That's what I think. Maybe before next year. Maybe this year. You won't be bringing in fish like this.' He looked very sad.

The authorities' failure to mitigate the impact of the dam was so severe that in late 2015, Brazil's Federal Public Ministry (MPF) decided to take action. After carrying out a lengthy study, which filled 50 volumes and included testimony from numerous experts, the MPF launched legal proceedings against Norte Energia, the Brazilian government, IBAMA, and FUNAI, accusing them of 'ethnocide' (destruction of a culture and way of life) against indigenous groups, such was the damage they had done to social organization, customs, language, and traditions (MPF, 2015).

What has happened at Belo Monte is not an isolated case, as Maria Eliete discovered when she went to a meeting of communities affected by dams:

> Various groups went. We met in Palmas [capital of the state of Tocantins] and we all gave a statement. Everyone had something to say. After listening to the others I thought, 'It's the same as in the Xingu! The same thing is happening! Different groups, different people, same story. They [the companies] are telling them the same things they told us. It's logical that they will do the same thing. They will listen and then speak to each group separately, each leader separately, until they get what they want.' Our role was to warn people about this strategy. I don't blame our leaders; their people [the company people] have been very well trained to persuade you that this is a good thing. Our leaders only have experience of dealing with their own people. They've never dealt with anything like this before and so it's very difficult.

Future prospects and resistance at Belo Monte

The damage may get worse in future years. Philip Fearnside, a renowned expert on hydropower, has long warned that the government will need to build more dams upstream if it is to regulate streamflow and increase the energy output of Belo Monte to anything close to the level required to make the plant profitable. Fearnside is not reassured by repeated government assurances that it is not planning to build any more dams. 'Denying these plans fits into a pattern in the history of Brazil's Amazonian dams', he commented drily (Fearnside, 2017).

Another harmful project is planned. The Canadian gold-mining company, Belo Sun, intends to open Brazil's largest gold mine beside the Volta Grande do Xingu stretch of the river. According to Juan Doblas, who works for the NGO Instituto Socioambiental (ISA), the mine wouldn't be feasible without Belo Monte's energy. Indeed, providing energy for this and other mining projects may have been one of the unpublicized reasons why Belo Monte was built in the first place.

The construction of Belo Monte was never seriously in doubt, as underresourced grassroots communities had engaged in a very unequal struggle against a US$20 billion project, backed by the Brazilian State. But neither local people, nor the social movements, nor the MPF have given up. While there is little hope of reversing Belo Monte, they can force the authorities to improve life for the evicted families and make it much more difficult for hydro-dams to be built in such a harmful fashion in future.

A significant victory occurred in April 2017. One of the reasons why the government has been able to push ahead with large dams in the Amazon without carrying out adequate environmental impact studies or proper consultations with affected communities is because it has invoked a legal instrument known as Suspensão de Segurança (Suspension of Security), which was widely used by Brazil's military dictatorship (1964–85). It allows the authorities to reverse any judicial decision by invoking national security, public order, or the national economy. This instrument was used 23 times in licensing dams on the Tapajós, Teles Pires, and Xingu rivers, and seven times with respect to Belo Monte.

One of the 'conditions' imposed on Norte Energia for the go-ahead for the dam was that it provide decent sanitation for the town of Altamira. It failed to do this and the government stopped all efforts to get it to comply through invoking Suspensão de Segurança. But in April 2017 the MPF managed to get the Suspensão de Segurança overruled in court. With this victory, Norte Energia was forced to close down the plant until it had provided sanitation for all the houses in Altamira.

Another important development has been among the *ribeirinhos*. Although there are thousands of them living by rivers in the Amazon, they are routinely ignored and widely misunderstood. At the end of 2016, they set up a Ribeirinho Council with representatives from the 22 affected areas. They are now demanding what the law guarantees them – to be settled on land that provides the same (or better) conditions than those they had in the areas they inhabited before. Aronor, who is a member of the Council, explains why:

> We're not objects; an object is something you take and place wherever you like. We're human beings; we have the right to choose what we believe is best for our lives and this must be respected. People need to speak up, tell the truth about what's happening, and ensure that the authorities defend their rights. We're Brazilian citizens and we have rights.
>
> They won't give us back the life we had, but they might at least give us something to make things easier, because everything we were working so hard to take care of was for our future. What is the future? It's our children, grandchildren, the islands, the rubber trees, the food for the fish, the fruit. They ruined everything! We lost everything, which was just the way they [Norte Energia and CCBM] wanted it! They picked us up and threw us away, plonked us down carelessly, saying, 'Oh, this is your little piece of land, this is where you live now. You'll be cosy here, we'll bring you wood and other materials for you to build your own home … ' No! We all had homes. They knocked them down!

It was not easy to form the Council because of how scattered the displaced *ribeirinhos* had become. But they managed, with support from some academics. 'They have been atrociously treated – their traditional knowledge has been scorned, their land has been invaded, and they have been evicted from their homes,' said Mauro Almeida, an anthropologist from Unicamp, the University of Campinas. 'But they have the right to regain traditional land' (Harari, 2018).

In February 2018 a delegation from the Ribeirinho Council went to Brasília to demand action from Norte Energia and IBAMA. For the first time in the history of dam-building in the Amazon, the *ribeirinhos* have had their rights as a distinctive social group recognized and are negotiating collectively. This will doubtless strengthen the position of *ribeirinhos* throughout the Brazilian Amazon.

This is not the only way the Belo Monte struggle has strengthened communities. In May 2013, together with *ribeirinhos*, representatives from eight indigenous groups, including the Munduruku, who inhabit the areas beside the Tapajós and Teles Pires rivers, occupied the Belo Monte building site. This action was not only a sign of solidarity with the beleaguered communities in the Xingu but also enabled the participants to see with their own eyes what was happening in the region. Many returned determined to fight to the death – and in the Amazon this is no metaphor – to prevent such a catastrophe happening to them.

Indigenous and *ribeirinho* mobilization seems to be working. After pushing through Belo Monte, the authorities turned their attention to the Tapajós River basin and quickly – and quietly – began building the Teles Pires and the São Manoel dams. São Luiz do Tapajós, by far the largest, was to be the next, and preparatory work began. But in 2016, IBAMA unexpectedly suspended the work. While this may be a consequence of Brazil's ongoing economic and political crisis, the scale of indigenous opposition was quoted as a key factor in this decision. And in late 2017, Paulo Pedrosa, the executive secretary of the Ministry of Mines and Energy, said that the era of big dams was coming to an end in the Amazon. 'We are not prejudiced against big [hydroelectric] projects,' he said, 'but we have to respect the views of society, which views them with reservations.' He also said that his ministry would 'no longer fight for the [São Luiz do Tapajós] project' (Branford, 2018). But the battle has not yet been won: by May 2018 Pedrosa and other like-minded officials had been removed from office by a new minister of mines and energy.

Organized resistance is growing in other Latin American countries too. Ismael Vega recalls a successful campaign from Peru:

> We managed to stop the massive Pakitzapango project, planned for the Selva Central of the Junín region. It was a long process, years of denouncing the project, explaining how it was going to affect the lives of ten thousand people, hundreds of communities, and how it was going to harm biodiversity, the rivers, and so on.

The Ene River, on which the Pakitzapango dam was to be built, is crucial for the Asháninka indigenous peoples, who depend on its fish resources and the fertile soils of its floodplains. In the end, Odebrecht pulled out, after being threatened with legal action. Asháninka leader Ruth Buendía Metzoquiari was awarded the Goldman Environmental Prize for her work in organizing opposition. On presenting the award, a Goldman spokesman said, 'Overcoming a history of traumatic violence, Ruth Buendía united the Asháninka people in a powerful campaign against large-scale dams that would have once again uprooted indigenous communities still recovering from Peru's civil war.'

International cooperation is growing. Ismael Vega said that at the end of 2017 CAAAP had helped organize a major event called the Pan-Amazonian Social Forum. 'It was the eighth such event, which brought together more than 1,500 people from different countries in the Amazon basin,' he said. In March 2018, 3,000 people – most of whom were Latin American – attended the Alternative World Water Forum in Brasília. They discussed many issues related to water, including fair access, conservation of watersheds, agriculture, and the impact of mega projects on rivers, underground water, and peoples' livelihoods.

Much more needs to be done but these are all important initiatives. With tears running down his cheeks, Aronor once said: 'We've always had the "before", the "now", and the "after". The before has gone, the now is a nightmare. And the after?' Perhaps it is not too late to hope that the future – both for Aronor and the Amazon region as a whole – will be better than the present.

About the authors

Marilene Ribeiro is an award-winning photographer and ecologist whose works investigate the relationship between human beings and nature concerning contemporary issues. She holds an MSc in Ecology and Wildlife Conservation and Management from the Federal University of Minas Gerais (Brazil), and a PhD in photography from the University of Brighton (UK). Marilene's works approach global issues seen through the lens of Brazil.

Sue Branford is a journalist who reported from Brazil for over a decade. A founding member of LAB's editorial team, she has worked for the BBC, the *Financial Times, The Guardian, and The Economist.* She has written five books on Latin America, mainly on Brazil. Her latest book, co-authored with Maurício Torres, is titled *Amazon Besieged: by dams, soya, agribusiness and land grabbing* (Practical Action Publishing and LAB 2018).

Interviews

Leonardo Batista, aka **Aronor** (Ribeirinho Council): interviewed in Altamira, Pará, Brazil, on 14 October 2016 by Marilene Cardoso Ribeiro. Transcribed by Karina Ribeiro and translated by Paula Coppio, Edgar Refinetti, and Diego Satyro.

Maria Eliete Felix Juruna (Paquiçamba Indigenous Reserve): interviewed in Paquiçamba, Pará, Brazil, on 6 November 2016 by Marilene Cardoso Ribeiro. Transcribed by Karina Ribeiro and translated by Chris Whitehouse.

Antônia Melo (Movimento Xingu Vivo para Sempre): interviewed in Altamira, Pará, Brazil, in early September 2015 by Eliane Brum. Translated by Hugo Moss.

Maria Rosa Pessoa Piedade (*ribeirinha* at Palhau): interviewed in Altamira, Pará, Brazil, on 2 November 2016 by Marilene Cardoso Ribeiro. Transcribed by Karina Ribeiro and translated by Alistair Clark.

Ismael Vega (CAAAP): interviewed via Skype on 11 and 12 January 2018 by Tom Gatehouse. Translated by Andrea Boehnert.

References

NB: All web references were checked and still available in May/June 2018 unless otherwise stated. All references are listed, with web-links, on the page for this chapter on the Voices website www.vola.org.uk

Aleixo, J. and Condé, N. (2015) *Quem são os proprietários das hidrelétricas da Amazônia?*, Instituto Mais Democracia, Rio de Janeiro.

Branford, S. (2016) 'BNDES has long history of loans to gigantic construction companies' *Mongabay,* 14 March, <https://news.mongabay.com/2016/03/bndes-has-long-history-of-loans-to-gigantic-construction-companies>

Branford, S. (2018) 'Brazil announces end to Amazon mega-dam building policy', *Mongabay,* 3 January, <https://news.mongabay.com/2018/01/brazil-announces-end-to-amazon-mega-dam-building-policy>

Brum, E. (2015) 'O dia em que a casa foi expulsa de casa', *El País*, 14 September, <https://brasil.elpais.com/brasil/2015/09/14/opinion/1442235958_647873.html>

Fearnside, P.M. (2015) *Hidrelétricas na Amazônia – impactos ambientais e sociais na tomada de decisões sobre grandes obras*, 2 vols, Editora do INPA, Manaus.

Fearnside, P.M. (2017) 'Brazil's Belo Monte dam: lessons of an Amazonian resource struggle', in McCoy (ed.), *Die Erde* Special Issue, 'Resource Geographies: New Perspectives from South America', <http://philip.inpa.gov.br/publ_livres/Preprints/2017/B-Belo_Monte_resistance-Die_Erde-Preprint.pdf>

FGV (2016) *Indicadores de Belo Monte – um diálogo entre condicionantes do licenciamento ambiental e o desenvolvimento local*, Câmara Técnica de Monitoramento das Condicionantes da UHE Belo Monte (CT-05), Fundação Getúlio Vargas and Centro de Estudos em Sustentabilidade (FGV-EAESP), Rio de Janeiro.

Harari, I. (2018) 'Ribeirinhos atingidos por Belo Monte exigem retomar seu território', Amazônia, 14 February <http://amazonia.org.br/2018/02/ribeirinhos-atingidos-por-belo-monte-exigem-retomar-seu-territorio/>

Hurwitz, Z., Millikan, B., Monteiro, T. and Widmer, R. (2011) *Mega projeto, mega riscos – análise de riscos para investidores no Complexo Hidrelétrico Belo Monte*, Amigos da Terra – Amazônia Brasileira and International Rivers, São Paulo, <https://www.banktrack.org/download/mega_projeto_mega_riscos/belo_monte__megarisks_portugese_0.pdf>

Instituto de Enghenaria (2010), 'Crítica ao Aproveitamento Hidrelétrico Belo Monte', Opinião, Jornal do Instituto de Enghenaria, Brasil, No.59, July,

<https://www.institutodeengenharia.org.br/site/wp-content/uploads/2018/02/arqjornalie41.pdf>

ISA (Instituto Socioambiental) (2016) *Belo Monte: um legado de violações*, <https://medium.com/@socioambiental/belo-monte-um-legado-de-viola%C3%A7%C3%B5es-43ea35c973b8#.oqwa42ifw>

Latrubesse, E.M., Arima, E.Y., Dunne, T., Park, E., Baker, V.R., d'Horta, F.M., Wight, C., Wittmann, F., Zuanon, J., Baker, P.A., Ribas, C.C., Norgaard, R.B., Filizola, N., Ansar, A., Flyvbjerg, B. and Stevaux, J.C. (2017) 'Damming the rivers of the Amazon basin', *Nature* 546(7658), 363–9.

Little, P. E. (2014) *Mega-Development Projects in Amazonia: A Geopolitical and Socioenvironmental Primer*, Red Jurídica Amazónica (RAMA), Derecho, Ambiente y Recursos Naturales (DAR), and Articulación Regional Amazónica (ARA), Lima.

MediaLivre (2011) 'Belo Monte derruba presidente do Ibama pela II vez', *YouTube*, 14 January, <https://www.youtube.com/watch?v=8utb4GTHlI4>

MPF (Ministério Público Federal) (2013) 'Ação civil pública no. 0000655-78.2013.4.01.3903', issued on 19 April 2013.

MPF (2014) *Plano Emergencial UHE Belo Monte*, video directed by Marco Paulo Fróes Schettino, MPF, Altamira /Pará, <https://youtu.be/pvyvyXVvmx0>

MPF (2015) 'Ação civil pública no. 3017-82.2015.4.01.3903', issued on 10 December 2015.

Pérez, M.S. (2015) 'Where the Xingu bends and will soon break', *American Scientist*, November/December, 395–403, <https://www.americanscientist.org/article/where-the-xingu-bends-and-will-soon-break>

Pontes, F. (2011) 'Belo Monte de violências'. *Piseagrama* 2, 16–20, <https://piseagrama.org/belo-monte-de-violencias/>.

Ribeiro, M.C. (2018) 'Dead water – a photography-based inquiry into the impact of dams in Brazil', University for the Creative Arts, Farnham [PhD thesis], slideshow: <www.marileneribeiro.com/deadwater>

Santos, S.M.S.B.M. and Hernández, F.M. (organizers) (2009) *Painel de especialistas – Análise crítica do estudo de impacto ambiental do aproveitamento hidrelétrico de Belo Monte*, 29 October, Fundação Viver, Produzir e Preservar (FVPP) de Altamira, ISA, International Rivers Network (IRN), WWF, FASE, Rede de Justiça Ambiental, Belém, <https://www.socioambiental.org/banco_imagens/pdfs/Belo_Monte_Painel_especialistas_EIA.pdf>

Sevá Filho, A.O. (2005) *Tenotã-Mõ – alertas sobre as consequências dos projetos hidrelétricos no rio Xingu*, IRN, São Paulo.

Sullivan, Z. (2016) 'Brazil's dispossessed: Belo Monte dam ruinous for indigenous cultures', *Mongabay*, 8 December, <https://news.mongabay.com/2016/12/brazils-dispossessed-belo-monte-dam-ruinous-for-indigenous-cultures>

CHAPTER 7
Mining and communities

Tom Gatehouse

Abstract

Mining has grown exponentially in Latin America in the last three decades. Massive new mining projects have had major socioenvironmental effects, including pollution, appropriation and contamination of water supplies, division and co-optation of communities, and in some cases their forced relocation. Communities are learning how to resist and some have successfully challenged government and company claims that large-scale mining projects can be safe, sustainable, and socially beneficial.

Mining in Latin America long predates the arrival of Europeans. There is evidence to suggest that organized and technologically sophisticated societies existed as early as 4,000–5,000 years ago and that they were engaged in mineral extraction. These activities were widespread and included most of Bolivia, Peru, and Chile (Bury and Bebbington, 2013). However, the voracious appetite of the Spanish and Portuguese for silver and gold changed history forever. It spurred on the colonial project and enslaved countless numbers of indigenous Americans and, later, Africans, while extracting vast sums of wealth and shipping it back to Europe. In the words of Uruguayan writer Eduardo Galeano:

> Gold and silver were the keys which the Renaissance used to open the gates of paradise in heaven and the doors of mercantile capitalism on earth. The saga of the Spaniards and the Portuguese in Latin America combined propagation of Christianity with the usurpation and wholesale theft of native treasure. European power reached out to seize the globe (Galeano, 1971).

It has been estimated that approximately 1,685 tonnes of gold and 85,991 tonnes of silver were extracted from Latin America between 1492 and 1810. At 2011 market rates, the combined value would have been US$210 bn (Bury and Bebbington, 2013). Over 60,000 tonnes of silver have been mined from Cerro Rico in Potosí, Bolivia, alone (Scott, 2016).

And the mining bonanza shows no signs of abating. Following the fall of the Cold War dictatorships and the debt crisis of the 1980s, many Latin American countries implemented World Bank and IMF approved reforms which privatized state-owned assets, slashed environmental regulations, and

http://dx.doi.org/10.3362/9781909014213.007

established incentives and favourable tax regimes for transnational companies and investors. With prices for many primary commodities, including
minerals, increasing steadily from the early 1990s, Latin American policymakers of all political persuasions saw the extraction of minerals and hydrocarbons as a motor for growth and a source of revenue (Bury and Bebbington,
2013). Capital poured into the region. While investment in mining exploration increased globally by 90 per cent from 1990 to 1997, in Latin America
it increased by 400 per cent and in Peru by a staggering 2,000 per cent
(Bebbington and Bury, 2013).

While on the one hand, these recent developments can be seen as the
continuation of Latin America's long history of mineral extraction, on the
other, a number of features suggest that they are part of something historically
unprecedented. Not only are vast new sums of capital flowing into the sector,
they are coming from new global actors such as China, South Africa, and
Canada. Moreover, technological advances permit landscape transformation
and environmental disruption that would have been inconceivable in the
days of the precarious underground shafts (Bebbington et al., 2013). This is
large-scale, open-pit mining, what is known in Spanish as *megaminería*. But
despite the vast wealth and power of the big mining multinationals, communities in Latin America have been mounting increasingly effective resistance
to their operations.

One key concept in the discussion of mining and other extractive industries in Latin America, which has been effectively employed by communities,
is the *socioambiental*, or socioenvironmental, aspect. As Lucrecia Wagner,
a researcher at the National Scientific and Technical Research Council
(CONICET) in Mendoza, Argentina, explains:

> It means people see the environment not just in terms of conservation,
> of saving the whales and the pandas – an image which prevailed for a
> long time amongst ecologists and environmentalists – but in terms of
> the effects on the place where one lives, which is something much more
> present for everyone.

The socioenvironmental effects of *megaminería* are inevitably drastic, and this
has caused increasing conflict between mining companies – often supported
by national governments – on the one hand, and local communities on the
other, as we will see below.

Socioenvironmental effects of *megaminería*

Latin America's history of mining has taken an enormous environmental
toll on the region. The Cerro Rico in Potosí is a vivid symbol of this – the
mountain's picturesque conical form ravaged by tracks, mine entrances, and
spoil heaps. Another historic mining site in Bolivia is Huanuni, home to the
country's largest underground tin mine, which dates back to the 19th century.

Oscar Roca works at the Centre of Support for Popular Education (CAEP), a local NGO which provides education and technical training to the community. Here he describes the pollution:

> Huanuni has a whole host of problems, all of which are interlinked. The most visible one is pollution. We are surrounded by every sort of pollution. The town really grew out of a mining settlement; there was never any urban planning. As you can see it's right next to all the mining activity and this creates many problems. There's pollution in the river, streets, valleys, and air. It's everywhere.

In a walk around the town, Oscar pointed out the mining dust in the gutters, the pools of rusty-coloured water by the roadside, and the river running through town, a toxic ribbon of grey sludge speckled with plastic bags and polystyrene fast-food boxes. As he says:

> I think there are very few prospects for Huanuni. Huanuni has grown around mining and mining is what sustains it, so I can't see what else it could do. It's natural that people look around and ask themselves, 'Who would want to stay here, make a life here, start a family, settle down?' It's an inhospitable, polluted place. It's not a suitable place to settle down. People are here either because they have a job in the mine or they provide a service to the mine, end of story.
>
> I'll give you a statistic. There used to be 5,000 workers in the mine, now there's 3,800. Of these 3,800, at least half don't live here. They live in Oruro, or in north Potosí, and they commute. They come here every day, do their work, and leave. Their families don't live here. Many of those who do live here send their children to study in Oruro once they reach a certain age. Part of the family live in Oruro, or Cochabamba, or occasionally in La Paz. And I would do the same.
>
> If mining is going to carry on for another 50 years or so here, then clearly the only hope that Huanuni has is to improve the general quality of life. But people have to get this into their heads. They have to say, 'OK, let's improve our quality of life, we live here, we work here, let's try and live well here.' But they just won't do it.

But, despite being subject to more stringent environmental regulation than the underground mines of the past and having access to more sophisticated technology, contemporary *megaminería* endangers the environment on an even greater scale, because of the sheer size of operations and the new technology and refining techniques involved (Brown, 2012). Camila Méndez is an activist with the Cajamarca Socioenvironmental Youth Collective (COSAJUCA) in Cajamarca, Colombia. She participated in a successful campaign to hold a *consulta popular* – a kind of local referendum – which ultimately rejected the installation of the La Colosa gold mine near the town by the South African company AngloGold Ashanti. By production volume it would have been the fifth-largest gold mine in the world (Colombia Solidarity Campaign, 2013) As she comments:

They wanted to cut down all the trees, open up the land, because in Cajamarca they have to mine open cast. The mineral is spread throughout the rock strata; it's not visible to the naked eye. According to the company's own data, for each tonne of rock they would extract one gram of gold or, to be more exact, 0.89 grams of gold. That means shifting an enormous amount of earth if they're to make it viable.

Camila Méndez.

Mining projects are often situated in ecologically sensitive areas, such as the Andean cordillera, home to all South America's glaciers, 82 per cent of which are located in Chile (Greenpeace Chile, 2016), where they are a vital source of fresh water. Around 75 per cent of the Chilean population relies on water supplied by melting ice (Jamasmie, 2013), a figure even higher in the arid regions of the north. Constanza San Juan is an environmental activist and member of the group Coordinación de Territorios por la Defensa de los Glaciares (CTDG). She lives in the Huasco Valley in the north of Chile, where local communities were threatened by Canadian mining giant Barrick Gold's Pascua Lama project:

You could say that the glaciers issue became visible at the national level because of the struggle in the Huasco Valley, when the people there realized that the mining project involved the destruction of glaciers, and that the mining companies had hidden this from them. The community had always been aware of the importance of the glaciers: farmers talked of being taken up into the mountains by their grandfathers and shown the glaciers, which they used to call 'perpetual banks' – perpetual water banks – because they knew that these glaciers provided the valley with water. In the valley it barely ever rains, so the water supply is clearly reliant on the glaciers; they are fundamental to the whole ecosystem. While at first the project was well regarded by some people, once they realized that it threatened the water supply and the survival of agriculture in the area, they started to fight it.

Though Pascua Lama straddles the border between Argentina and Chile, most of the project is on the Chilean side. It was suspended in 2013 due to environmental violations, and in January 2018 the Chilean environmental authorities ordered its definitive closure, with the opposition of NGOs, civil society organizations, and community groups having been a key factor. Stefanía Vega is a friend of Constanza and fellow member of CTDG. For her, as for many others, Pascua Lama was a watershed moment:

> Although I'm from the Aconcagua Valley, where we've had the giant that is CODELCO [Chile's state-owned copper mining corporation] operating for such a long time, since before I was born, for me it was also the Pascua Lama project that made me question the existence of the mining industry. It made me question its costs and what it does to the areas it operates in. For us, it leaves behind waste, pollution, tailings ponds, pits, drought, and an insecure and polluted water supply – while they leave with all the money. For me the Pascua Lama project meant all those things, it meant the destruction of a completely rural community, it meant the huge Canadian mining industry bringing 'progress' to these poor people, and that's why I decided to join a campaign group.

Clearly, *megaminería* has the power to fundamentally alter and even destroy traditional cultures and ways of life. Rogelio Ustate is a poet and activist from the Afro-Colombian community of Tabaco where, in 2001, 1,200 people were forced off their land by hundreds of police and armed security personnel to make way for the expansion of El Cerrejón, the largest open-pit coal mine in Latin America (Sankey, 2014). El Cerrejón has brought with it a whole host of negative environmental effects, as Rogelio explains:

> Whether from deforestation or the loading or unloading of materials, the atmospheric pollution here is damaging the whole region – not just in Albania, Barranca, and Hatonuevo. The dust causes breast, skin, cervical, oesophageal, throat, and lung cancer. It damages DNA structure and causes deformities. That's why today there are so many children with special needs. It's a huge problem, but it's permitted by the state and no one's doing anything about it. Also, if you go to any town in Guajira, from Albania down to San Juan, you'll see that all the houses are cracked, due to the blasting. The earth shakes.

There have also been negative social consequences:

> Multinationals are expanding across the globe, and ethnic groups like ours, particularly black, Raizal, and Palenquera communities, have suffered waves of displacement due to mining. In turn, that's also produced extreme poverty because, without land to work on and crops to grow, many people move away from their ancestral lands to other places where they can't find work. Many fall into destitution, hoping that someone will give them a helping hand to survive. They end up selling any old thing and many of them suffer discrimination for doing this in urban public spaces. Crime has also grown very quickly, because when people don't have work they consider bad options, like prostitution. This is something which didn't previously exist in our territory, but now you

see it more and more often. When people don't have access to education and proper housing, their desire for a better life means they end up choosing the wrong path. They lose their habits and customs.

For rural communities, this can be intensely traumatic. It is a forced severance from their culture, the destruction of a society that may go back for hundreds of years (Thorp et al., 2012). In the Tabaco case, there is effectively no chance of return, as Rogelio acknowledges:

> The struggle here with the multinationals has been so direct because their actions have resulted in forced displacement. In fact, it's worse than displacement: it's an uprooting, because with the former you still have the possibility of return. But those of us displaced by the mining industry can't return to the land.

Another emblematic case is that of Caimanes, a small Chilean township around 250 km north of Santiago, consisting of dusty, unpaved streets lined mostly by modest, one-storey houses with corrugated iron roofs. Since the early 2000s, this has been the site of a conflict between the company Minera Los Pelambres (MLP), its parent company Antofagasta PLC, and the local community. The principal cause is the nearby El Mauro tailings dam – a vast reservoir of mining waste which is the largest of its type in Latin America. Caimanes is in a region of high seismic activity and residents argue that the dam is unsafe. The second point of conflict relates to water. To build El Mauro, MLP diverted the river which once flowed through the Choapa Valley, where Caimanes is located, and appropriated underground water flows. As a result, the river in the town is now completely dry and 80 per cent of the water in the valley has been lost, all but destroying local agriculture (Gatehouse, 2017a). Esther González – a member of the Comité de Defensa Personal de Caimanes (CDPC), the main group opposing MLP – describes what happened:

> Before, people grew crops. But now there's no water for crops. I don't know if you saw the river, but it's dry. I was born and grew up here, just like my father, and I've never seen anything like it. In all the years I've lived here, the river had never dried up. They have to bring water in from Los Vilos by tanker. The company came and because they cut the aquifers, the water decreased. Basically, they stole our water.

Her statement is supported by Lucio Cuenca, director of the Latin American Observatory of Environmental Conflicts (OLCA), an NGO based in Santiago which has followed the conflict since the beginning:

> The area in which Pelambres is located is in the Norte Chico, which is a semi-arid area, where there is a major water supply problem. There has been a drought in recent years; there was no water for agriculture. But the Pelambres mine never had a problem. It always had a guaranteed water supply, despite being a major consumer of water.

Dried up river-bed in Caimanes.

Caimanes is a community divided. Esther lives in a simple house, much like most of the others in town, with a small veranda and plants climbing up the outside wall. The black flag of the CDPC flies above her gate; others, often faded to grey, billow above houses throughout the town. In contrast, just across the highway is an imposing, modern house, which Esther said had been built with MLP money. Indeed, some residents have prospered, accepting money from the company and setting up businesses providing goods and services to its staff (Gatehouse, 2017a). One such individual is Angelo Herrera. Involved in the resistance initially, he was persuaded to switch sides and now owns and manages El Corral, the largest restaurant and hotel in town, which is constantly busy with MLP staff. He describes how this happened:

> After we got the money I thought to myself: how can we stay in Caimanes, while taking advantage of what we have? I didn't see any point in saying that we were going to win this, when we knew perfectly well that everyone had been bought off. So my mother and I reconciled with Claudio [his brother, who worked for MLP] and we decided to set up an eight-bed hostel. After building the hostel we needed more space, so we acquired rooms in private houses. We were providing accommodation to a lot of people. Then they began to ask us to do meals. Out of that came the restaurant. Now we have a hotel with twenty rooms. We've been providing this service to the company since 2013 – just three years.
>
> Our thinking was: let's try to obtain some economic benefit before it all rots, before Caimanes is completely lost. Our days are numbered. They say that the dam at El Mauro has enough capacity for another ten years of mine tailings. After that, it'll take them another ten years

to close it down. So in 20 years, we will have no work, no workers, no means of maintaining the town, no water, no resources ... this is the future for us.

It used to be a very united community. Caimanes is renowned for what it achieved. For example, the first drinking water was installed thanks to the work of the community – the government only got behind it later. Likewise, the community raised money for a generator, which was turned on from 7 p.m. until midnight. Again, the government only helped out afterwards. We always worked together to achieve things. But the mine has divided the community. Sometimes people avoid one another. Some of them won't so much as look at each other, greet each other.

Here Lucio Cuenca offers his assessment:

The various ways in which the community has sought to resolve the conflict have turned out badly, with many people hurt. In this fight between David and Goliath, Goliath is in fact crushing David, despite the heroic efforts of many people who remain opposed on the basis of deeply-held convictions. But the company has destroyed the town socially and culturally, it has broken it into a thousand pieces. And there is no possibility of repairing that damage.

People will continue to live there and adapt to the conditions imposed by the company, the security measures that the company alleges are necessary, the supply of water by lorries. Some people may be able to move elsewhere. In the end, though, I think the company has destroyed the community, with all the pain that implies.

What all the voices throughout this section express is the 'irreversibility' of the socioenvironmental effects of large open-pit mining operations. They threaten the physical existence of communities by diverting and contaminating water supplies, building potentially dangerous tailings dams, and in some cases removing the community altogether. At the same time, the influence of the company often divides communities, playing residents off against each other and causing breaches which may never heal.

The Bento Rodrigues dam disaster

On 5 November 2015, the Fundão tailings dam at the Germano mine complex collapsed near the town of Mariana, in the state of Minas Gerais, in the south-east of Brazil. A tidal wave of toxic sludge was released, destroying the nearby village of Bento Rodrigues, killing 19 people and leaving around 700 homeless. Forty-five million cubic metres of mine tailings flowed into the nearby Doce River and eventually reached the Atlantic Ocean, over 600 km from the dam, with catastrophic effects for the river basin and the communities which live there, an area roughly the size of Austria. The episode is widely considered to be Brazil's worst ever environmental disaster, and globally it is the biggest tailings dam failure of this kind.

The Germano mine complex is owned by the company Samarco, a joint venture between the Anglo-Australian mining giant BHP Billiton and the Brazilian company Vale. Following the disaster, BHP and Vale created Fundação Renova in an agreement with the Brazilian State, the aim of which is to oversee the recovery of the affected area and compensate resident families, including resettlement of those who lost their homes. However, critics point to delays in registering those affected, overly bureaucratic procedures, and unilateral 'take it or leave it' offers of compensation. None of the 375 families who lost their homes has yet been rehoused (Gatehouse, 2017b).

Strategies of the mining companies

How, when the medium- and long-term effects of *megaminería* appear to be so negative, do companies manage to obtain consent for their operations at all?

Alfredo Gallardo, a founding member of the CDPC, recalls the arrival of MLP in the Choapa Valley:

© Tom Gatehouse 2016

Alfredo Gallardo and Esther González

In 2000 they started applying [for a mining permit] and by 2002 they were practically operating. In 2004 they made a pledge to the village, basically to the whole community. That includes the whole of the Río Choapa region, so Salamanca, Illapel, Canela, Los Vilos. There were consultations in all these places to see if they agreed with the installation of El Mauro, because they'd already bought the site for the tailings dam. And these communities all gave their approval. Many people here in Caimanes also agreed to it.

The pledge was that we'd have a road, and an ambulance, plenty of work. They promised scholarships to all the children who wanted to study elsewhere. In the end, we got the ambulance, and they are giving scholarships, but for the last seven years the value has been the same: 600,000 pesos a year, which isn't enough to pay the rent. You spend a million pesos just on rent if you go to Santiago, La Serena, Viña del Mar, or Valparaíso, which is nearer. The parents have to make up the rest.

The promise of work is often particularly effective, especially in rural communities where employment is scarce and young people tend to migrate to the larger towns and cities in search of opportunities. Constanza San Juan describes how this presents an obstacle for the anti-mining movement in her municipality of Alto del Carmen in the Huasco Valley:

It's still difficult because of the issue of jobs. For example, in a small village called Chollay – the one most polluted by the project [Pascua

Lama] – Barrick turned up offering jobs to all the young people, and unfortunately this ends up being effective as there aren't any jobs in the valley. The local council isn't interested in creating another vision, finding another way to develop the area, nor is the regional government, nor the state. They accuse us of not offering any alternatives, so on top of fighting against the project we have to propose solutions as well!

However, not only do companies tend to exaggerate their promises of work, but the kind of unskilled or semi-skilled labour these rural communities are most able to provide is only of use during the mine's installation phase. Once it is up and running, these workers are usually laid off and the company depends on a much smaller contingent of engineers and technicians, most of whom come from elsewhere. The La Colosa project in Cajamarca, Colombia, would have created no more than 500 jobs, most of which would have gone to outsiders (Sankey, 2014).

Carina Jofré is an activist and researcher at CONICET San Juan, Argentina, who has supported community resistance in the town of Jáchal to Barrick Gold's Veladero operation, where the local assembly Jáchal No Se Toca (Hands Off Jáchal) have maintained a camp opposite the town hall since 2015. This consists of a large tent full of posters, banners, and photos, including one on the outside showing Pope Francis holding up a T-shirt reading 'El agua vale + que el oro' ('Water is worth more than gold'). Carina describes how the lack of sustainable employment contributed to local opposition:

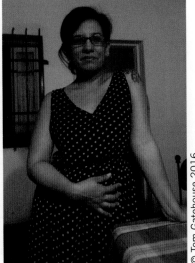

© Tom Gatehouse 2016

Residents began to see that the development model based on mining, which had initially provided work for the community, is cyclical. In other words, when they're installing the mine they need 5,000 workers but then once it's up and running they only need 10. They didn't tell us that 10 years ago. They said that the mine was coming and it would provide jobs forever. So, people started to see, after 10, 20 years of *megaminería*, that while the company polluted more all the time, the jobs became increasingly scarce. Meanwhile there was more division in the community and local institutions Carina Jofré. had been co-opted by the mining company. So, the resistance in Jáchal today is the result of 20 years of accumulated discontent.

© Tom Gatehouse 2016

The camp at Jáchal: 'Hands off Jáchal'.

Another common strategy is to offer goods and services that the community lacks, often as part of Corporate Social Responsibility (CSR) programmes, a method Barrick has deployed heavily in Jáchal and other towns in the north of San Juan near Veladero. As Carina comments:

> There's another interesting aspect to the new, 21st-century *megaminería* which can be seen clearly in San Juan. It's this corporate monster coming to supplant the traditional welfare state. In other words, the company provides everything, from the syringes in the hospital to your child's school rucksack, all within the framework of Corporate Social Responsibility, which is essentially a policy of governance.

Lucrecia Wagner echoes Carina's assessment:

> Other means have included co-optation of the communities, trying to obtain social licence to operate by offering services that should be the responsibility of the state. This is clear in Jáchal, where health and recreation services are being provided by the mining companies. They help the schools, institutions, churches, playing a kind of paternal role within communities which have often been neglected by the provincial governments, as they are in remote places which are difficult to access.

Offering such services can be highly effective. In remote rural communities, residents may quickly become dependent on the company, particularly the elderly, children, and other vulnerable individuals. In such a climate, dissenters may struggle to convince their neighbours that the eventual costs will outweigh any short-term benefits.

Rodrigo Péret and Thiago Alves da Silva have worked with communities affected by the Bento Rodrigues dam disaster near Mariana, Brazil (see box).

For Rodrigo, of the Churches and Mining Network, 'The first method of dividing communities – and this is common to all the companies – is to ensure that all negotiations are conducted individually, to break the possibility of community initiative and thinking in common.' Thiago, of the Movement of People Affected by Dams (MAB), describes the efforts of Samarco to achieve this:

> There are companies contracted on the ground to do this work. They are special consulting firms, which set up offices in the communities, hiring people – sometimes from the community, sometimes not. Normally they're young, good-looking, well-educated, and manage to gain access to people's houses. They're responsible for what they call 'social dialogue', working as mediators between the company and social movements. The aim is to demobilize the resistance to the company, create confusion in people's minds. I've seen it happen first-hand.

This is an essential point: communities which have successfully resisted the installation of large mining projects are those which remain united. Communities which become fragmented are almost always unable to prevent companies from achieving their objectives in the long term, though they may succeed in making it more difficult for them to do so. Companies therefore devote energy and resources to intelligence gathering within communities, to assess what the community lacks and who might be susceptible to offers of cash, goods, and services. Camila Méndez recalls how AngloGold Ashanti went about this in Cajamarca, Colombia:

> It came out in the press that one of the largest gold deposits in Latin America had been discovered in Cajamarca, Tolima, and that it was going to be exploited for the common good of our country. That was early in 2007, when it was announced publicly, but the company had already been present in the area for some time in the guise of another company called Sociedad Kedahda. It had been doing assessments, socioeconomic surveys, interviewing people, handing out questionnaires, exploring the whole area without asking permission. Once it became public knowledge, we found out that the company behind it was AngloGold Ashanti.

When all else fails, companies can always rely on the power of hard cash – both licit, in the form of compensation to affected communities, and illicit, in the form of bribes to politicians and other public officials. Money has certainly been a decisive factor in shaping the outcome of the Caimanes conflict in Chile, as Angelo Herrera comments:

> Five million dollars was distributed amongst the community, amongst the opponents of the mine. So it wasn't a battle we were fighting as a community and I didn't end up feeling that I had sold out. What I did feel was that I had done everything in my power to stop the building of the dam. Through the sale of the land we made a profit and in the end I

Anti-MLP graffiti in Caimanes: 'MLP – one of the most privileged copper mining companies in Chile – what safety measures have the inhabitants of Caimanes been notified of? We don't know the likelihood of a natural disaster, living as we do in an earthquake zone, and with huge global changes taking place. We demand an early warning system that we can trust, covering the whole area. Power to the Comité de Defensa Personal!'

stepped aside. It wasn't for me. I wasn't going to continue fighting when it was clear that the mining company had bought the support of lawyers and judges and was buying our support as a community.

As Lucio Cuenca says, 'Basically, Pelambres has used money to resolve things, though not even that much. They are under some pressure not to establish a precedent for other companies, so they're not going to meet all the community's demands, even though they have the money to do so.'

MLP has also been implicated in recent corruption scandals in Chile. Lucio describes how MLP was discovered to have been making illicit payments to the politician Jorge Insunza:

He [Insunza] was president of the mining committee in the Chamber of Deputies. He voted with the right, despite being of the left, to block legislation which aimed to regulate mining companies' water consumption. It then transpired that over the course of five to seven years, he had received a monthly sum of about $4,000 for providing fictitious services, which is quite a lot of money. This was while he was still a deputy. The money was channelled through a company in which he is the majority shareholder and it was paid by Pelambres.

This is only one of many egregious examples of complicity between mining companies and the state. In the Argentine province of San Juan, the provincial government has taken an extremely aggressive pro-mining stance, the effects of which are described by Lucrecia Wagner:

> There are people who've reported direct harassment – threats, being followed, being told they're going to lose their jobs. Provinces with a high proportion of public sector workers are always more vulnerable to this kind of repression. There's also censorship. Programmes aired on national television which took a critical stance on mining were censored in San Juan. A few years ago, there was a case that became notorious in [the neighbouring province] Mendoza. The newspaper *Los Andes*, which is produced in Mendoza but distributed also in San Juan, ran a piece critical of mining in a supplement back in 2008 or 2009. But in San Juan, the newspaper was distributed without the supplement. Someone took them all out before distribution. In the university I have colleagues who tell me that it's not possible to discuss mining. There's a pact of silence.

This complicity became particularly obvious following a spill at Veladero in 2015, in which 224 cubic metres of a cyanide solution leaked into the Potrerillos River, a tributary of the Jáchal River. This remains Argentina's worst ever environmental disaster caused by mining. As Carina Jofré recalls:

> The residents in Jáchal have been bringing cases against Barrick since 2011 for environmental crimes, but it wasn't until 2015 when the spill happened that these cases really took off. They became more visible, they even got media coverage. After the spill it was no longer possible for the media to claim that *megaminería* didn't pollute. And the authorities handled it all in such a revolting way – there's really no other way to describe it. The company lied about the spill. It denied the spill 10 times; first it would say one thing, then another. And the provincial government never once came out to contradict what the company was saying. People saw clearly the complicity between the company and the government. And that made the credibility of *megaminería* collapse.

In Colombia this complicity between government and the mining sector is particularly serious, given the country's recent history of armed conflict. Álvaro Uribe, president from 2002 to 2010, introduced a whole swathe of measures to attract mining companies to Colombia and increased the military presence in mining areas. Emboldened paramilitary groups also moved into these regions, supported by US counterinsurgency operatives, national politicians, and local businessmen (Sankey, 2014). Camila Méndez describes receiving threats for her opposition to La Colosa:

> We have received threats from groups operating outside the law: for opposing development projects there have been generalized threats from paramilitary groups like the so-called Black Eagles, who declared that anyone would be a military target who opposed these development projects or who opposed particular companies, among them AngloGold Ashanti.

In 2014, 74 per cent of human rights violations in Colombia occurred in mining and oil regions, though these spanned just 32 per cent of national territory (Sankey, 2014). Unsurprisingly, guerrilla groups such as the Revolutionary Armed Forces of Colombia (FARC) and the National Liberation Army (ELN) have targeted mining operations; FARC bombed El Cerrejón's railway in 2013 and in the same year the ELN kidnapped five geologists and a mining executive from a gold mining operation by the Canadian company Braeval Mining. This is the violent climate in which opponents to mining in Colombia have to operate, despite the peace process between the Colombian State and the guerrillas. As Camila comments:

> It's supposed to be peacetime, a time when people can participate and communities can make their voices heard. But what we find is that the government is responding only to the interests of the extractive industries. The largest guerrilla army has demobilized and handed over their weapons, but there are new outbreaks of conflict, more displacement, more murders, and it's all thanks to the extractive industries.

Another tool available to companies is the Environmental Impact Assessment (EIA). Ostensibly, the aim is to identify the likely environmental consequences of the work, so the authorities can take them into account when deciding whether to grant a licence and the company can take steps to mitigate them. However, it is the companies themselves which carry out these assessments, so from the outset there is an obvious conflict of interest. Carina Jofré used to work in the mining sector writing EIAs:

> I got a job doing the Environmental Impact Assessment at Filo Colorado, a mining project which was eventually abandoned due to local resistance in Andalgalá. I also did some exploratory work for a Rio Tinto project, which also failed. Through this experience I got to see the whole market of the EIAs from the inside, as a professional. This was how I realized that the state is unable to control the mining industry effectively. Mining companies tend to operate high up in the mountains, where implementing such control is very difficult. The state simply isn't capable, it doesn't have enough qualified professionals to read the EIAs that the mining companies submit. So they put whatever they want in these assessments. There is a whole chain of small consultants – they're vultures – who tell you what to include and what to leave out. It's a culture which is highly patriarchal, autocratic, and *machista*. They hire you to write what they tell you to, and if you won't do it they just hire someone who will. This is how the EIAs work, and as a result I broke with my profession and the academic environment which I inhabited at that time.

It is not just that EIAs are an ineffective form of regulation: they are a propaganda tool, giving mining projects a veneer of scientific and political legitimacy in order to pre-emptively defuse any potential conflicts (Veltmeyer and Petras, 2014a). As Carina says:

> I stopped doing EIAs. I am against them. They're just part of the apparatus that legitimizes *megaminería*. The aim of EIAs is to clear an area ahead of a mining project. What's hard is that lots of my colleagues still don't understand this. They say, 'The only way we can conduct mining responsibly is through carrying out EIAs'. But if you're receiving money for this work, to clear an area ahead of mining exploration, what possible resistance can there be?

That said, the fact that companies are obliged to publish EIAs opens up a key space from which communities can mount opposition to mining projects, as we will see in the following section.

The people fight back

One of the most effective weapons with which communities have opposed mining projects is the *consulta popular*. This mechanism has been used successfully in several Latin American countries, including Guatemala, El Salvador, Colombia, Peru, and Argentina, with each new victory serving as a model for other communities threatened by mining interests. Marcelo Giraud, a member of Mendoza's Asamblea Popular por el Agua, recalls how a 2002 *consulta* held in Tambogrande, Peru, came to influence the opposition to mining in Argentina, particularly in Esquel, Chubut, where they held a successful *consulta* on installation of a gold mine by Canadian mining company Meridian Gold, the following year:

> Our assembly in Mendoza is, if you like, the child of the assemblies out in the province, which are themselves the children of the assembly in Esquel. This, in turn, has its origins in Tambogrande, Peru, where they organized a *consulta popular* rejecting mining activity, the first of its kind in South America. Of course, the Peruvian government dismissed it at first, but after a long struggle, in which someone died, the government was forced to bow to popular pressure. The assembly in Esquel took the Peruvian experience as a direct example and held a *consulta* which was key in preventing the Meridian Gold project from going ahead.

Likewise, as Camila Méndez says of the *consulta* in Cajamarca, Colombia, 'Our *consulta* is in a way a replica, within our own national context, of what happened in Esquel, Argentina.' Here she describes what happened:

> It meant going door to door, farm to farm, person to person. We told them the date of the ballot and explained why they should vote, because people were very confused. We stressed how important it was: the vote was to give guarantees to our children and grandchildren that they would be able to enjoy a healthy environment, land, food produced in Cajamarca, the rivers and ravines, the whole campesino culture. That's

what we focused on in those two weeks. It was a huge task, working with communities to encourage them to take part.

On 26 March, we were finally able to hold our *consulta popular*. After so long, so much effort, the tension that day was indescribable. We were confident that we had done everything that could be done, but it still felt like anything could happen. A lot of police arrived, and the atmosphere became very tense. Fortunately, the voting went off normally, without incident, and turnout was high. Then we waited for the results. For the *consulta* to be valid, 70 per cent of the registered electorate had to vote. We needed 5,500 people to vote. To win, we needed a simple majority. You can imagine the tension we felt. When the results came in, 6,175 'No' votes were counted. Well, first of all it was a relief to know that enough people had voted to make the *consulta* valid. Then, of those votes, 98 per cent were for 'No' to mining.

That's when we started to celebrate. It had been 10 years of suffering, difficulties, accusations, threats ... so that moment was the climax. It was on national and international news. And in the community, it was the satisfaction of knowing that we had held our *consulta popular*, and we had said 'No' to mining.

The Argentine province of Mendoza is another good example of successful opposition. For Lucrecia Wagner:

Mendoza has one of the strongest resistance movements [in Argentina], along with Famatina, Chilecito, and Esquel. It's a provincial network with its own internal organization and is seen as an example by the other assemblies; it's highly respected. Moreover, Mendoza is one of the provinces which has a law specifically restricting mining with toxic substances, Law 7722. And it's not just that Mendoza has obtained this law, but it actively defends it. Last year [2015] the mining sector tried to get it overturned, arguing that it was unconstitutional, but the provincial court ruled against them.

Significantly, the local assemblies in Mendoza were quick to understand the importance of appropriating specialist knowledge on the issue. Lucrecia continues:

For me, as someone with a degree in environmental management, one of the most impressive things has been to see how people have appropriated the EIAs. In these conflicts you have retired people, housewives, professionals in other areas, but they read the EIAs and they're capable of discussing them with a representative from a mining company or someone from the government.

In almost all mining conflicts, both in Argentina and elsewhere, the mining companies, and also governments to a large extent, argue that the subject can only be understood by geologists, mining engineers, and other specialists. Mendoza is one of the cases where the assemblies attempted to dispute this specialist knowledge. They did this using the knowledge of the common citizen – for example, I remember the people of Uspallata saying, 'How can they tell us the water quality of the river is no good, if we can see fish?' But they also got hold of the EIAs, read them, and produced a lot of information off the back of this. Each assembly built up their own knowledge, in order to dispute or cast doubt upon that of their opponent. This was particularly effective not so much against the mining sector but against local authorities. They acquired a knowledge of the issues which the civil servants working on these cases didn't have, that became very clear.

While universities are sometimes co-opted by mining interests, which can offer employment and funding, they also provide important spaces for criticism of the sector. In Mendoza there is a strategic relationship between the opposition to mining and local academia. This was clear in the rejection of the San Jorge copper mine in Uspallata, as Lucrecia describes:

The San Jorge project was risky, given that it was located upstream. The EIA was very poor, with misinterpreted scientific data and outright lies. Three researchers – two from CONICET – blew the whistle on this, showing how the company had claimed the soil was more permeable where they needed to draw water and less permeable where they wanted to put the tailings ponds, to give you an example. One of the greatest successes of the assemblies has therefore been to expose all these attempts to obtain environmental permission by any means. They also showed how, though provincial civil servants might talk a lot about environmental controls, they have no way of enforcing them and no real understanding of what mining activity actually means.

One major victory for the Coordinación de Territorios por la Defensa de los Glaciares, in Chile, was the failure of Michelle Bachelet's administration (2014–18) to pass a proposed law on glaciers, under which, according to Constanza San Juan, 'Most glaciers in our country would remain unprotected, and … dangerously, what the legislation actually did was legalize and enable their destruction.' The Glaciers Bill was eventually withdrawn by the Piñera government in June 2018. As Constanza says:

We've managed to make quite an impact, for example the day of the Supreme Court's ruling was like a mini-victory for us. It backed up our claim that Bachelet's law didn't protect a single glacier. For the Supreme Court to say the same thing – this was like, 'Wow! What we said is right, the Supreme Court are saying it too!' The same sort of thing happened with the guys from the Universidad de Atacama when they released their report, as well as the good reception we had at the forums we've held. So I think we managed to achieve our primary objective, which was to establish that the Glaciers Law was a load of shit and didn't protect a single glacier.

Input from the scientific community helped add weight to the campaign against the legislation, as Stefanía Vega says:

> Although for the March in Defence of Glaciers we didn't get the numbers we wanted...it started a very interesting process whereby a lot of glaciologists came out making statements about why the draft legislation was bad. This is significant because the mining companies carry out environmental impact studies and they depend on scientists and other experts. But the scientists are supporting what we in the territories are saying, and this has been fascinating. More and more glaciologists are coming out on our side and ultimately, in doing so, throwing away the possibility of a job with these powerful groups.

As Lucrecia says, paraphrasing Gabriela Merlinsky, another Argentine researcher, 'It's a dispute about knowledge, about who has the right to an opinion'.

Networking is another key factor, allowing what may only be small local movements to achieve national and international projection. One event of note in Argentina is a regular conference known as the Union of Citizen Assemblies (UAC), which brings together local assembly movements from all over the country, as Lucrecia describes:

> In 2006, the Union of Citizen Assemblies was held, a national event which brought together all the assemblies and other social organizations in Argentina which were fighting against the plunder of our natural resources and the pollution of our environment. It's not just about mining. There were organizations against the pulp mills on the Uruguay River; people against building developments and polluting factories in the cities; people against the building of motorways; peasant and indigenous organizations representing people affected by the advance of agribusiness and the evictions that have come with it. There was a vast range of environmental problems, and one organization from Córdoba began to push the idea that they should all get together. Since 2006 these meetings have been held in different places across Argentina, every three or four months.

Such networking may go beyond national borders. Camila Méndez describes how opponents of La Colosa in Cajamarca, Colombia, were influenced by a trip they made to the Peruvian region of the same name, which is home to the massive Yanacocha project, the fourth-largest gold mine in the world:

> The people who were able to go and see what was happening in Cajamarca, Peru, echoed the voice of the communities there. What they told us was that when Yanacocha arrived and started work there, they told everyone that they would be bringing employment, progress. And people accepted it – who doesn't want a better quality of life? But as time went by they began to realize they had been duped. For example,

they now have access to water only when the company wants to give it to them. And as for their crops ... they became dependent on mining and were no longer able to maintain their other activities. It was about amplifying the voice of these communities, who were telling us, 'Please, don't make the same mistake! Don't let them go ahead with this project.'

Likewise, Marcelo Giraud discusses the links between the assembly in Mendoza and similar movements outside Argentina:

We've had direct contact with Tambogrande, and with other assemblies in the country, through the UAC. Also, because of the Pascua Lama project, many groups in Chile. When we first started – I can't remember which month – we hosted some comrades who had been working in Brazil with the groups Affected by Vale and the Movement of People Affected by Dams. Just this year in fact, two lawyers from this collective came here from Brazil. And some of our people have been over there two or three times.

But arguably what most provides communities with ammunition to use against the mining sector are the companies themselves. Camila Méndez describes how AngloGold Ashanti contributed to its own expulsion from Cajamarca:

When the company arrived, they were saying they would provide jobs and bring development. Many people didn't know, didn't understand what was happening. We had to hold so many events to provide information, to publicize what was happening in other areas, and that began to generate a level of consciousness among the people.

But at the same time the company itself began to undermine its own image and reputation, specifically thanks to the way they hired labour. They used a cooperative to contract workers for fixed three-month terms, but made no payments for healthcare, and fired them all at the end of the term. Then they'd hire another group of workers and do the same. That began to provoke discontent in the community, giving rise to the feeling that they were just toying with us. Another example was a transport company which provided services. Eventually [AngloGold Ashanti] got rid of them and set up its own transport company. It became clear that they weren't investing in the people here. People began to complain about this, a lot of them were angry. They began to realize they were being lied to.

On top of this discontent, people were saying that there would be problems, pointing to the social harm the companies do, the irreversible environmental impacts. These factors then came into play. And the company's own reputation worked in our favour. This is a company eminently open to question, all over the world, because of all the things they have done, especially in Africa.

And with each environmental disaster, it becomes increasingly hard for companies and governments to argue that *megaminería* is safe, clean, or sustainable.

Lucrecia Wagner describes the influence of the 2015 spill at Veladero and the Bento Rodrigues dam disaster in Brazil (see box) on the decision of Mendoza's Supreme Court to uphold Law 7722:

> The Mariana [Bento Rodrigues] disaster happened just a few months after the spill at Veladero, which had reignited the whole debate about the effects of mining in Argentina. In Argentina there aren't very many big active mining projects. Of those that do exist, several are in Patagonia, in very remote areas where nobody knows what's going on. The spill at Veladero was the first time there had been an accident on this scale in Argentina, and it happened in a very pro-mining province [San Juan]. This meant that in society and the media mining was now seen as a problem. It was already a controversial activity, and here was proof of an accident. There was a lot of criticism of how the company and the government managed the situation, and this was all still very fresh when the disaster at Mariana happened. Meanwhile, there were provinces in Argentina which were taking decisions on mining regulation. Clearly, it had an influence.

* * *

For the communities, the evidence overwhelmingly suggests that the costs of large open-pit mining operations outweigh the benefits (Veltmeyer and Petras, 2014b). The reason companies and governments try so hard to convince them otherwise lies in the extraordinary profits to be made. BHP Billiton (part owner of El Cerrejón in Colombia and the Germano complex in Brazil) posted revenue of $38.285 bn in 2017, while Glencore, one of its partners in El Cerrejón, reported a massive $205.476 bn the same year. But the days of this bonanza are numbered. Not only is mining for non-renewable natural resources inherently unsustainable physically, it is becoming increasingly unsustainable socially too. In a context of climate change and drought, the effects of *megaminería* – particularly on water supply – will generate increasing conflict with communities, and popular rejection of the sector is only likely to increase. It is already becoming a hard sell for policymakers, as has been the case in Mendoza, as Marcelo Giraud recalls:

> In 2011 we feared the San Jorge project would be approved by the legislature. One of the candidates for governor, Francisco 'Paco' Pérez, from the Justicialist Party (PJ), had had a long association with the mining industry. He's a lawyer, and in his law firm he had been a friend and partner of the president and representative of the mining company. He'd approved the project as a minister himself, and so as governor we expected him to be very pro-mining. The project had to go through the legislature and the pressure was growing. The opposition were against it, and popular rejection of the project was increasing. Polls showed that 70 per cent of the population was against it. At the last minute, Pérez backtracked. He realized that if he pushed on with it he risked being voted

out. So he told his deputies to vote against it. Two months earlier it had looked as if 60 per cent of the legislature would back it, but it ended up being rejected unanimously. Why? Because 2011 was an election year.

The most spectacular success, however, has been in El Salvador where, following a 12-year campaign by local communities, the Catholic Church, and the Central American University, a law was approved on 29 March 2017 banning all metal mining in the country. However, presidential elections in 2019 could lead to a reversal if the right-wing ARENA candidate wins (McKinley, 2018).

Proponents of *megaminería* typically argue that the industry brings employment and prosperity, with dissenters often accused of opposing local development. Following AngloGold Ashanti's departure from Cajamarca, Colombia, the mayor suggested that increased unemployment was leading to a social crisis in the town, as Camila Méndez describes:

> After a while, the mayor started going around saying that here in Cajamarca we were starving to death and lots of people had lost their jobs. And this was what was being reported nationally. We just carried on with our work, in agriculture, because here it's an agricultural economy. Our main product is *racacha*, which is a root vegetable like a carrot. Our municipality is the world leader in *racacha* production. We also produce beans, coffee, bananas, and other fruit and vegetables. As the campesinos say, whatever you plant will grow – literally. So it was a lie, what the mayor was saying. It's true that the few remaining employees of the company ended up out of work, but in Cajamarca there is employment on the land, and most of us carried on with our usual work in family agriculture.
>
> On 26 November [2017], eight months after the *consulta*, we held an event in the park at which we distributed around 2,000 plates of *sancocho*, a traditional soup made with maize, plantain, potato, cassava, and meat, which we often eat in Colombia. Thanks to the solidarity of the campesinos, we cooked this *sancocho* to show the whole world, and specifically the mayor of Cajamarca, that we weren't starving; on the contrary, after eight months, there was still plenty of food for everyone. It was a symbolic act to prove that the true wealth of our area, Cajamarca, is not gold, not a mine, but our agriculture, which is what we want to work at.

The point here being that there are alternatives. Residents in Esquel successfully argued that any jobs brought by the mine would only last for a decade at most, while investments in the town's expanding ecotourism industry would be far more sustainable (Miller, 2010). Likewise, Constanza San Juan describes some alternative activities being developed by rural communities in Chile:

> I have a bit of hope because I can see that people understand that the struggle isn't just about doing things that make a big impact but also about the day-to-day struggle of trying to find new ways of doing things,

new economic models, new ways of getting along with your neighbours. An example of this is the number of markets and fairs beginning to reappear in our territories. It's about rescuing cultures, traditions, artisan crafts, and showing that there are alternatives to mining. Another example is the increasing number of winemaking cooperatives that produce *pajarete*, a wine local to the Huasco Valley, showing how instrumental the water from the glaciers is in its production. This is their way of showing that they want to live in the valley and this is the way of life they want to lead, and in order for them to do this it's important that the glaciers remain unpolluted and unthreatened.

While such community initiatives are encouraging, we should not romanticize resistance to mining. The struggle is not necessarily noble, picturesque, or progressive. The scale of *megaminería* operations is such that they may galvanize a wide range of different actors with diverse motivations and agendas (Bebbington et al., 2013). Though this may provide resistance groups with greater social legitimacy, it also produces challenges. It can make resistance easy to fragment and consensus difficult to obtain, as Carina Jofré acknowledges:

> The assemblies are tough spaces, spaces of confrontation, where the residents come up face-to-face against power. The aim is for horizontality but in practice this is very difficult to maintain. There's always someone who takes the initiative and as such they can be very conflictive. They wear you out. For people without experience of political activism, they're exhausting.

Resistance does not always spring from deeply held political beliefs or ethical principles. It may simply be a case of self-preservation. Carina continues:

> What motivates me is pain. One doesn't just decide to be an activist. It's something that happens to you, that hurts you, that mobilizes you. I was born and brought up here. I have a daughter and I'm expecting another child. I want to raise my family here. But I can see – and it hurts – that the future is very uncertain.
>
> I find it hard to talk about participation, because that implies that there is an isolated space and time in which one participates. But it's not like that. You live somewhere and you're involved; there's no way of being neutral. This is what it means to live somewhere, in a province, where our days are numbered. That's how it feels to live where a decision has been made to pursue this model of development. You can't say, 'Tomorrow I won't participate.' No, it affects you in every way.
>
> The spills in the north of the province – and there are studies proving this – are affecting the whole water basin. Sooner or later the environmental problems in the north are going to start affecting the centre of the province as well. San Juan has already declared a state of emergency

due to water shortages. The flow of water is no longer the same. The water quality is no longer the same. Studies commissioned by the assemblies have shown that water quality in the province is not good.

So you can't just decide to participate for a while and then leave, no. The only way of not participating would be, I don't know, to go and live in London, somewhere they don't have *megaminería*. It's impossible.

Whatever the motivation, opposition to *megaminería* can and does work. This depends on several factors: proactive organization, effective political campaigning based on sound technical knowledge, a strong sense of community togetherness, and perhaps also a healthy dash of good luck. Most of all, communities must believe that their resistance is not futile – even if the odds appear to be massively stacked against them. As Camila Méndez says of the Cajamarca *consulta*:

> Cajamarca has become a beacon of hope. We faced down a lot of adversity; many outsiders thought that we wouldn't succeed. There was a lot of tension. Once we had achieved it and shown that we, a campesino community, proud of who we are but with limited resources, really could confront this monster, one of the world's biggest gold producers – that fills people with hope.

About the author

Tom Gatehouse is a writer and translator who has lived in Argentina, Spain, and Brazil. He holds an MPhil in Latin American Studies from the University of Cambridge. He has written for LAB and Red Pepper, amongst other outlets, while his translations have appeared in *Folha de S. Paulo*, Agência Pública, and *Tales and Trails Lisbon*, a recent collection of short stories and other writings. He lives in London.

Interviews

Lucio Cuenca (OLCA): interviewed in London on 23 May 2017 by Tom Gatehouse. Transcribed by Tom Gatehouse and translated by Chris Whitehouse.

Marcelo Giraud (Asamblea Popular por el Agua): interviewed in Mendoza, Argentina, on 17 November 2016 by Tom Gatehouse. Translated by Hebe Powell.

Esther González and **Alfredo Gallardo** (CDPC): interviewed in Caimanes, Chile, on 24 November 2016 by Tom Gatehouse. Translated by Francis McDonagh.

Angelo Herrera (Hotel manager): interviewed in Caimanes, Chile, on 25 November 2016 by Tom Gatehouse. Translated by María Boniface and Mike Gatehouse.

Carina Jofré (CONICET San Juan): interviewed in San Juan, Argentina, on 17 November 2016 by Tom Gatehouse. Translated by Tom Gatehouse.

Camila Méndez (COSAJUCA): interviewed in London on 30 November 2017 by Tom Gatehouse. Translated by Mike Gatehouse.

Rodrigo Péret (Churches and Mining Network) and **Thiago Alves da Silva** (MAB): interviewed in London on 19 October 2017 by Tom Gatehouse. Translated by Tom Gatehouse.

Oscar Roca (CAEP): interviewed in Huanuni, Bolivia, on 30 November 2016 by Tom Gatehouse. Transcribed by Alan Williams and translated by Rachel Toogood.

Constanza San Juan and **Stefanía Vega** (CTDG): interviewed in Santiago de Chile on 26 November 2016 by Tom Gatehouse. Translated by Matty Rose.

Rogelio Ustate (Tabaco community): interviewed in Hatonuevo, La Guajira, Colombia, on 7 January 2017 by Emma Banks. Transcribed by Elizabeth Pillares and translated by James Scorer.

Lucrecia Wagner (CONICET Mendoza): interviewed in Mendoza, Argentina, on 16 November 2016 by Tom Gatehouse. Translated by Tom Gatehouse.

References

NB: All web references were checked and still available in May/June 2018 unless otherwise stated. All references are listed, with web-links, on the page for this chapter on the Voices website www.vola.org.uk

Bebbington, A. and Bury, J. (2013) 'Political ecologies of the subsoil', in A. Bebbington and J. Bury (eds), *Subterranean Struggles*, pp. 1–26, University of Texas Press, Austin, TX.

Bebbington, A., Bury, J. and Gallagher, E. (2013) 'Conclusions', in A. Bebbington and J. Bury (eds), *Subterranean Struggles*, pp. 267–88, University of Texas Press, Austin, TX.

Brown, K. (2012) *A History of Mining in Latin America*, University of New Mexico Press, Albuquerque, NM.

Bury, J. and Bebbington, A. (2013) 'New geographies of extractive industries in Latin America', in A. Bebbington and J. Bury (eds), *Subterranean Struggles*, pp. 27–66, University of Texas Press, Austin, TX.

Colombia Solidarity Campaign (2013) 'La Colosa: a death foretold', Colombia Solidarity Campaign, London, <https://www.colombiasolidarity.org.uk/attachments/article/612/LA%20COLOSA_A%20Death%20Foretold.pdf>

Galeano, E. (1971) *Open Veins of Latin America*, tr. C. Belfrage (1997), Monthly Review Press, New York, NY.

Gatehouse, T. (2017a) 'Antofagasta: the Goliath which is crushing Caimanes', Latin America Bureau (LAB), <https://lab.org.uk/antofagasta-the-goliath-which-is-crushing-caimanes>

Gatehouse, T. (2017b) 'After the flood: two years on from the Fundão tailings dam disaster', LAB, <https://lab.org.uk/after-the-flood-two-years-on-from-the-fundao-tailings-dam-disaster>

Greenpeace Chile (2016) 'Greenpeace: El proyecto de Ley de Glaciares es malo y no protege a los glaciares', <http://www.greenpeace.org/chile/es/noticias/

Greenpeace-El-proyecto-de-Ley-de-Glaciares-es-malo-y-no-protege-a-los-glaciares>

Jamasmie, C. (2013) 'Chile's proposed glaciers protection law worries miners, investors', MINING.com, <http://www.mining.com/chiles-proposed-glaciers-protection-law-worries-miners-investors-15134>

McKinley, A. (2018) 'El Salvador: first anniversary of the mining ban', LAB, <https://lab.org.uk/el-salvador-first-anniversary-of-the-mining-ban>

Miller, H. (2010) 'Esquel community opposes to gold mining, Argentina, 2002–2006', Global Nonviolent Action Database, <https://nvdatabase.swarthmore.edu/content/esquel-community-opposes-gold-mining-argentina-2002–2006>

Sankey, K. (2014) 'Colombia: The mining boom: a catalyst of development or resistance?', in H. Veltmeyer and J. Petras (eds), *The New Extractivism: A Post-Neoliberal Development Model of Imperialism of the Twenty-First Century?*, pp. 114–43, Zed Books, London and New York, NY.

Scott, P. (2016) 'Review of Cerro Rico – the silver mountain', London Mining Network, <http://londonminingnetwork.org/2016/08/review-of-cerro-rico-the-silver-mountain>

Thorp, R., Battistelli, S., Guichaoua, Y., Orihuela, J.C. and Paredes, M. (2012) 'Extractives-based development and developmental outcomes', in R. Thorp et al., *The Developmental Challenges of Mining and Oil: Lessons from Africa and Latin America*, pp. 168–211, Palgrave Macmillan, Basingstoke.

Veltmeyer, H. and Petras, J. (2014a) 'A new model or extractive imperialism?', in H. Veltmeyer and J. Petras (eds), *The New Extractivism*, pp. 21–46, Zed Books, London and New York, NY.

Veltmeyer, H. and Petras, J. (2014b) 'Theses on extractive imperialism and the post-neoliberal state', in H. Veltmeyer and J. Petras (eds), *The New Extractivism*, pp. 222–49, Zed Books, London and New York, NY.

CHAPTER 8
State violence, policing, and paramilitaries
Mike Gatehouse

Abstract

Policing in Latin America has been increasingly militarized in recent years. Not only has this failed to reduce crime, it kills and injures many innocent people, including children. This violence disproportionately affects the poor, as well as black and indigenous communities. Migrants are frequent targets. Both state forces and non-state actors such as paramilitary groups may be deployed to protect the operations of extractive industries such as mining, oil drilling, and agribusiness.

Many Latin Americans are accustomed to view the coercive forces of the state as routine perpetrators of violence, rather than as guarantors of civic peace, protectors of borders, and their defence in war. The history of state violence against civilian populations in Latin America goes back to the colonial era, but the perversion of the role of the state was given fresh impetus from the 1950s onwards by the various military dictatorships which adopted models of 'national security' that prioritized the battle against 'the enemy within'. These ideas were integral to the officer training programmes funded and organized by the Pentagon for officers from most of Latin America's armed forces, especially at the US Army School of the Americas in Panama.

While the dictatorships and the more extreme of their doctrines have now ended, much of the thinking they embodied survives within military and police institutions and in the attitude and practice of civilian governments. Military, paramilitary, and armed police solutions are routinely sought for social problems such as narcotrafficking, gang violence, and smuggling, as well as the policing of key infrastructure projects, often on behalf of private corporations and owners. The weakness and corruption of civil institutions, especially the courts and regulatory bodies, leads politicians to argue for the deployment of the armed forces as being the only agents with the power, honesty, and efficiency to protect civil society. Such a rosy view of the military is seldom supported by the facts. Military training is no preparation for policing civilians, soldiers are no less prone than civilians to succumb to bribery, and the result is a corrosion of military institutions themselves.

The role of the United States has changed since its unapologetic promotion of military coups and dictatorships during the Cold War. However,

http://dx.doi.org/10.3362/9781909014213.008

support for authoritarian government remains evident in the policies and practice of successive US presidents (both Democrat and Republican), the State Department, and the Pentagon. It is manifest, for instance, in the military-backed coups that ended the democratically elected governments of Manuel Zelaya in Honduras (2009) and Fernando Lugo in Paraguay (2012); in the more than US$7 bn in US military aid channelled through Plan Colombia from 2000 to 2010, and continued for a further five years after that on the pretext of the War on Drugs (Huey, 2014); and in Mérida Initiative funding for the Mexican government's militarization, since 2006, of action against the drug cartels. The US was directly complicit in the Honduran coup and the abortive coup against Hugo Chávez in Venezuela in 2002, and again today, as the Trump administration threatens the 'military option' against the Maduro government.

State violence in the region is now most acute in two arenas: in the effort to control the narcotics trade, both in urban areas where drugs are distributed and consumed, and in the rural areas where they are produced and transported; and in the expropriation of land, coercive regulation, and policing required by the large extractive projects (hydroelectric dams, mines, road building, forest clearance, and monocultures such as soya and palm oil) to which Latin American governments have become increasingly committed in the past 30 years. In both these arenas, the violence is often perpetrated by paramilitary forces, militias, and private security guards who are nominally independent of the state, but often act with the complicity and protection of local or national government officials and in many cases are staffed by former or even serving members of the armed forces and police. This has been starkly evident in Mexico, Brazil, and Colombia.

Security and police forces are also routinely deployed not only against political or criminal groups deemed a threat to 'national security', but against social groups, especially of black and indigenous peoples. The governments of both Guatemala (1975–85) and Peru (1980–95) deployed the military in full-scale operations against indigenous groups. In Guatemala between 1980 and 1983, 'the army destroyed 626 villages, killed or "disappeared" more than 200,000 people, and displaced an additional 1.5 million, while more than 150,000 were driven to seek refuge in Mexico' (Holocaust Museum, n.d.) This was deemed genocide by the Commission for Historical Clarification (CEH) established by the UN (CEH, 1999). In Peru, military operations in the Andean highlands against the Sendero Luminoso guerrilla group often led to indiscriminate killings of civilians by army units such as the Colina Group, responsible for the Barrios Altos massacre in 1991 and other killings (Burt, 2012). Meanwhile, indigenous peoples and *quilombo* communities in Brazil, Chile, Ecuador, and Argentina have suffered disproportionate numbers of their people killed by the police, military, or paramilitary groups protected by government, usually in disputes about land rights and incursions by land thieves, loggers, and mining and energy companies.

Migrants are a particularly vulnerable group. The threat of deportation puts them at risk of coercion, extortion, blackmail, enslavement, and killing. In Mexico especially, migrants from Central America heading overland to the US are targeted by gangs, the police, the army, and immigration officials, sometimes acting in concert. They are robbed, raped, imprisoned, and disappeared.

Brazil: racism and poverty

Contemporary state violence in Brazil is largely a legacy of slavery and the country's historically troubled relationship with race. Most state violence occurs in marginalized communities, primarily the favelas and poor neighbourhoods in the urban *periferias*, which are disproportionately inhabited by black and mixed-race Brazilians.

Police in the state of Rio de Janeiro killed more than 8,000 people between 2006 and 2016, three-quarters of whom were black men. They typically invoke what is known as *autos de resistência* – indicating legitimate self-defence or that a suspect was resisting arrest. Such cases are hardly ever investigated. Rio de Janeiro is undoubtedly a very difficult environment to police effectively and officers face very real threats. Criminal organizations in the state are armed with high-powered rifles, machine guns, grenades, and even rocket launchers. Nonetheless, many of the killings are cases of extrajudicial execution. Police shoot unarmed civilians, including children. They shoot people in the back as they are running away. They execute people whom they have detained and arrested. And they routinely manipulate crime scenes and stage cover-ups (Human Rights Watch, 2016).

From 2008, the Rio state government introduced Police Pacification Units (UPPs), in an attempt to 'cleanse' the favelas and destroy the power of the criminal gangs which control the drug trade. Up to 40 were in place by 2014, covering 231 favelas. The programme was intensified in 'clean-up operations' prior to the World Cup in 2014 and the Rio Olympics in 2016. While UPPs may enjoy some short-term success in driving the gangs out of one area, these merely move their operations elsewhere and they then return as soon as the UPP winds down. Meanwhile, many innocent people are caught in the crossfire, arrested, and sometimes killed by the police. The vast majority are black males under the age of 30. The February 2018 decision of the Temer government to place the policing of Rio under military control threatens to exacerbate the situation.

Ana Paula Oliveira and Fatima Pinho are founder members of Mães de Manguinhos (Mothers of Manguinhos), a group of mothers from the Manguinhos favela in Rio de Janeiro who have lost children to acts of violence committed by the local UPP. As Fatima explains:

> [My son] Paulo Roberto died on 17 October 2013. He was killed by several police officers here in Manguinhos, but only five were charged. It

Ana Paula (left) and Fatima, with a banner of some of the young men killed in Manguinhos

happened because he stood up to them. He had a record and he had been arrested before by a policeman who happened to be from the UPP base here. This policeman recognized him and began to follow him around the favela, though he had no legal reason to do so. Paulo confronted him, he wanted to fight this policeman but couldn't while he was in uniform. Paulo said, 'Take off your uniform, let's have it out, your problem with me is personal.' This policeman ended up leaving the favela. But he told his colleagues about Paulo – that he objected to their approach, that he was the rowdiest kid here. So they thought Paulo was a problem.

On 17 October, he saw the police carrying out an operation here and went over to ask them what they were doing. It was a little past two in the morning. He went down the alley, and when the policemen saw him they dropped what they were doing and went after him and the three boys he was with. They didn't do anything to the other boys, just put guns to them, threatened them, but they piled on top of my son and assaulted him. During the assault, my son grabbed one of their vests and fell back, bringing two policemen down with him. They called for reinforcement and in the end there were more than 15 policemen in the alley beating him up. They suffocated him. He was 18 years old.

Ana Paula explains what happened to her son and several other young men and boys in Manguinhos:

> Johnatha was passing Fatima's front door when he got shot; she saw it happen. It was just seven months after Fatima's own son was killed by police here in Manguinhos. Her loss was still so recent, when she witnessed another young man get shot for no reason. Fatima says Johnatha was passing and her [other] son was at the door. There were a few people around. When she heard the shots, she ran downstairs to grab the children, because it was around four in the afternoon and they were playing outside. Everyone ran home because it was kicking off between residents and the police. That kind of violence had become the norm since the UPP arrived here in Manguinhos. Residents didn't take kindly to their heavy-handed approach and would stand up to them, swear at them. It always ended up with someone getting shot.
>
> Johnatha was the third victim of the UPP in Manguinhos. After him, there were four more victims, so there have been seven so far. The last one was in April this year [2016]. The boy was in his house and was shot in the head. In 2014, there were two: Johnatha, and a month later, Afonso.
>
> In 2015, Christian was killed in September. It happened on some wasteland here. There used to be houses there but they knocked them down and now it's all overgrown. Apparently, the police were hiding out there, shooting. I was at my house. It was around 10.30 or 11 a.m. when I heard the shots. Soon after, my phone rang, and they asked me to call people, because the police had come in and shot a boy. They sent me a photo of Christian on the ground, and people were saying that it was the grandson of Dona Graça, an elderly, well-known resident who had a guesthouse. And then I realized that I knew the boy, because Dona Graça had been my neighbour here on the next street. I panicked and started calling the human rights people, like Marielle [see box], who had helped me when Johnatha died. I called the staff from the Fórum Social de Manguinhos, the independent media.
>
> And Caio Daniel and João were both killed this year. We've noticed that when they kill somebody, they move the officer who did it to another favela that has a UPP. So they just transfer the problem. We know that in other favelas like Borel, mothers have got police arrested, through group efforts. We know another mother, Marcia Jacinto from Lins, who managed to get the policeman who killed her son convicted, through her own investigation. When Paulo died, Fatima had support from the Fórum Social. And when Johnatha died, Fatima and the Fórum Social were there for me. Fatima came to Johnatha's 7th day Mass, and told me about the Fórum, invited me to participate and join her in the struggle. She said, 'My cry will be stronger with yours, we can fight and bring together other mothers too.'

Marielle Franco

Marielle Franco, who helped Ana Paula after the death of her son, was elected to Rio's city council in the 2016 elections with the fifth-highest number of votes among 70 councillors. Black, lesbian, and a feminist, Marielle was born in Maré, a favela complex in the north of the city which was occupied by the military for 15 months in 2014–2015. She was an outspoken critic of the UPPs and of military intervention in the city's favelas.

In March 2018, Marielle publicly denounced police operations in the Favela de Acari. 'We need to scream so that everyone knows what is happening in Acari right now. The 41st Battalion of the Military Police in Rio de Janeiro is terrorizing and violating the rights of the residents of Acari. This week two young men were killed and thrown in a ditch. Today the police have been patrolling the streets and threatening residents. This happens all the time but since the intervention it has become even worse.'

Marielle Franco.

© Mídia Ninja - Flickr, CC BY-SA 2.

Shortly afterwards, on 14 March, Marielle was being driven home through central Rio after attending an event on black women's empowerment. A car with two men pulled up alongside hers and fired nine times. Marielle was hit three times in the head, once in the neck. She died at the scene. Her driver was also killed. It was a targeted assassination, and the bullets were stolen from a consignment purchased by the federal police in 2006.

Ana Paula explains how these killings led to the formation of Mães de Manguinhos:

[After Christian was killed], Fatima came to see me and I said, 'Let's go, there's going to be a demonstration, a meeting of mothers.' I ended up giving her that kick-start, that drive she still has today. She started coming up with ideas to go to places, meeting the Mães de Maio [see box below], and so on.

Our first trip together was to Brasília, to the launch of the Amnesty International Jovem Negro Vivo [Young, Black, Alive] campaign ... They needed as much support as possible because there were several movements present on the day that Bill PL 4471 on *autos de resistência* was on the agenda. They said they would pay.

PL 4471 is a bill which was presented by Workers' Party (PT) Deputy Paulo Teixeira in 2012 to enforce proper investigation of all deaths at the hands of the police and military and ban the use of the blanket term *auto de resistência*. It has not yet been approved and is opposed by right-wing presidential candidate Jair Bolsonaro. Ana Paula continues:

> We met the Mães de Maio when we were invited to São Paulo. It was to mark nine years of their struggle. There we received a medal as the Mães de Manguinhos, and that was when we had the idea of bringing together other mothers from the favela ... We liked the name. There are already the groups Mães de Acari and Mães de Maio in São Paulo. So I thought we should start our own movement, using that name.

Mães de Maio

In May 2006, after prison authorities in the state of São Paulo decided to transfer 765 prisoners to a maximum-security prison, the First Capital Command (PCC) – one of Brazil's two largest criminal organizations – organized riots in 74 prisons, as well as launching attacks on police stations, fire stations, public vehicles, prisons, and other public buildings. The violence was a response not only to the prisoner transfers, but to an extortion racket by members of the Civil Police of São Paulo, who were threatening families of prisoners and even kidnapped the stepson of Marcola, the PCC boss.

In response to the attacks, police death squads took to the streets. The population, terrified, stayed indoors. Businesses, schools, and universities remained closed. The streets of the largest city in the southern hemisphere were deserted. Ultimately, 564 people were killed: 509 civilians, 59 agents of the state. Eight of every ten killed were under 35, 96 per cent were male, and well over half were black or of mixed race. Just 6 per cent of them had a criminal record. As the researcher Camila Dias says, 'The reaction [of state security forces] was to kill indiscriminately in the *periferia*, to send the following message: "never do that again". It was a totally disproportionate response by the Military Police of São Paulo' (Cruz, 2016).

The mothers and relatives of the victims joined to form a movement called Mães de Maio [Mothers of May]. Like Ana Paula and Fatima, they are women who have channelled their grief into the struggle for justice, demanding that such atrocities are never repeated.

Police who kill unlawfully in Brazil almost always escape justice. In 64 cases between 2006 and 2016 in Rio de Janeiro and São Paulo analysed by Human Rights Watch, only eight went to trial and only four resulted in convictions. In 36 cases, prosecutors did not even seek indictment, despite credible evidence of police cover-up (Human Rights Watch, 2016). This makes Ana Paula's and Fatima's persistence all the more remarkable. As Ana Paula says:

> Generally, what prevents mothers from getting involved is their health. At least two of the victims were raised by their grandmothers, like Mateus, the first victim, and Afonso. The elderly don't have the health for this struggle; they prefer not to talk about it. However, many people

don't get involved because they just don't believe in the justice system – they think they'll only end up dwelling on their losses and nothing will happen. That might have been the case in the beginning, but now people have seen that the cases of Paulo and Johnatha were investigated thanks to our perseverance. In Paulo's case, the public prosecutor rejected the murder charge, claiming that the police didn't intend to kill him. They beat him repeatedly but didn't intend to kill him, apparently. Even so, the case is with the review board of the Military Police. The lawyers say that the best that we can hope for is that the officers responsible are fired.

In Johnatha's case, we've already spent over two years fighting for justice ... There was an investigation and they summoned witnesses as soon as the case was passed from the police station to the Public Prosecutor's Office. The court official told me that though she'd been working in Manguinhos for a long time, she'd never seen one of these cases go to court, and she'd never seen so many witnesses come forward. She summoned seven. Usually witnesses don't want to get involved, they're afraid.

Some of the media were there at the first hearing – it made the news. That's something that encouraged me to keep fighting, and still does today. A few days beforehand, a reporter asked me what I expected now that Johnatha's case had made it to court. I said that the least a mother could want, when her son had been murdered so cruelly, was justice. Then he asked if I knew the name of the policeman, so I gave his full name. I told him that the weapons had been apprehended at the scene and the ballistics examination confirmed who it was. This was on a Friday.

Before I left the house for the hearing on Monday, I received messages and links to the interview in the newspaper, *O Dia*. This reporter had managed to find things out about this policeman that not even the lawyer on Johnatha's case knew. It turned out that he had already been involved in a triple homicide and two attempted homicides in the Baixada Fluminense and had spent a month in prison in 2013. But the case was shelved due to lack of witnesses. Baixada Fluminense is a dangerous place, where there are death squads and militias. It's very hard for a family to pursue justice in that environment. When I found out that the policeman had faced charges before, I was appalled. Why hadn't the courts done their job?

It's the questions they ask. I have seen the same thing at other hearings: 'Does narcotrafficking occur in the favela where you live?' and 'Was your son involved in trafficking?' This shows their prejudice. The person on trial isn't the policeman, the murderer, but the victim. They spend the whole time trying to justify the killings. The way we see it, there is no justice for us, the poor, who live in the favelas. We only see the agents of justice when they come to arrest and punish us. Otherwise justice is non-existent. People ask me if I believe in justice, if I believe the policeman will be convicted. I believe in my struggle, and the struggle of the mothers. It will get results. Johnatha's case made it to court, thanks to the residents who had the courage to go and testify, and thanks to my efforts with the other mothers. That's why. It's not because the justice system is kind. I've always said that I never wanted revenge. I want justice. I want Johnatha's case to be an example to residents, so that they can believe that if you fight for it, justice will be done. We have to fight. We have to know and understand our rights. I want Johnatha's case to be an example to Manguinhos, and to so many other mothers.

It is notable that, as in Chile and Argentina during the 1970s and 1980s, many of the most active campaigns against state violence in Latin America today are led by or consist wholly of women (Ruge, 2017). Ana Paula comments:

After Johnatha's death, my partner didn't support my work, but now he sees that I feel better when I can scream, get my pain out. He was afraid something would happen to me for speaking out. He used to say it was no use, that I'd just exhaust myself. He thought that nothing would come of it, just like in all the other cases we've seen. Today, he still worries, but I think he sees things differently, because he's seen the impact, how much people are talking about it. So today he supports me and lets me get on with it.

As with so many of the voices in this book, while they may be working in very small, local organizations, contact with others engaged in similar campaigns, often via social media, is vitally important:

We live in Manguinhos, but if there is a mother who needs us in another favela, we go to her. Social networks have been a good tool for bringing mothers together. The other day a mother from Mossoró, Rio Grande do Norte, contacted me on Facebook. The police had murdered her son too. She had been looking for other cases and came across my posts. She wrote, 'I see your posts, your struggle, and it makes me sad because I want to do that too, but we don't have a group of mothers here. I really want to talk about my son. His case is still going nowhere. It was the police who killed him as well.' ... Today, that woman in Mossoró is in our mothers' WhatsApp group for Rio and São Paulo.

Moreover, these links go beyond Brazil's borders. As Ana Paula says, 'this struggle is going global':

This year, there has been the Black Lives Matter movement, and it came to Rio. I think the fight has to be international. People from here and the US gave testimonies. They came to Manguinhos, along with the Mães de Maio. It was great to exchange our experiences. In October, Amnesty International invited me to Washington DC, to attend a seminar to talk about the relationship between sporting mega-events, violence, and human rights violations. Dona Maria da Penha from the Vila Autódromo went to talk about the forced evictions from the favelas, and I went to talk about police violence. There's a marked increase when there are mega-events.

We had some time to visit Amnesty International's headquarters, then we had a meeting with some of the social movements in Washington, like Black Lives Matter. At the meeting, I found out that there was a protest the following day, led by a mother whose son had been murdered by the police in Washington. She was called Beverly Smith, and her son was Alonso. I told them I wanted to go and support her and share my experiences too. I left the seminar early to get there. We got an interpreter, and I put on the Mães de Manguinhos T-shirt. It was very emotional. I never imagined where this struggle would take me. I never imagined leaving Manguinhos, let alone going to Europe or the US.

The struggle of the Mães de Manguinhos is more than just a legal battle for justice for their children. Half of the Brazilian population agrees with the phrase 'bandido bom é bandido morto' ('the only good criminal is a dead criminal') (Jardim, 2018), and at the time of writing the current frontrunner for the 2018 presidential elections is the far-right congressman Jair Bolsonaro. In 2017 he was asked about an investigation into 20 officers of the Rio de Janeiro Military Police suspected of involvement in over 350 killings. 'They should be decorated,' he replied. 'Police who don't kill aren't proper police' (Roxo, 2017). The Mães are therefore engaged in something much bigger, a cultural battle against racism, classism, and punitive attitudes regarding criminal justice, says Ana Paula:

> It's all the prejudice, all the racism that is rooted in society, in the whole system, the judiciary, the media. Every time we can talk, we scream, and tell our story of pain and struggle. And I'm sure that at least one person will be moved by what we say, when perhaps before they had thought of everyone in the favelas as poor black criminals who deserve to die. When a mother speaks about her struggle, even if this has an impact on just one person, things begin to change. People begin to reflect on their beliefs. That's why I think it's so important for us to speak out.
>
> And we've had so many setbacks. Things are getting worse. This is not only a fight for justice for Johnatha. The mothers' struggle is not just about getting justice for our children. It is a struggle for survival. It's a struggle for the right to life. Because we are poor, black, and come from the favela, society thinks that the right to life doesn't apply to us. We don't have the right to go to the beach because there will be muggings. They say 'bandido bom é bandido morto'. But the National Congress is full of white-collar criminals, thieves, and society's not calling for them to be killed. And neither am I. I'm fighting for life, but everyone's life, including those of people who live in the favelas.

Mexico and the War on Drugs

In Brazil, state violence is justified because people in the favelas and *periferias* are labelled as criminals and regarded as 'other'. In Colombia, as we will see later, military and paramilitary violence in rural areas is justified in the context of the war against the guerrillas of the Revolutionary Armed Forces of Colombia (FARC). In Mexico, the language is that of an openly avowed 'War on Drugs', launched by President Felipe Calderón in December 2006, when he sent 6,500 troops into the state of Michoacán.

Mexico has not acted alone – it has relied on huge quantities of US aid, justified to the US public as a means of halting the torrent of illegal narcotics flowing northward to the larger and far wealthier US market. Since 2006, the US Congress has authorized $2.8 bn for the Mérida Initiative, the first phase of which funded the purchase of equipment to support the efforts of Mexico's federal security forces (military and police), including $590.5 m for aircraft and helicopters. Under Obama, some aid under the initiative was designated for institution building and the rule of law, while under Trump the focus has switched back to military and policing programmes and equipment (Seelke and Finklea, 2017).

Javier Treviño Rangel is an assistant professor at the Drug Policy Programme of the Centro de Investigación y Docencia Económicas (CIDE), based in Aguascalientes in central Mexico. Here he discusses the work of a CIDE colleague who is studying prisons and incarceration:

[She is] analysing how the people who are in jail are not the big *capos* but, you know, ordinary Mexicans who smoke marijuana. Most of them are poor; this War on Drugs is helping to get rid of poor people, to put them in jail. She has also found that we don't have due legal process and the use of torture is a systematic practice. If you're caught smoking marijuana in the street, you have a 40 or 50 per cent chance of being tortured by the police or military. Electric shocks, waterboarding, and so on.

Javier Treviño Rangel.
© María Cortina 2015

[Two other CIDE colleagues] are working on some databases of people who have been killed in the last few years. What they have found is that when the military intervene, instead of diminishing violence, they create violence. It's incredible, terrifying. Sometimes, when the military patrol the streets with the police, they basically just kill people, for no reason. No investigations, no nothing – just killing. They are like death squads.

'What do you think is the main problem nowadays in Mexico in terms of human rights?' Javier asked a friend who had been working on human rights in Mexico for more than 20 years. 'Without hesitation, she replied "disappearances."' According to Amnesty International there were at least 27,600 people officially registered as 'lost or disappeared' between 2006 and 2016, of whom 3,425 were reported in 2015 alone (Amnesty International, 2016).

Javier's own cousin is one of them. 'He was illegally detained by traffic police ... back in September 2012, and he hasn't been seen since.' Here he describes his aunt's attempts to find her son:

> My aunt, the mother of my cousin, went to the police, but they didn't do anything. So she went to see the military in Durango, because, you know, despite everything, the military have a good reputation in Mexico. I understand that in countries like Spain, Argentina, Chile, or Colombia, to talk of the military on the street is unthinkable, but in Mexico the military enjoy a good reputation. But they told her, 'Just forget about what happened, you won't achieve anything: just forget about it and move on.' ...
>
> When the War on Drugs began, and human rights organizations and experts on violence and security started criticizing President Calderón, he responded by arguing that the killings were criminals killing each other. No good people were dying; there was no collateral damage. It was justified, because we needed to get rid of all these people. This discourse was very contagious, very popular. It was stupid and simplistic and false, but it helped society make sense of what was happening. Ten bodies found in a mass grave? No problem, just the bad guys killing each other. This discourse explained everything.
>
> So when this happened to my cousin, the assumption was that he must have been mixed up in something. My aunt was no longer a victim; she was polluted, stigmatized. On top of that, there was the threat that if she made a fuss, something might happen to her as well ... My aunt's family asked her to stop investigating. And everything stopped there. This is the story of my cousin.

Javier also mentions the Ayotzinapa case, the most notorious case of disappearance in Mexico:

> [Ayotzinapa] forced the international community to pay attention. It's the most investigated case in Mexican history, with the international mass media watching it ... And still, the prosecutor who led the investigation had eight out of the ten suspects tortured, according to the Inter-American Commission on Human Rights. Eight out of ten! This wasn't some local prosecutor out in the countryside; he was a federal attorney. Despite the presence of the global media and an international group of experts, he still felt free to allow the torture of most of the suspects back in 2015.

A March 2018 UN report concluded that at least 34 of the 63 individuals prosecuted in the case had been tortured (UN News, 2018).

Ayotzinapa

On 26 September 2014, more than 100 students from the Raúl Isidro Burgos Rural Teacher Training College in Iguala, in the state of Guerrero, commandeered several buses for an event in Mexico City a few days later commemorating the 2 October 1968 Tlatelolco massacre. This was a school tradition and had been largely tolerated by the bus companies and local authorities. Students would borrow the buses for the event and then return them afterwards (Semple, 2016).

However, on this occasion, police set roadblocks for the students and pursued the buses. At one point they opened fire. Two students were shot dead, along with the driver of a bus carrying a local football team and one of the players (their bus was presumably mistaken for one of those taken by the students). A woman in a taxi was also killed. Another student, who had fled when shooting began, was found dead the following morning, his body mutilated. During the chaos, 43 students disappeared. What exactly happened is still unknown. The Mexican authorities claim that corrupt local police arrested the students and handed them over to the Guerreros Unidos criminal gang. They were then murdered, the bodies incinerated in a skip at Cocula, and the remains thrown in a river.

However, after a year-long forensic investigation, a group of experts appointed by the Inter-American Commission on Human Rights concluded that it was scientifically impossible for 43 bodies to have been burned in a skip in the conditions described by the authorities. Satellite images of the area showed no signs of a significant fire. An investigation by the University of California blames the Mexican Federal Police and the military for the mass disappearance (Hernández and Fisher, 2014). Remains of at least some of the bodies were recovered, but only two have been identified. The fate and whereabouts of the other 41 remain unknown.

It is clear that in the context of the War on Drugs, the lines between state security forces and criminal organizations have been becoming increasingly blurred, as Javier recognizes:

> The discourse of some security experts is that organized crime is co-opting or conquering the state. They argue we have to fight back, the Mexican State has to fight back. One of the most brutal criminal organizations is called Los Zetas. Well, this organization was formed by four main members of the Mexican military. So it's not that Los Zetas are conquering the military, it's that these organizations were created by the military ... So, who is conquering whom? Who is learning from whom? Are members of criminal organizations learning how to torture from us, from the state? Or is the state learning how to torture from criminal organizations? That's my point: it's too simple to say that these criminal organizations are conquering the state; maybe it's the other way around.

The targeting of migrants

The toll of those disappeared and killed in Mexico includes many migrants, most of them from Central America. Javier recalls two notorious cases from 2010 and 2011, known as the San Fernando massacres:

> Seventy-two undocumented migrants from Central America were killed and found in a mass grave on a ranch in Tamaulipas, in the north of Mexico ... The immediate response of the government was to claim that the victims were involved in organized crime. What little evidence there was, because the government tends to conceal evidence in these cases, revealed that these guys were kidnapped from ordinary passenger buses. They were detained – not kidnapped – by members of the Mexican State, police or immigration officials. They were detaining undocumented migrants and handing them over to criminal organizations. Not for thousands of dollars: sometimes they were handing them over for a six pack of beer, a bottle of whisky, 500 pesos – which is what, $25? So, it was in 2010 that we began to understand that the atrocities that are happening now in Mexico cannot be explained if we don't take into account the active involvement of the state.
>
> Some months later, more than one hundred people, I think even close to two hundred bodies were found. Again, in Tamaulipas. Again, they were undocumented migrants. I interviewed Mercedes Doretti, the head of the Argentine Forensic Anthropology Team, which I think is the most prestigious organization working on forensic issues in the world, which has been working on these issues since the end of the Argentine dictatorship. She posed the following question: how is it possible that more than a hundred bodies were found in the very same place where 72 migrants had been killed some months beforehand?

Ana Enamorado, a Honduran woman living in Mexico and working with the Movimiento Migrante Mesoamericano (MMM), says:

> There are thousands of migrants from El Salvador, Guatemala, Nicaragua, and Honduras who have gone missing in Mexico. We try to find them and reunite them with their families. That is our work. Fortunately, we have found over 200 people, almost 300. I think we will pass 300 this year, God willing. We don't look for people believed to be dead, but because of the situation here in Mexico, we have to look in the mass graves with the Mexican families looking for their loved ones. As we say, Mexico is a graveyard.

Ana's own son disappeared while she was still in Honduras. She was put in touch with the MMM, and they invited her to participate in La Caravana de Madres (The Mothers' Caravan). Here she describes the movement's origins:

> La Caravana de Madres came about in 2000. A group of Honduran mothers got together to look for their children, whom they hadn't heard from

Ana Enamorado, with a photo of her son Oscar Antonio.

© Francisco Elías Prada/ojos ilegales 2012. From the photo essay *Transmigración en Movimiento*

in years ... It was a small group, without resources, without money. They knew nothing about Mexico and had never really left their homes. But they made it all the way to Tapachula on the Mexico–Guatemala border, walking and hitching rides ... Eventually they got into Mexico with the help of [MMM president] Marta Sánchez Soler and her husband. Afterwards, the MMM managed to get border control to grant families permission to enter Mexico ... The first formal caravan took place in 2006, and it went to various states, visiting the prisons. They now had the strength to demand that the government tell them the truth about what had happened to their children. Since then, we have held La Caravana every year in November.

We get no [support] from the government, absolutely nothing ... We're supported by civil society in the states we visit – social organizations, NGOs, migrant hostels, and so on. And sometimes the local residents are waiting for us with food or somewhere to stay. It isn't easy. Sometimes we have to sleep on mattresses on the floor. But you get used to it. When you go out into the countryside you sleep wherever you can, it doesn't bother me. But it breaks my heart to see these mothers, a lot of whom are elderly, sleeping on the floor. Their love and their need to find their children is so great, they don't care what they have to go through. I wish that it were easier for them, but that's how it is. We stay in the hostels sometimes and we eat there. Sometimes we stay in hotels too. Sometimes the mayor of a town we visit will help with everything and we get to stay in a hotel, which makes us feel safer. More than anyone though, it's civil society which helps and supports us.

Ana explains that La Caravana has become untouchable. It is accompanied by the National Human Rights Commission (CNDH) and by border control, state, and federal police:

They come because they have to by law. Also, La Caravana is high-profile, it gets a lot of attention both nationally and internationally. Also, we ask for their support as sometimes we have to go to very dangerous areas. The CNDH always comes with us alongside other organizations and puts pressure on these state institutions to accompany us. Of course, if a mother tried to do this on her own she wouldn't receive the same support. It makes me angry when we arrive in a town and some state official welcomes us because they want the publicity. They hug the mothers and are very attentive because the media is there. I know from personal experience that this is false, because if a mother arrives alone then she receives no help at all ... They only behave the way they should when the cameras are there, so I don't trust them.

La Caravana only travels for 18 days at most. During these 18 days the mothers report the disappearance of their children to the police. We go out into the countryside, walk along the train tracks, visit the migrant hostels, and pick up clues as we go. People come and look at the photos and tell us they saw the missing person working in a market, in a restaurant, or wherever. We take down all the information, including the details of the person providing it. This is the work of La Caravana. When it's over, the family goes back to Central America and we spend the rest of the year following up on the clues. Often these are accurate; sometimes not, perhaps the person made a mistake. But we follow up all of them.

The work that we do is the responsibility of the state, but we know they will never assume this responsibility. In fact, the state does the opposite, it interferes with the process. It doesn't look for anyone, it doesn't do any investigation, it hides information from us. It's abuse. It tries to intimidate us, we receive death threats to make us stop looking and investigating.

But those who are most to blame are the Central American governments, because if people had everything they needed there, like basic security, work, and study opportunities, then they wouldn't need to migrate. Why would you leave your home? Why would you abandon your family? These are not easy things to do. The Honduran government cynically says that the country has got better, that there isn't so much migration, but it isn't true. Every day hundreds of Hondurans migrate, sometimes whole families that are being threatened, unaccompanied children, mothers carrying small babies, children of five, two, or three years old forced to flee for their lives. The migrants say they would prefer to die on the journey than die in their country.

Once, when I went to see the offic... lawyer, at the Regional Prosecutor's Offic... a gun and placed it in front of me, to intim... my son's case, the they think they're all-powerful. I'm a woman, ...arta, he took out not from here, so he asked me, 'Aren't you afraid... is illegal, but So I said, 'No, I'm not scared.' So he said, 'Great, ...ne, and I'm but the cemetery is full of the brave.' Imagine! So of cou... one here?' me. I'm scared I might be killed or disappeared. I prefer no... ate you, I don't even tell people where I'm going. If one day something ...out, scared to me, then so be it. But I'm not going to keep quiet, and I'll car...s denouncing what is happening wherever I need to. I've travelled outsi... the country to say it, and I'll carry on saying it wherever is necessary: in Mexico there is no respect for human life. In Mexico there is no respect for human rights, and especially not for migrants. They see migrants here as scum. How many are there in the mass graves?

Colombia: paramilitaries and extractivism

Throughout Latin America in recent years there has been a proliferation of socioenvironmental conflicts, in which local communities oppose development projects promoted by the state. These include roads, dams, mines, drilling for hydrocarbons, and agribusiness. In exchange for promises of employment and revenue to finance social goods such as healthcare and education, governments have agreed to the demands of large corporations for confiscation of land, forced displacement of communities, and control of water resources. Community opposition has often been violently repressed, not only by police forces and civil guards, but also by non-state actors such as private security guards and paramilitaries. The state is usually willing at least to turn a blind eye to the activities of these actors, and in some cases offers support, protection, and funding.

Colombia, emerging gradually from the continent's longest civil war, has been plagued by new waves of violence, where criminal gangs move into areas formerly policed by the FARC guerrillas (Ni Bhriain, 2016), and where mining and oil companies expand operations into areas formerly considered too dangerous (Mortensen, 2017; Chohan, 2017). Government policy post-2000 has been massive expansion of the country's extractive sector, with a corresponding increase in military and paramilitary presence in these regions. As part of his Democratic Security policy, former president Álvaro Uribe sent two-thirds of Colombian troops to defend mining and oil infrastructure (Sankey, 2014). Local people and communities are often treated like 'overburden' – the vegetation, soil, and rock the mining company must remove before they can extract the mineral ore (LAB, forthcoming).

Rogelio Ustate is an Afro-Colombian from the community of Tabaco, which was violently displaced in 2001 by police and private security guards to make way for the expansion of El Cerrejón, a vast open-pit coal mine (see Chapter 7)

...can (an Anglo-South African company), BHP Billiton co-owned by ... Glencore (Anglo-Swiss):

(Anglo-Aus... Rogelio Ustate Arro-
... representative of the
...r black council of Tabaco
...ational delegate for prior
...sultation of black, Raizal, and
...alenquera communities. I have
been displaced as a result of mining
in the community of Tabaco and I
am involved in the ongoing struggle in defence of the rights of black
communities both within the territory and across the region.

Rogelio Ustate Arrogoces.

© Emma Banks 2017

After 2001, with the black communities here in the Guajira territory suffering indiscriminate displacement, we started defending our economic, political, social, and environmental rights ... Through publications at home and abroad, including my poetry, we have denounced the frequent violations of the rights of ethnic communities, which occur with the permission of the state. Thanks to the NGOs, we have crossed borders to denounce the violations carried out by multinational companies in our territory.

The state ignores Law 70, Decree 1745, and [ILO] Convention 107, which are based on black community councils and on the fundamental principle of collective land ownership. The multinational wants to mine, so the state gives its permission and removes people by force. Anyone who resists is beaten and removed by the riot police. The state disrespects the constitution itself, since in Article 79 it clearly states that everyone has the right to a healthy environment. This is incompatible with granting multinationals the right to deforest and contaminate the whole of the Guajira territory, committing an ecological crime against the land, water, air, and communities. And in Article 7 it talks about respecting and protecting black communities, which the state also ignores. Uprooting someone from their land is an act of disrespect, a violation of the communities. The day that the state starts playing by its own rules, things will be different. But as long as the state sees natural resources in economic terms, then they will carry on with such violations. They need to think about them in terms of ancestral value.

Colombia is the country where paramilitary groups have been particularly numerous and active. They act as agents of powerful landowners, politicians, and companies involved in extraction and agribusiness. Sometimes they act directly for the state, alongside or in place of police and military units. Forced displacement on a massive scale has been the consequence.

As Gabriela Díaz, from the group Hijos e Hijas por la Memoria y contra la Impunidad (HIJOS) (Sons and Daughters for Memory and Against Impunity), explains, such forced displacement has a long history in Colombia:

> Historically, forced displacement is a strategy that has been used extensively all over Colombia, to clear land for farming and monoculture crops. In the context of the [2016] Peace Accords, we wanted to contribute participatory research on the conflict, in which we identify factors that appear and reappear, such as state crime, which has been going on for decades. There are obvious links between certain powerful figures and strategies of forced displacement, involving clear discrimination against marginalized, ethnic, and impoverished groups.
>
> We're also working with a community in La Esperanza, in the department of Antioquia. Their relatives were kidnapped about 20 years ago, while they have been displaced from their land. And now, concessions are being granted for the construction of a hydroelectric power plant on the river that runs through the area. There are also natural resources in the mountains nearby ... Others were interested in the resources in that territory, and the locals represented a barrier to their exploitation. There were also armed groups active in the area.

HIJOS is fighting for justice for the victims of the country's long and brutal civil war, aiming to ensure that the victims are remembered and that those

© Ricardo Robayo Vallejo

Hijos and Hijas – sons and daughters of those forcibly disappeared – put on a play in memory of their loved ones, 20 August 2016.

responsible for human rights violations face justice. In particular, it aims to highlight the historical links between the state and illegal paramilitary groups in Colombia, which have come to light in recent years. A report by the Colombian Prosecutor General revealed that it investigated a total of 519 elected state officials for links to paramilitaries, narcotraffickers, or guerrillas between 2006 and 2016 (Gill, 2016). Dozens of politicians have been convicted of conspiring with paramilitaries in a scandal which touches close relatives of former president Álvaro Uribe. Uribe's cousin received a jail sentence, while his brother spent two years in preventive detention and remains under investigation. Nonetheless, ties continue to exist. Gabriela describes how HIJOS came about:

> Álvaro Uribe came to power in 2002. During his first term he passed the Justice and Peace Law (2005), supposedly to facilitate the demobilization of the paramilitaries in Colombia. These are illegal groups, which were armed by the state and committed massacres throughout the country. They were used to clear lands for projects, expelling the people who lived there. There were also targeted assassinations, disappearances, and extrajudicial executions. It was an illegal armed apparatus that was obviously funded by businesspeople and politicians. They clearly aimed to target social leaders and organized communities in general. So, Uribe's peace process was more of a demobilization process, in which paramilitary leaders who confessed to their crimes would receive just an eight-year prison sentence, though some were extradited.
>
> The demobilization of the paramilitaries was a decisive factor in the emergence of HIJOS. During the peace and justice process, there were public trials. Members of the paramilitaries faced their victims and other members of the public, and had to answer truthfully. That was the one condition of their having access to reduced sentencing. You might have killed 1,000 people, but if you answered the questions honestly, you'd get a prison sentence of just eight years. However, those trials were characterized by half-truths. The paramilitaries didn't expose the whole state-run system behind all of this. State crimes weren't included.
>
> In 2006, there were elections to the House of Representatives and the Senate. Many candidates had ties with paramilitary groups. In 2005, the National Movement of Victims of State Crime (MOVICE) emerged as a response, hoping to ensure that the paramilitaries wouldn't go unpunished for their crimes, which were committed with the complicity and support of the state. This movement consisted not only of victims but also organizations, associations, and other movements that faced discrimination for their social background or struggle. That was what brought us together as Hijos e Hijas ... There was a need for unity at the time, to fight together against the impunity that the state wanted to impose.

The Colombian HIJOS group is very much part of a broad Latin American movement. Founded in 1995, HIJOS Argentina was the first, and has become famous for its *escraches*, a type of demonstration in which the group publicly shames former members of the police and military involved in human rights violations during the 'Dirty War', usually outside their homes. HIJOS Guatemala emerged four years later, founded by exiles and family members of people disappeared and executed during the country's 36-year Civil War. There are also HIJOS organizations in Brazil, Uruguay, Chile, Paraguay, Peru, and Mexico. However, the dynamics of each group are influenced by local context:

> HIJOS was inspired by groups of the same name elsewhere in Latin America, especially in Argentina, where it appeared as a legacy of associations such as the Mothers and Grandmothers of the Plaza de Mayo …
>
> The Colombian HIJOS group was different to the others because we've always believed that the fight for memory is everyone's battle. Our first slogan as an organization was 'Hijos Somos Todos' ['We Are All Sons and Daughters']. We've always thought that the task of remembering the political violence of our country is the task of all young people. Of course, many of the people that joined at first were victims, as their mothers and fathers had disappeared or been murdered. Others, like me, had parents who were persecuted or imprisoned for taking part in opposition political groups. More and more people kept joining the group, and there came a point when it was clear that many of them weren't victims as such. However, they liked this task of rebuilding the memory of what had happened in Colombia, because at that time there was a strategy to delegitimize, persecute, and stigmatize people of dissenting political views, anyone who thought differently or opposed the status quo.
>
> HIJOS also puts a strong emphasis on this generation. We're a generation that wants to stop war and conflict. We're a generation that wants change. Not through guns or violence but through truth, memory, and organizing different cultural and academic events, as we've inherited decades and decades of internal conflict. One of the main differences between the Colombian HIJOS group and the others was that we were born in response to a conflict that was still ongoing. In the case of Guatemala or Argentina, or even Chile or Brazil, the groups emerged as a response to dictatorships which were no longer in power.
>
> We were inspired by other HIJOS groups from different countries and after HIJOS Colombia emerged, similar movements appeared in countries such as Peru, Brazil, and Uruguay. At one point we decided to come together. We met in Mexico and Argentina. It was very interesting to learn about other experiences. In the case of HIJOS Argentina, as in our case, there was a division between those who were children of victims and those who weren't.

We would bring drums and cymbals and we would make up slogans to chant in the Bogotá marches. This injected some fresh energy into the leftist and social movements, which were very shocked. HIJOS was known for its association with musical groups, theatre groups, and artists, for disturbing this sense of lethargy ... Our biggest achievement was to remember creatively, in a lively manner. It wasn't about producing books or documents to be filed away forever. Our activities are physical; it's about putting memory in movement. I think that was one of our greatest achievements, as it succeeded in waking up some of the other groups.

We want to expose the businesspeople, landowners, and farmers who funded the war, as well as the local party-political structures that were involved and figures like governors and mayors. There are also other, less visible groups involved, such as the Church. We need to talk about these connections and that's why we launched this campaign. We also want to challenge the view that the only reason the guerrillas have been around for so long is the drug trade. This is a completely short-sighted notion of what's happened in this country.

'There are no paramilitaries in Colombia,' said Colombian defence minister Luis Carlos Villegas in 2017. 'To say otherwise would be to grant political recognition to groups dedicated to common and organized crime' (El Colombiano, 2017). Such declarations are part of a historical strategy of the Colombian State to deny the existence of paramilitarism, thus obscuring its own role in the problem. But paramilitarism is clearly not a thing of the past in Colombia. As Gabriela says:

It's also worrying that there's been an increase in the number of murders of social leaders, especially in zones where there are fewer guerrillas and more of a military and police presence. This is something we've highlighted in our campaign. There have been more than 116 targeted assassinations since the [Peace] Accords were signed ... They're ramping up the military presence in the poor neighbourhoods on the outskirts of the cities and in more distant regions. It's like we're going back to the paramilitary environment of the 1990s and 2000s. It's already a tense climate and on top of that, we've got elections coming up. It's very complex.

There's a theory put forward by human rights activists and social movements that Uribe's demobilization of the paramilitaries wasn't genuine. They've just given the paramilitary groups new names, what they call in the media the *bancrims* [criminal gangs]. This removes the political connotation – they're represented exclusively as criminal organizations. They keep changing their names, but it's exactly the same type of organization that has been occupying the territories this whole time. This is one of our biggest challenges. I don't want to call it a defeat, as if we'd already lost. The fight continues. But state and parastate criminality are still ongoing, even after everything we've done and all the networks that we've been building. It's incredibly worrying.

* * *

This chapter has brought together just a handful of people who are, in various ways, contesting state violence, whether it is the killing of young black men in Brazilian favelas, the disappearance of protesters and migrants in Mexico, or forced displacement and targeted assassinations in Colombia, often linked to the expansion of agribusiness and extractive projects. What is most impressive is that, despite facing a widespread lack of justice for victims, impunity for perpetrators, and in many cases considerable personal risk, these individuals and organizations continue to stand tall, speak out, and retain a sense of optimism. Perhaps the last word should be Ana Paula's:

> I feel closer to my son, when I'm near these mothers. Every time I do something good, I feel closer to Johnatha. It does me good; it gives me strength. You would love him if you met him, because he was such a charming boy. I wanted to be like him, because I was always so shy. I never liked going out much. Not Johnatha. He lit up everywhere he went, and brought joy, happiness. Today my house is so sad. I would wake up, and he'd already be dancing about, I could tell him off and he'd still find a way to make me smile. He was always joking, you know? So bright. I'm so proud to be his mother.
>
> This violence, the absence of love that we see in the world, people's selfishness – it can bring you down sometimes. In spite of it all, I still believe in the power of people. I have faith in humanity.

About the author

Mike Gatehouse lived in Chile in 1972-3 and worked for 15 years in London for Latin America solidarity and human rights organizations. Co-author of LAB's *Soft Drink, Hard Labour - Guatemalan workers take on Coca Cola* and *In the Mountains of Morazán - Portrait of a returned refugee community in El Salvador*, he is an editor at LAB.

Interviews

Gabriela Díaz (HIJOS): interviewed via Skype on 24 February 2018 by Ali Rocha. Translated by Ingrid de Almeida.

Ana Enamorado (MMM): interviewed in Mexico City on 14 August 2017 by Carol Byrne. Translated by Carol Byrne.

Ana Paula Oliveira and **Fatima Pinho** (Mães de Manguinhos): interviewed in Rio de Janeiro on 8 December 2016 by Ali Rocha. Translated by Catherine Morgans.

Javier Treviño Rangel (CIDE): interviewed in Aguascalientes, Mexico, on 28 February 2017 by Francesco di Bernardo. Transcribed by Andreea Tudose.

Rogelio Ustate (Tabaco community): interviewed in Hatonuevo, La Guajira, Colombia, on 7 January 2017 by Emma Banks. Transcribed by Elizabeth Pillares and translated by James Scorer.

References

NB: All web references were checked and still available in May/June 2018 unless otherwise stated. All references are listed, with web-links, on the page for this chapter on the Voices website www.vola.org.uk

Amnesty International (2016) *"Treated with Indolence" – The State's Response to Disappearances in Mexico*, Amnesty International Report, <https://www.amnesty.org/download/Documents/AMR4131502016ENGLISH.PDF>

Burt, J. M. (2012) 'Quest for human rights justice in Peru suffers serious setbacks', Foreign Policy in Focus <http://fpif.org/quest_for_human_rights_justice_in_peru_suffers_serious_setbacks>

CEH (1999) 'Guatemala: memory of silence', Report of the Commission for Historical Clarification, Conclusions and Recommendations, English summary, <https://www.aaas.org/sites/default/files/migrate/uploads/mos_en.pdf>

Chohan, J.K. (2017) 'Colombia: incompliance, continued violence and crop eradication', LAB, 31 October, <https://lab.org.uk/colombia-incompliance-continued-violence-and-crop-eradication>

Cruz, E. (2016) 'Crimes de Maio causaram 564 mortes em 2006; entenda o caso', Agência Brasil, <http://agenciabrasil.ebc.com.br/direitos-humanos/noticia/2016-05/crimes-de-maio-causaram-564-mortes-em-2006-entenda-o-caso>

El Colombiano (2017) '"En Colombia no hay paramilitarismo": Ministro de Defensa', 11 January <http://www.elcolombiano.com/colombia/en-colombia-no-hay-paramilitarismo-dice-ministro-de-defensa-luis-carlos-villegas-IX5734390>

Gill, S. (2016) 'Colombia state ties to paramilitary groups alive and well: Report', Colombia Reports, <https://colombiareports.com/paramilitary-links-still-present-colombia-politics-report>

Hernández, A. and Fisher, S. (2014) 'Iguala: la historia no oficial', *Proceso*, <https://www.proceso.com.mx/390560>

Holocaust Museum (no date) 'Genocide in Guatemala, 1981–83', Holocaust Museum, Houston, TX, <https://www.hmh.org/la_Genocide_Guatemala.shtml>

Huey, D. (2014) 'The US war on drugs and its legacy in Latin America', *The Guardian*, 3 February, <https://www.theguardian.com/global-development-professionals-network/2014/feb/03/us-war-on-drugs-impact-in-latin-american>

Human Rights Watch (2016) '"Good cops are afraid" – the toll of unchecked police violence in Rio de Janeiro', Human Rights Watch, <https://www.hrw.org/report/2016/07/07/good-cops-are-afraid/toll-unchecked-police-violence-rio-de-janeiro>

Jardim, L. (2018) 'Ibope: 50% dos brasileiros acham que 'bandido bom é bandido morto', *O Globo*, 4 March, <https://blogs.oglobo.globo.com/lauro-jardim/post/ibope-50-dos-brasileiros-acham-que-bandido-bom-e-bandido-morto.html>

LAB (forthcoming) *Overburden: Community Resistance to Mining in Latin America*, Latin America Bureau (LAB) and Practical Action Publishing, Rugby.

Mortensen, T. (2017) 'Colombia: peace, but maybe not the peace we hoped for', LAB, 27 November, <https://lab.org.uk/colombia-peace-but-maybe-not-the-peace-we-hoped-for>

Ni Bhriain, N. (2016) 'Colombia: the dark side of peace in Tumaco', LAB, 20 September, <https://lab.org.uk/colombia-the-dark-side-of-peace-in-tumaco>

Roxo, S. (2017) '"Policial que não mata não é policial", diz Bolsonaro', *O Globo*, <https://oglobo.globo.com/brasil/policial-que-nao-mata-nao-e-policial-diz-bolsonaro-22118273>

Ruge, E. (2017) 'Mothers of kids killed by police speak out at launch of "No tanks!" campaign against police operations', RioOnWatch, 15 December, <http://rioonwatch.org/?p=40794>

Sankey, K. (2014) 'Colombia: the mining boom: a catalyst of development or resistance?', in H. Veltmeyer. and J. Petras (eds), *The New Extractivism: A Post-Neoliberal Development Model of Imperialism of the Twenty-First Century?*, Zed Books, London.

Seelke, C.R. and Finklea, K. (2017) *U.S.–Mexican Security Cooperation: The Mérida Initiative and Beyond*, US Congressional Research Service, 29 June, <https://fas.org/sgp/crs/row/R41349.pdf>

Semple, K. (2016) 'Missing Mexican students suffered a night of "terror", investigators say', *New York Times*, 25 April, <https://www.nytimes.com/2016/04/25/world/americas/missing-mexican-students-suffered-a-night-of-terror-investigators-say.html>

UN News (2018) 'Mexico: UN report points to torture, cover-ups in probe into disappearance of 43 students', <https://news.un.org/en/story/2018/03/1005022>

CHAPTER 9

Spaces of everyday resistance: the right to the city

Antonia Burchard-Levine

Abstract

Latin America has witnessed unprecedented levels of urbanization over the past few decades, which has produced informal processes and urban conflicts. Urban spaces are more than just physical infrastructure: they are the site of class struggles, collective initiatives, and confrontations, in which citizens demand access to public services, urban resources, and dignified living from the sources of political and economic power.

> *'But, if the city is the world which man created, it is the world in which he is henceforth condemned to live. Thus, indirectly, and without any clear sense of the nature of his task, in making the city man has remade himself.' – Robert Park*

Recent decades have brought profound changes in the spatial distribution of the global population. More than half of the world's population now lives in cities (54 per cent by 2014 and 66 per cent projected by 2050, according to the UN). Latin America today is a predominantly urban region, with an urbanization rate of 80 per cent (Jaitman, 2015). While this rate is comparable to those of high-income countries, most cities across the region continue to struggle to provide the infrastructure and services necessary for their inhabitants to enjoy a decent quality of life.

Latin America absorbed 450 million new urban dwellers between 1930 and the early 21st century (Green and Branford, 2013). Many of these are migrants from rural areas and their descendants, who have seized or occupied an estimated 70 per cent of the urban space to set up their homes and the infrastructure needed to ensure access to basic services (Bauwens, 2018). The rapid pace of this urbanization has produced many informal processes and phenomena. Unlicensed transport, street vendors, and shantytowns exist alongside upmarket developments, imported cars, and tourist resorts, leading Felix Guattari to observe that 'Latin America is Africa, Asia and Europe at the same time' (McGuirk, 2014). The negative consequences of this process have, in turn, led to some innovative, imaginative, and sometimes violent measures in the pursuit of remedies.

http://dx.doi.org/10.3362/9781909014213.009

Aerial images testify to the unequal spatial distribution of urban space in Latin America. The periphery, with minimal access to public services and the life of the city, tends to be reserved for the poor (though there are also some upmarket suburbs and gated communities located in peripheral areas). The middle and upper classes tend to live closer to the city centres. In some cities (particularly in Brazil) the historic centres themselves are neglected, poor, and unsafe, with the more fashionable and affluent neighbourhoods located around them. Different social classes have different holds on the land, raising the question of the 'right to the city', a term first coined by Henri Lefebvre more than 50 years ago and still pertinent today. As he wrote, 'Today more than ever, the class struggle is inscribed in space.'

Urban space is the arena in which class struggles are manifest, particularly the political action of minorities and marginalized groups (Lefebvre, 2014). From small, local protests to vast citywide demonstrations, these are everyday battles to claim the right to the city and demand dignified living. These do not always arise from complex ideologies, but rather from basic survival needs (Bauwens, 2018). And they don't always involve conventional political actions, such as being a member of a party, knocking on doors and going to meetings. Instead they invoke a sense of the collective, a feeling of belonging to the city, and a shared desire to have a say in its functioning and change it for the better (Merrifeld, 2017).

While taken from a diverse range of contexts, the voices in this chapter all express exactly this sense of shared purpose.

More than a roof over one's head

Latin America has long suffered from a lack of housing, magnified by the speed of urbanization. Supply has consistently failed to keep up with demand, resulting in the proliferation of shantytowns. Variously known as *favelas* in Brazil, *villas miseria* in Argentina, *callampas* in Chile, or the more euphemistic *pueblos jóvenes* (literally, 'young towns') in Peru, these settlements lack established legal tenure and mostly consist of precarious structures built by residents themselves. They have poor access to public services and substandard living conditions.

In Brazil, more than 80 per cent of the population resides in urban areas and around 20 per cent of Brazilians are settled in favelas, with some of these housing as many as 60,000 people (Boyer, 2005). Efforts to improve them have proven highly problematic, as have resettlement programmes, which often involve the forced removal of residents to more peripheral areas of the city. Families and individuals may find themselves dispersed far from their previous neighbourhood and place of work, with all the financial, social, and emotional consequences this implies.

São Paulo is Latin America's largest city by population and the largest metropolitan area in the southern hemisphere. Throughout much of the 20th century, it absorbed vast numbers of migrants, mostly from rural areas and particularly from the north-east of Brazil. One of these migrants was Luiz Gonzaga da Silva, better known as Gegê:

> I'm Gegê, of the Housing Movement of the City of São Paulo (MMC), part of the Congress of Popular Movements (CMP) of Brazil. I came here from Paraíba in 1974, the darkest years of the dictatorship, and when I got to São Paulo I went to live in a favela called Vila Olímpia. There I went back to my work as a militant, this time in an urban environment. In the favela we began fighting for its urbanization [council recognition and services], water, electricity. And I've been involved ever since, never stopped.

The Vila Olímpia favela burnt down in suspicious circumstances; such fires continue to occur in São Paulo even today:

> The way I see it, it was arson. A favela burns down, and capital comes along and establishes itself in that physical space. To this day there are fires in favelas and it's clear they are started deliberately. Organized crime will even do it just to get in with the police. They start fires at specific points in the favela and then scarper.

After the fire, Gegê went to live in a *cortiço*, a large, inner-city tenement, which was the prevalent type of slum housing in São Paulo until the favelas began to spread and expand in the 1980s. *Cortiços* differ from favelas in that favela

© Julien Jatobá Karl 2018

Luiz Gonzaga da Silva, aka Gegê.

residents generally own their property, even if legally speaking they are considered squatters, whereas the *cortiços* are mostly private-sector rentals, albeit precarious and dilapidated. For Gegê:

> *Cortiços* are some of the worst sort of housing possible for human beings. They're enormous buildings, subdivided into small spaces. You pay more for the cost of living in a *cortiço*: you pay for water, electricity, rent, and council tax, but the housing is inadequate and unhygienic.
>
> I lived for a while at a *cortiço* called Cama Quente [Hot Bed], where you were allowed to live from 6 p.m. to 6 a.m. You slept at night and when you got up in the morning another person came to sleep in your bed. [You kept your stuff] in your bag, just your bag. When I went to work I'd leave my bag there with my things, but you couldn't keep much. You'd only get robbed … There were two things that made me leave Cama Quente. One day I got back and everyone who worked nights had been robbed, except me. I had nothing to steal, just the clothes on my back. But everyone else, who had watches, radios, record players, they'd all been robbed, every single one. Also, I was seeing a girl and she couldn't visit, I wasn't going to take her there. To give you an idea, in my bedroom at Cama Quente there were 24 other people in a space three metres by four. Twelve square metres. Twelve people on one shift and twelve on the other. So I decided to leave and went to another *cortiço* on Rua Albuquerque Lins, where I paid rent for a tiny space, really cramped. I'd lock my door but there was never any security in the *cortiços*. Anyone who tells you they had security in a *cortiço* is lying.
>
> They were favelas in a different format. When Luiza Erundina was mayor of São Paulo (1989–93), the Municipal Planning Department (SEMPLA) did a study showing that the city had over two million people living in *cortiços*. A quarter of a population of eight million. So they began shutting them down and moving people on. By the end of Erundina's term a lot of people were no longer living in *cortiços*.
>
> Many of the people in the *cortiços* went to live in favelas or neighbouring cities. A lot went to live in Jandira, Osasco, the poor peripheries of the poor periphery, places like Itaquaquecetuba. It was a very difficult time for the people who had been in *cortiços*. They worked in the centre and found themselves living a really long way out – Itapevi, Barueri.

Today, the MMC leads occupations of abandoned buildings in the centre of São Paulo and campaigns for their renovation and regularization. Gegê describes what these occupations involve:

> The common areas have a cleaning rota. If I do it today, you do it tomorrow, regardless of whether I'm a man or you're a woman, we take turns. We all take responsibility for the upkeep of the units. I'm against paying for a cleaner; we're not a business, we're a movement occupying a building. Likewise, I'm against having a porter. We can keep someone on the

door, but with everyone taking turns. That's how we live in the squats. You can't have a squat with a hired cleaner. Or a security guard, a porter.

There can be no drugs, guns, or prostitution in a squat. Out on the street you can do whatever you like with your body, but not in there. Drugs, alcohol, and guns are the main elements you want to avoid. If someone comes into a squat with a gun, the first little thing and he'll start threatening people. Likewise, anyone drunk or high is bound to pick fights with the others.

The fight for decent housing in the city of São Paulo isn't at all easy. It would be if it were just this city, but now it's everywhere, the country has a housing shortage of nearly six million new housing units, with over 10 million units in need of renovation. The state of São Paulo has a housing shortage of 1.5–2 million, and 2.5–3 million properties requiring renovation. The city of São Paulo alone has a housing shortage of almost 1 million and nearly 2.5 million properties needing renovation, and this isn't being done.

In order to tackle this shortage, in 2009 the administration of Luiz Inácio Lula da Silva launched Minha Casa Minha Vida (My House, My Life – MCMV), an ambitious house-building programme. By 2016, it had placed 10.5 million low-income people in 2.6 million new housing units (Pacheco, 2016). While it has undoubtedly helped to ease the housing shortage, it has been criticized for putting quantity before quality and producing vast numbers of homes which are not only poorly built but poorly located and connected. MCMV has also been a victim of the change in the political climate in Brazil since the impeachment of Dilma Rousseff and her replacement by Michel Temer in 2016, as Gegê acknowledges:

> Temer will do with MCMV the same thing he did with health, education, and culture: freeze everything. Funds are short, there's no money, so everything will get held up with paperwork, bureaucracy, you'll have to provide endless documentation. If you present a project to Caixa [the state-owned bank which administers MCMV], they'll have to analyse it, but they'll be overly critical and drag their feet. Then you become the incompetent one, unable to present a decent project, ready to be implemented. That's what they're doing. The first thing Temer did was do away with MCMV. That's gone. In December we delivered some documentation to Caixa, and the boss there, Cíntia, told us, 'I'm sorry, but although I can see it's in order, for them it won't be right. When it reaches the ministry, it'll get stuck. For sure.' We've had to redo it.

For Gegê, housing is much more than a shelter and a roof over one's head:

> Our struggle was always for the recovery of citizenship and human dignity. Because for us at the Movement, a citizen with no address can't be treated like a citizen. And an address can't be a favela, a *cortiço*. You need to be able to say, 'Today I'm going home, with my key I'll walk into

my home. This is where I can receive a neighbour, or a letter through the post.' It's where every citizen's dignity and citizenship are manifest. For us the home is where the life story of each citizen begins, men and women.

In other words, housing is an inherently political issue, and there is an ongoing conflict between the notions of housing as a home, as understood by Gegê, and housing as property or investment. This is clear from the following statement by Emília Maria de Souza, vice president of the Residents' Association of Horto, a Rio de Janeiro favela threatened with removal:

> As members of the community we aren't fighting for property. We don't want deeds. We don't want any documents that will undermine us further down the line. We need the Housing Concessions (CUEs), because this instrument limits and inhibits real estate speculation. It gives families the perpetual right to live there and use the property, but they can't sell or rent it. We don't want to open the door to land regularization where the resident is able to sell the property. We want to benefit from the land, but we don't want to take it.

There is a clear need to innovate in terms of housing models, especially for vulnerable populations and those whose needs are not addressed by the conventional real estate market. Such models are beginning to appear, including the Community Land Trusts (CLTs) in Mexico, community-led housing developments that seek to ensure housing remains affordable in the long term, based on community members' incomes. There are also some alternative ownership scenarios such as Cooperative Housing in Uruguay, as well as the CUEs described by Emília above.

When housing is left to the whims of the market, gentrification and land price speculation become a major threat to many, especially those on lower incomes.

Gentrification and expulsion

For the distinguished urban geographer David Harvey, gentrification is 'a process of displacement and dispossession', arising from capitalist processes in urban spaces (Harvey, 2012). Residents having documentary title and the right to sell land can bring problems later, as Emília warns, but lacking title deeds can be much worse. Displacement and dispossession are a cruel reality for many people in cities across Latin America, particularly those in informal communities such as favelas, where many have no means of proving legal ownership. In Rio de Janeiro, the gentrification process has been accelerated by the city playing host to two sporting mega-events: the World Cup of 2014 (the matches took place all over Brazil, with the final played at the Maracanã in Rio) and the Olympic Games of 2016. Preparations for these two events involved Rio's largest and most ambitious urban reform in decades, with billions of reais spent on new infrastructure. Over 22,000 families were rehoused, and the legality of this process has been called into question by human rights organizations, the Displacement Research and Action Network at the Massachusetts Institute of Technology, and the UN's Special Rapporteur on adequate housing (Gatehouse, 2016).

Marcello Deodoro of the Tijuca Indiana Community Residents' Commission in Rio de Janeiro is a retired navy veteran who settled in the Tijuca Indiana favela in 1992 with his wife Inês. Their three children were born in the community. He describes how the city announced plans for the removal of the favela, in the guise of a federal urban regeneration programme:

> The Indiana community was formed around 1957. Occupation of the foothills of the Morro do Borel in northern Rio de Janeiro, which includes the Tijuca Indiana favela, began more than 50 years ago.
>
> In 2009, the then municipal housing secretary, Jorge Bittar, announced plans to demolish Indiana in preparation for the urbanization of 13,754 square metres of land along the banks of the Maracanã river. They wanted to create a public square and rehouse residents in new homes in the area under the Minha Casa Minha Vida federal housing programme. In an interview, Bittar claimed he had reached an agreement with the residents' association to carry out the project. At the beginning of 2010, the city government announced plans for the removal of 119 favelas, including Indiana, by the end of 2012. Housing department employees started going into people's houses and taking photographs, saying it was related to the planned modernization of the community.

Marcello believes that the lack of clear communication between the city authorities in Rio de Janeiro and local residents was deliberate:

> The lack of a connection between the survey and the removal plans announced by the city government are an example of one of the many state strategies during removal programmes. It wasn't always clear why officials were taking photographs of rooms or measuring the dimensions of buildings, so residents didn't feel they were being fully informed about the ultimate objectives of the government's policies.
>
> The first meetings with the housing secretary in Indiana led to many disputes among residents. This was part of a strategy to facilitate the removal by weakening community resistance. The lack of clarity about the objectives of certain official initiatives and the stirring up of internal conflict created a confusing scenario, full of ambiguities, doubts, and disputes, undermining action taken by the social movements that emerge at critical times like this. The residents often can't understand what the government is trying to do, because officials contradict each other, in both words and actions. The situation then becomes more attractive to the dominant political and economic groups, as they see the possibility of weakening the resistance and accelerating the removal.

The influence of powerful interests – be they political, financial, or of the media – is particularly clear in the case of the Horto community, as Emília Maria de Souza describes:

> The struggle for the right to housing here in the community began when the value of the land in Horto began to increase. This was in the 1980s. Until then, Horto had been completely neglected by the authorities and the economic elite. Nobody knew this place existed. It was inhospitable and very difficult to get to. There was no public transport here. Residents had to walk to the Rua Jardim Botânico. Later, they put in a bus service and it became easier for residents to get to the main street. Until the 1970s and 1980s Horto was a very quiet and peaceful place. It was like the countryside, but in the Zona Sul [Rio's affluent South Zone, home to many of the city's major attractions]. Then, at the end of the 1970s and beginning of the 1980s, the area started to develop, and the establishment of Rede Globo [South America's biggest media conglomerate] caused a boom in real estate speculation. With the arrival of Rede Globo, several big businessmen, intellectuals, and artists discovered Horto and began to move to this part of the city. That's how the land started to increase in value and property speculation began.
>
> Our struggle here is mainly against the economic elite. It's also against government agencies, such as the Ministry of the Environment. They don't think poor people have the right to live in an area with a special environmental status. They accept, cover up, and regularize the environmental crimes and the invasion of the rich, but they criminalize the traditional poor population who also have the acquired right to live in these areas.
>
> It's mainly the people at the top, those who have a lot of economic power. These are the people at the forefront of the battle against the community. We've noticed their prejudice getting more obvious over time. They do more and more to undermine and disqualify the rights of residents. We've also noticed that a lot of the people at the top of the organizations that want to get rid of the community are managers at Rede Globo, as well as bankers and big businessmen involved in construction and real estate. They are the ones who have the economic power here in the Zona Sul. They are the ones who are most interested in getting rid of the community. One of them, one of the owners of the Banco da Bahia [today known as Banco BBM], is insisting on getting rid of the community because he thinks that our presence devalues his property. If the community is made to leave, his property will immediately increase in value because there won't be a favela nearby.
>
> It's class discrimination. They think that poor and black people shouldn't live in the Zona Sul, because it's a very affluent area. They think the community should leave so that the area and the properties in it can increase in value. It's social and racial discrimination.

Such gentrification is hardly unique to Rio or to Brazil. In Bogotá, Colombia, Mayor Enrique Peñalosa attempted to upgrade an area of the city centre formerly home to the notorious drug- and crime-ridden neighbourhood El Cartucho, which is described here by the urban consultant and documentary film-maker Andrés Chaves:

> It was a neighbourhood of colonial architecture, but as the slums pro-liferated the old houses deteriorated and living conditions became very precarious. Over the 1980s and 1990s, these buildings became *fumaderos*, places where people went to smoke *basuco* [a highly addictive form of smokable cocaine, similar to crack]. Little by little, dealers appropriated these buildings for the drug trade. At the same time, there was massive consumption of drugs in public spaces. The control of the space exer-cised by the dealers and mafiosi was such that the police and author-ities could not enter. Well, the police could enter, but they had been co-opted; they were part of the business. It was well known that you could go there both to buy and consume drugs freely at any time of day. It was a permanent party 24/7. You could take drugs on the street or in the *fumaderos*. The area was completely run by mafia.
>
> By the 1990s, the decay was complete and El Cartucho was notorious as a place for drug use. Then Peñalosa became mayor. His programme involved constructing new infrastructure and rebuilding public spaces, for which he got much international recognition. One of his propos-als was the complete demolition of El Cartucho. The people living in El Cartucho fought against it; there were years of conflict. However, in the end, he got his way: the area was completely demolished. Peñalosa didn't even want to keep any of the old colonial mansions. He destroyed absolutely everything, about 35 or 40 blocks altogether. In its place he built Parque Tercer Milenio, which won many prizes, including at the architecture biennale in Venice. I spoke to many of the architects involved in its design. The original idea had been to com-bine the park and the old houses, conserving some of the buildings of greater architectural value. But Peñalosa refused; he just wanted to knock it all down.

In 2017, Andrés launched the documentary *Cartucho*, in which the park is portrayed as a desolate and empty space. He also argues that the demolition failed to deal with the problems underpinning El Cartucho:

> Not everyone living in El Cartucho was a criminal, there were also some more traditional families, traders, and all kinds of people who lived there despite its reputation. There had to be a negotiation with the homeown-ers, so they could go somewhere else. But the problem of drugs and destitution was never properly dealt with, either by Peñalosa or his suc-cessors. With the demolition of El Cartucho, many of the mafias just moved to surrounding areas or other parts of the city.

And so, very close to the new park, two new neighbourhoods were formed. One was known as El Bronx or La Ele; the other as San Bernardo. They just reproduced what we had seen in El Cartucho. When Peñalosa became mayor again [in 2016], he decided to demolish these neighbourhoods as well. El Cartucho is an expression of a phenomenon that has persisted since the 1940s. Through architectural or urbanistic interventions, city authorities always try to sweep these social issues under the carpet, but there has never been a clear response to the problem. The phenomenon just repeats itself. At the moment, the issue of destitution and drug use and the proliferation of the areas we call *las ollas* [pots], places where drugs are sold, is bigger than ever. The responses have only ever been banal or insignificant and the phenomenon has only grown. It's a serious problem which is getting worse, and we have no solutions.

Some consider the park an urban regeneration achievement of tremendous potential for Bogotá. Others consider it a classic case of gentrification, the replacement of a poor population with a wealthier one.

Some also argue that the installation of transport infrastructure is a catalyst for gentrification, and this is often the case when projects are planned without considering the needs of the most vulnerable populations. One of the legacy projects of the 2016 Rio Olympics is a new Bus Rapid Transit (BRT) system – a network of dedicated and integrated bus lanes with special high-capacity vehicles. Rio is currently Brazil's most congested city (Carvalho, 2017) and has long been in dire need of better transport infrastructure. The BRT, however, has proven controversial. Not only did its construction involve the wholesale removal of entire communities, but its design has been much criticized. Rather than providing for the major daily flows of commuters from the north and west of the city to the city centre and the Zona Sul, where most of Rio's formal employment is located, the BRTs instead all run through Barra da Tijuca – the site of the Olympic Park and the centre of current property speculation in Rio (Johnson, 2014).

However, while the BRT system in Rio may have been misconceived, such infrastructure – when properly and holistically planned – can be a vital element in social mobility, allowing citizens to claim their right to the city.

Connecting and getting around

Urban transportation and mobility networks serve as the veins and arteries of a city; they are crucial to its effective functioning and constitute a major determining factor in urban quality of life. All over the world, dominant modernist planning ideologies throughout much of the 20th century allowed cars to invade the city and gave insufficient priority to pedestrians, ultimately leading to the erosion of city life. Latin America is no exception to this; however, what is particularly problematic is that, despite being one of the most motorized regions of the world, it ranks relatively low in terms of transport infrastructure, having both low road density and a very low percentage of paved roads (Jaitman, 2015).

The road safety and urban mobility activist Jorge Cáñez discusses Mexico City's car culture:

> Well, we all know the story of cities and how we fell in love with the car. It's a great machine. The car manufacturers and governments got together and it seemed like the car was the future, that everyone would have one. This is the all-pervasive culture which still exists amongst citizens and in government. It's hard to make people understand that the car isn't the future of cities any more. The future is walking, cycling, and public transport. Another obstacle is the great inequality in Latin America. Rich people have more cars, and they are the ones who have a voice. They dominate public opinion; they are the political classes. It's the mode of transport of choice for the powerful, whether in media or politics, and so they always advocate building more infrastructure for cars. It's very difficult to convince both the elite and the population at large that we have to change our mentality.
>
> People are dying from respiratory conditions caused by pollution, and motorized vehicles are the main culprits. Even efforts to reduce the pollution they cause – by bringing in electric vehicles and hybrids – is no good because cars continue to occupy too much space. Our cities are still being built to make space for cars and we keep missing opportunities to build cycling infrastructure.

A turn away from car-oriented cities would have a fourfold effect in making cities more lively, healthy, sustainable, and human-centred (Gehl, 2010). But as Jorge says, this change is not easy to achieve, requiring not only a shift in preferences and customs, but also a radical reassessment of current government spending and policy:

> The government wastes loads of money building bridges and flyovers for cars but won't invest in safe spaces for pedestrians and cyclists. This is the essence of our fight. We need to be more considerate of the disabled, children, and the elderly. These people should be able to get about the city, but it's chaos. You can't walk on the pavements because they are all broken, full of potholes and full of obstacles like vendors' stalls, posts, and public telephones. Nobody can walk in the city and it's even worse for people in wheelchairs or if you're a parent with a pram.

Salvador Medina is an urban economist and activist, who also lives in Mexico City. He shares Jorge's feelings:

> I spent a year studying in Madrid. When I got back to Mexico City, I had a new perspective on things; I saw things with a bit more distance.

Things were happening in Mexico City that I had also noticed taking place in other parts of the world. The government was implementing policies that had nothing to do with the official justification. For example, they would say that the construction of a new urban highway was the best way to combat pollution. More highways mean more cars, and as a user of public transport it made no sense to me that they were investing so much money in new highways, flyovers, and so on. I began to pay attention to what was going on. As an economist, I could see that government policy didn't correspond with a cost–benefit analysis.

These kinds of policy were manifest in the area where I was living. Firstly, with the construction of a flyover during the administration of Andrés Manuel López Obrador [head of Mexico City's government, 2000–05]. There was a lot of disruption and ultimately it was a disaster. It didn't help at all; it only made the traffic worse. A few years later, Marcelo Ebrard [López Obrador's successor] proposed constructing a subterranean tunnel from Reforma to Santa Fe, which was just ridiculous. He also proposed building more superhighways, including plans for another tunnel from Santa Fe to San Jerónimo, and extending the flyovers. I hadn't been that bothered until then, but I began to look into the projects in more detail. The Reforma–Santa Fe tunnel never happened due to the economic crisis, but the Santa Fe–San Jerónimo project did. The way they went about it was very nasty; they wanted to expropriate houses in working-class neighbourhoods and build over a number of parks, all to make a high-speed connection to Santa Fe because of the property developments there.

However, cities across Latin America are slowly beginning to move away from car-oriented policies and improve infrastructure for cyclists and pedestrians. According to Jorge, cycling has increased by 50 per cent in Mexico City in the last 10 years. However, despite some improvements, it remains 'extremely dangerous':

> Twice vehicles have hit me and twice I've been doored. I have friends who've ended up in hospital. Fortunately, nobody I know has died, but it's terrible to see that one cyclist per month dies here, more or less. It's very dangerous, though it was even worse 10 years ago.

Even the simple act of walking through the city is a battle, as he describes:

> Mexico City is a hostile environment for walkers. With all the cars it's a very dangerous place: at least one pedestrian dies every day here. The city is designed for cars, it's dirty and you're in constant danger. Walking is an extreme sport. To cross the bigger roads, you have to run.

To remedy this, Jorge has taken on another persona: Peatónito [a play on words on the Spanish *peatón*, pedestrian, and *atónito*, astonished]. Peatónito wears a cape and a *lucha libre* wrestling mask, taking his battle to the streets of Mexico City, where he heroically defends the rights of the pedestrian. Here Jorge recalls how he became Peatónito:

> One day I went to a *lucha libre mexicana* [LLM, Mexican professional wrestling] event. I was with my best friend and I said, why don't we buy masks and go out onto the roads dressed like the traditional *lucha libre* fighters, to defend pedestrians? LLM is a very traditional sport in our country and it remains very popular. The masks and characters of the fighters are a big part of the culture and they are very well known and loved. So this was a really creative way of taking our fight onto the streets. We took the atmosphere of the ring, the spectacle, onto the streets, where the battle is for a better city. It's a fight to protect pedestrians, reduce the number of casualties on the roads, and start constructing the city on a more human scale.
>
> Many people know Peatónito. Every time I go out there are people who recognize him, and he has had some impact in the press ... Drivers are sometimes annoyed but most of them respond with a smile. Sometimes, when drivers stop on pedestrian crossings, I push them out of the way. When they park on the pavement, I walk over the cars, which is the most controversial thing I do. I never damage any private property though, I just walk over them to show that the pavements are for pedestrians. Of course, that's when drivers get most annoyed, but I show them that I've not damaged their car, I've not scratched it or dented it, and

© Héctor Ríos 2012

Peatónito at work.

I explain to them that they're breaking the law. Then they calm down. These are the reactions for the most part. I also paint zebra crossings and pavements where they don't exist. People support me and sometimes help me paint. The police occasionally stop me but sometimes they support me, though that's rare.

Although Jorge is upbeat about many of the improvements in Mexico City, he acknowledges that they continue to reflect the unequal distribution of the city. They tend to be concentrated in the more affluent city centre, while there is still much work to do in the periphery:

There is a Harvard study that says the main condition for getting out of poverty is to have a means of transport that gets you to work. It should be subsidized, though ideally with a staggered fare structure. At the moment the Metro in Mexico City is highly subsidized and the fare is very low: just five pesos, which is the equivalent of 25 American cents. My idea is that it should be double the cost for those who can afford it. Those who can't – the unemployed, single mothers, the disabled, students – should have access to the subsidized price. But everyone else should pay more so that we can maintain the system and invest in a quality public transport system across the whole city. This is so important for people on very low incomes, who tend to live in the outskirts of the city, three or even four hours away. This is to do with the way the city has developed. Everything is very centralized; everyone comes to the centre to work. But the city has sprawled outwards and we need a system of public transport that serves the whole metropolitan area, providing a better quality of life for those who live on the outskirts, using all the means available to us: the Metro, buses, cycling, and park and ride schemes. This way, people will spend less money and have access to dignified transport. After road safety, this is the most important issue.

Overall though, he is optimistic:

This is where we are. It's a fight for our right to walk, a fight for a more human city, a fight for better air quality. A fight for a city where we can get about more safely and efficiently, with reduced use of the automobile. Somewhere pedestrians and cyclists are treated with respect and public transport is dignified and safe to use. I am a pedestrian activist working within a bigger activist community, which includes cyclists, and we've achieved great things, both in civil society and the government. We hope to bring about a revolution in better mobility.

I think we've turned a corner. It looks as if the elite are moving in this direction and they are taking the rest of the population with them. We are starting to change the discourse – and the law. That said, it's still a problem in some parts of the media and with certain politicians. There is still a lot of discrimination and hatred against pedestrians and cyclists. It's a dispute about communication.

Taking matters into your own hands

Tired of empty promises and waiting for bureaucrats to act, local citizens, activists, and neighbourhood groups have resorted to taking matters into their own hands. Like Peatónito, many other activists and civil society organizations are intervening in urban space in playful and creative fashion. A major influence has been the former mayor of Bogotá, Antanas Mockus. Trained as an educator, Mockus turned Bogotá into a classroom, using entertaining and cost-effective tactics to encourage civic education and improve urban behaviour. This approach met with great success: Mockus managed to cut the homicide rate by 70 per cent and traffic fatalities by more than 50 per cent during his first term (Marsh, 2013). Jorge discusses Mockus' influence on his work as Peatónito:

> This has been inspired by the ex-mayor of Bogotá, Antanas Mockus. He's a strange character who almost got to be president of Colombia. Well, he sacked all the traffic police in Bogotá one day and got in a group of mime artists to direct the traffic. He wanted to shape the culture of the city and it is creative acts like these which people really remember. So, occasionally there are times when other people put on masks with me and we make *cultura vial* [road culture] on street corners across Mexico City. I also get invited to other cities in Mexico, where there are other masked fighters for pedestrian rights. In La Paz, in the north, there is Dante Caminante. Then in Querétaro there is Caminatubela. In Comarca Lagunera, also in the north, there is Peatón Lagunero. And this is just in Mexico.
>
> There are also fighters in other parts of Latin America, for example: Super-Ando from São Paulo in Brazil and Super Urbana – a woman – also from Brazil. In Quito, the fight for pedestrian rights was going on long before anything started in Mexico City. There they have Peatón Man and the first-ever pedestrian 'army': Capitán Zapato and his Ejército Zapatista de la Liberación de la Vereda [a wordplay on the Mexican guerrilla group the Zapatista Army of National Liberation]. It's an informal, very grassroots network of pedestrian activists.

Here Jorge explains how his activism began:

> I started this journey when I joined Camina Ciudad, a group of young activists who painted pavements and zebra crossings illegally. Then pedestrian groups spread across the country, united in an organization called the Liga Peatonal [Pedestrian League]. Now I work with a group called Camina [Walk] and we do projects, workshops, and consultation sessions. There are just three of us – an architect, a teacher, and me. I'm the political/public relations guy. I do this separately from my work in the government. When I go out onto the streets in my fighting get-up I am nearly always alone, though I take other masks with me in case anyone else wants to join in. We want to shape the culture of the streets and protect pedestrians.

The painting of pavements and zebra crossings is a good example of what is known as tactical urbanism. This is defined as a 'citizen-led approach to neigh-bourhood building using short-term, low-cost, and scalable interventions to catalyse long-term change' (Tactical Urbanism, n.d.) As Salvador Medina comments:

> Activism in Mexico City can be very confrontational, and often it has to be, but I didn't think this would be much use to us. I proposed more playful interventions. One thing we did was an idea that we borrowed from Guadalajara, where the authorities were going to build a flyover in a residential neighbourhood. Locals organized an intervention using paint. They painted a cycle lane and with the help of residents they converted an old railway line into a park. This had a very positive result. They uploaded a video to YouTube, which went viral, and as a result the construction work was halted. We took this idea and made similar inter-ventions in Santa Fe. We painted a pavement, because the authorities never give a thought to the pedestrian; they only think about cars. These tactics are what is known as 'tactical urbanism'.
>
> We started with fun interventions, silly stuff, which the authorities didn't know how to deal with. For example, in areas where there were road traffic accidents we would paint zebra crossings. We said: what the government won't do, we'll do ourselves, with our own time and money. These interventions attracted a lot of media attention and the response wasn't negative – we were just doing what the government wasn't, so people couldn't really complain.

The do-it-yourself spirit of tactical urbanism is also manifest in other, more long-term community initiatives. In São Paulo, the recovery of a long-aban-doned park was taken on by a group of determined citizens, despite bureau-cratic obstacles. Luciana Cury of Coletivo Ocupe e Abrace [Occupy and Embrace Collective] describes what happened:

> We started around June 2013. At first, it was just people who lived in the neighbourhood who wanted to get the park back into shape. Praça da Nascente – also known as Praça Homero Silva – is a huge green space, the biggest in the neighbourhood of Pompeia in São Paulo. It's 12,000 square metres, on the side of a hill, and was urbanized some 20 or 30 years ago. When we decided to set up the group, the park was completely abandoned. Parts of it were flooded. We wanted to recover it, so we went around knocking on doors close to the park. But peo-ple would only say, 'That's a very dangerous place, you shouldn't go there, people have been raped and murdered there.' But if we hadn't started going to the park, it would have stayed like that. We had to start going there.
>
> So we started talking to the neighbours and we didn't get much sup-port. They were like, 'I've been living here for 40 years and it's always

Luciana Cury (right) and Miriam Melo Franco at the Praça da Nascente.

been like that.' It was all overgrown and full of rubbish, people would just throw their waste there. Parts were flooded; there were mosquitoes. A really bad vibe! The smell was bad. People used to go and pee there. Homeless people used to sleep there and did whatever they needed to. We decided we wanted to do something. So we went to City Hall and asked them to do something about it. They wouldn't listen. So we decided to do it ourselves. We got everyone together at the park, put some gloves on and started to pick up the rubbish.

For everyone in the group it was liberating, an important step towards feeling like more of a citizen. Towards feeling like we belonged to the city and could do something to improve it. We were doing it for ourselves, but the side effect was that it was good for others too. We started to be interviewed by TV and the newspapers, and they would always say, 'Oh, you're very altruistic people. You donate time and effort, you pick up the spade and so on.' But we started to realize that we do this for ourselves. And for our kids, our parents, you know? We want to live in a better environment and if they won't do anything to provide this for us, then we'll do it ourselves. And the side effect is that the city benefits from this as well.

One of the girls in the group, who is a Tai Chi instructor, put up a sign in the park which read, 'Cuidar de si, é cuidar do outro' ['Caring for oneself is caring for others']. We were like, 'That's perfect, you know!' Whenever we had an interview, we'd say, 'There's a sign in the Praça – go there and take a picture. You can put the picture in your article.' Because if everyone takes care of themselves the way they should, then they're also taking care of others. So we cut out this altruistic bullshit! No one wants to be good. If I'm taking care of the Praça, I'm doing it for myself.

In similar fashion, communities develop their own forms of decision-making and problem-solving in order to deal with the challenges they face day to day. Johans Rodriguez is president of the 1st Brigade of Polvorines, which has built a bottom-up strategy for community resilience, minimizing risks for inhabitants of the shantytown Los Polvorines, in Piura, Peru. Johans explains:

We are members of the 1st Brigade of Polvorines, the first trained and certified brigade from the shantytown of Los Polvorines in the new district of 26 de Octubre … We have a certificate that [the NGO] Practical Solutions (SP) got us through the Ministry of Education and we're accredited by the district of 26 de Octubre, which has recognized us as the first brigade of the district. They count on us as the first response for any emergency that could happen in 26 de Octubre.

In meetings with other shantytowns, we've always been clear that what we do isn't political or to make money. It's all voluntary. All the resources we receive are discussed at meetings and everyone can see where it goes. If we don't have trust and honesty, which are the values that should reign in society, we won't go far.

We formed one group to focus on risk and disaster management and to form a civil defence platform. Through meetings with residents, we elected a president, a secretary, and a treasurer. As people recognized my leadership skills, my ability to bring people together and the work I had already done, I was voted in as president, out of four candidates.

Johans and the other members of the brigade have conducted surveys to gather key information, in order to safeguard the lives of the most vulnerable, ensure effective strategy, and prioritize certain areas:

Our database helps us to prioritize areas in the event of a risk. It's easy to say, 'Children first', but we don't know how many there are, who is most vulnerable, or where they are. In some houses there might be up to four children under the age of five, in which case that becomes our priority. It also helps us to analyse what kind of help we need, for example with medicine. If we know that there is a person with chronic asthma or hypertension, then we should bring someone who can help. It's also been helpful to know what jobs people do. We have drivers, nurses, policemen, and technicians, who we can count on as human resources to help us mitigate an emergency. If we explain we're from the platform, they'll be glad to help in the event of a risk. It helps us to work calmly and know that we can partially control any risk.

It brings me happiness, because I can show all the other residents that it's not necessary for people to applaud you. All our work has been very low profile. We did our work raising awareness in the community, going out with our megaphones, without anyone asking us. It brings me happiness to repay people's trust in me. And above all it's a big responsibility, because everyone knows that there's a brigade in a shantytown that is at risk.

Cities for citizens

For urbanists such as Jan Gehl and Jane Jacobs, the human life flowing through the physical infrastructure is what truly builds the urban space. They have criticized the ways in which current planning practices overlook this human dimension, obliterating city spaces that might serve as places for meetings and encounters. Likewise, for Andrés Chaves, there is an emotional aspect to urban planning which all too often is absent. He began making documentaries to capture this more human side of cities and urban development:

> I became concerned that a whole series of perceptions and emotions generated in contemporary cities were not being expressed in the projects on which we urban specialists work. There is an emotional component to these issues, which is lacking, and which in my opinion is fundamental when it comes to experiencing a city. I got interested in photography at first and then in documentary film-making. That's how I came to make my first documentary, *La Hortua*, which was filmed in Bogotá. It looks at how workers of a hospital abandoned by the Colombian government in 1997 decided to appropriate this space and make it their home. I met the people who lived there and decided to make a documentary about it.
>
> There have been publications, academic work, and other audio-visual work about El Cartucho, but the inhabitants – the poor people who are the soul of the neighbourhood – are always absent. My documentary aimed to allow them to speak and to do so freely and openly. I hope this film will show an urban phenomenon that persists. When it comes to urban planning, in Colombia, and especially in Bogotá, we tend to have very short memories. There have been interventions in the neighbourhoods that appeared after El Cartucho, San Bernardo, El Bronx, and others, but people forget that the strategy of demolition has already been tried, we've done it twice. It hasn't worked, and I hope this documentary will help to remind people. I think it also tries to reconstruct memories from a certain perspective. It seeks to collect disparate materials in one place, to tell the story of a neighbourhood that hadn't been told before and was in danger of being lost. It's an audio-visual legacy. Nobody had tried to do this before.

The film has had quite a strong impact on me, as an urban planner. I wanted to show the other side to urban planning, the human side, the side we don't normally see. I went a long way into this with the documentary, right into its innards. As an urban planner, I am concerned with space, and El Cartucho is a space where there was a symbiotic relationship between the architecture and the people who lived there. I went through a kind of crisis, exploring this, because it became very clear to me that most urban planning happens from a desk. In terms of governance, it is very top-down. Everything comes down to plans, images, visualizations, and perspectives, with the human, emotional side missing or being forgotten. Humans become mere data. I think that as urban planners we are very disconnected from people, from what I've seen.

Ciudad Emergente is an urban laboratory located in Santiago de Chile, which promotes human-centred and participatory tactics to improve cities. Kurt Steffens, their urban strategies coordinator, sees social cohesion and the building of trust as a cornerstone of urban development:

While it might seem obvious that cities are developed around and for people, this isn't necessarily the case. As an organization, we dedicate ourselves to looking for evidence, exposing the political motives behind urban interventions – like a highway going through the middle of a community, for example – which are presented simply as technical decisions. What we do is make these political motives evident and question the supposed technical justification, using tactical urbanism interventions. These are immediate, short-term actions, to challenge, influence, or modify things in the long term. Obviously, this implies influencing public policy.

One of the initiatives by Ciudad Emergente which has received significant positive feedback is an event called El Gran Malón, as Kurt explains:

Malón is a Mapuche term in origin, but for Chileans it means a meal to which everyone brings their own food or contributes something. It can take place in a public space, or at home. What our initiative has aimed to achieve is for communities in Chile to start to get to know and trust each other, via self-management, via the action of sharing a meal out on the street.

Why is this so important in Chile? Because according to OECD data, only 12.6 per cent of people trust their neighbours, which is worrying. A lack of trust completely precludes the organization of cohesive communities. We consider this to be of great importance for Chile's development. If Chile wants to feel it has become a middle-class country, it needs – amongst many other things – to be a country in which neighbours and citizens trust one another.

We held our first *malón* on 8 April 2017, where we invited all Chileans to go out to the street on the same day. We invited neighbourhood

© Ciudad Emergente 2018

La Gran Mateada – a local version of El Gran Malón in Salamanca, Chile.

associations, foundations, and so on to put a table out onto the street, or in a plaza, and share a meal over a topic that united them. We asked them to discuss the question, 'What do you think Chile needs?' We wanted people to get together to answer this question, but mostly just to get together and get to know one another. We wanted people to talk about things that affected them as a community. Things like security, parking, crime, waste, as well as more complex issues like migration, which is an issue of increasing importance in Chile. Around 11,500 people participated, in 11 out of Chile's 15 regions. More than 40 communes [Chile's smallest territorial subdivision] in total. More than 111 *malones* took place, proving that there was a real need for people to gather and meet their neighbours and other members of the community.

Kurt and the team at Ciudad Emergente are happy that their work has put issues of trust and community cohesion onto the public policy agenda:

Many local governments have found this an effective way to get in touch with some of the most difficult communities. Some local mayors are *maloneros* and publicize the event on social media. They use it as a means of community outreach, and this makes us extremely happy. El Gran Malón also has a particular style or aesthetic, for example the use of little flags, which has spread throughout Chile. This makes us happy, as it's something that's happened so quickly.

The second Gran Malón was celebrated throughout Chile on 7 April 2018, and Kurt has ambitions for future *malones* beyond Chile's borders. 'We hope that one day Latin America will be celebrating getting to know each other on the street, reclaiming public spaces,' he says. 'We hope it becomes part of the calendar, instead of a North American celebration like Halloween, for example.'

* * *

For David Harvey:

> The right to the city is, therefore, far more than a right of individual or group access to the resources that the city embodies: it is a right to change and reinvent the city more after our hearts' desire. It is, moreover, a collective rather than an individual right, since reinventing the city inevitably depends upon the exercise of a collective power over the processes of urbanization. The freedom to make and remake ourselves and our cities is, I want to argue, one of the most precious yet most neglected of our human rights. How best then to exercise that right? (Harvey, 2012)

This is not an easy question to answer. The Latin American city is a diverse and complex ecosystem, a polarized and contested space. It is more than its visible highways, buildings, and structures: it is class struggle, politics, and competition for the resources needed for dignified living.

Migration from the countryside to the city in Latin America will continue. Rural populations, all too often neglected by government, continue to believe that the city provides better job opportunities, public services, and quality of life, however disappointing the reality may be for many. Yet, to ensure a better future, cities must provide adequate conditions. While city authorities and national governments have a crucial role to play, there is also an onus on communities and citizens to organize and represent their needs effectively (Green and Branford, 2013).

While architects give physical shape to spaces, activists define what happens within them. This might take the form of organizing a brigade for emergencies, coordinating residents to resist evictions, painting zebra crossings, getting neighbours to share a meal, or even dressing up as a superhero to defend people's rights. The voices of this chapter build and give shape to their urban spaces as much as the architects and engineers responsible for the physical materialization of a city. As Jorge Cáñez/Peatónito says, 'I've learnt that a revolution is possible. Street corner by street corner, pavement by pavement, block by block, neighbourhood by neighbourhood, we can change the city. It starts locally with your neighbours, all the way up to planning for the whole city.'

About the author

Antonia Burchard-Levine specializes in urban transportation and mobility, urban land development, housing and livelihoods, and infrastructure financing. She is particularly interested in urban social movements, issues of access to the city and its resources, and the range of processes that shape cities and their inhabitants. Antonia is currently based in Berlin and consults on international development projects as an urban development specialist.

Interviews

Jorge Cáñez, aka **Peatónito** (urban mobility and road safety activist): interviewed via Jitsi Meet on 23 February 2018 by Tom Gatehouse. Translated by Hebe Powell.

Andrés Chaves (urbanist and film-maker): interviewed via Skype on 11 January 2018 by Antonia Burchard-Levine. Translated by Antonia Burchard-Levine.

Luciana Cury (Coletivo Ocupe e Abrace): interviewed via Skype on 12 February 2018 by Antonia Burchard-Levine. Transcribed by Tom Gatehouse.

Marcello Deodoro (Tijuca Indiana Residents' Commission): interviewed via email on 18 December 2017 by Jennifer Chisholm. Translated by Chris Whitehouse.

Luiz Gonzaga da Silva, aka **Gegê** (MMC): interviewed in São Paulo on 21 December 2016 and 28 January 2017 by Ali Rocha. Translated by Hugo Moss.

Salvador Medina (urban economist and activist): interviewed via Skype on 8 February 2018 by Antonia Burchard-Levine. Translated by Antonia Burchard-Levine.

Johans Rodriguez (1st Brigade of Polvorines): interviewed in Piura, Peru, in late January 2016 by Kary Stewart. Translated by Kary Stewart.

Emília Maria de Souza (Horto Residents' Association): interviewed in Rio de Janeiro on 29 January 2018 by Jennifer Chisholm. Translated by Theo Bradford.

Kurt Steffens (Ciudad Emergente): interviewed via WhatsApp on 20 March 2018 by Antonia Burchard-Levine. Translated by Antonia Burchard-Levine.

References

NB: All web references were checked and still available in May/June 2018 unless otherwise stated. All references are listed, with web-links, on the page for this chapter on the Voices website www.vola.org.uk

Bauwens, M. (2018) 'People in defence of life and territory: counter-power and self-defence in Latin America', P2P Foundation, <https://blog.p2pfoundation.net/people-in-defence-of-life-and-territory-counter-power-and-self-defence-in-latin-america/2018/04/09>

Boyer, H. (2005) 'Urban land and housing challenges in Brazil', Lincoln Institute of Land Policy, <https://www.lincolninst.edu/publications/articles/urban-land-housing-challenges-brazil>

Carvalho, S. (2017) 'As 9 cidades brasileiras com o pior trânsito', Circuito D, <https://www.circuitod.com.br/single-post/As-9-cidades-brasileiras-com-o-pior-transito>

Gatehouse, T. (2016) 'Brazil's Olympic flames', Red Pepper, <https://www.redpepper.org.uk/brazils-olympic-flames>

Gehl, J. (2010) *Cities for People*, Island Press, Washington DC.

Green, D. and Branford, S. (2013) *Faces of Latin America*, 4th edn, Latin America Bureau (LAB), London.

Harvey, D. (2012) *Rebel Cities: From the Right to the City to the Urban Revolution*, Verso, London and New York, NY.

Jacobs, J. (1961) *The Death and Life of Great American Cities*, Vintage Books, New York, NY.

Jaitman, L. (2015) 'Urban infrastructure in Latin America and the Caribbean: public policy priorities', *Latin American Economic Review* 24: 13 <https://doi.org/10.1007/s40503-015-0027-5>

Johnson, S. (2014) 'Rio's BRT system: a tool for legacy or fragmentation?', RioOnWatch, <http://www.rioonwatch.org/?p=15531>

Lefebvre, H. (2014) *The Production of Space*, 18th edn, Blackwell, Oxford.

Marsh, S. (2013) 'Antanas Mockus: Colombians fear ridicule more than being fined', *The Guardian*, 28 October, <https://www.theguardian.com/public-leaders-network/2013/oct/28/antanas-mockus-bogota-mayor>

McGuirk, J. (2014) *Radical Cities: Across Latin America in Search of a New Architecture*, Verso, London and New York, NY.

Merrifeld, A. (2017) 'Fifty years on: the right to the city', in A. Merrifeld, *The Right to the City: A Verso Report*, Verso, London and New York, NY.

Pacheco, P. (2016) 'Brazil: My House, My Life', World Policy, <https://worldpolicy.org/2016/07/07/brazil-my-house-my-life>

Tactical Urbanism (no date) 'What is Tactical Urbanism?', <http://tacticalurbanismguide.com/about>

CHAPTER 10

The new journalism: now the people make the news

Mike Gatehouse

Abstract

While mainstream media, especially print and television, are mostly owned and controlled by large companies and rich families, new forms of journalism are proliferating across Latin America. Web-only news sites, blogs, Facebook newspapers, YouTube video, and Twitter have empowered a whole generation of new journalists, photographers, and video-makers – professional, self-taught, and amateur – often working closely with social movements.

Concentration and control

The press, radio, and television in Latin America have long been dominated by huge media conglomerates such as Globo in Brazil, Grupo Clarín in Argentina, and Televisa in Mexico. Grupo Globo owns Rede Globo, the free-to-air TV network, and is the largest media company in the region by advertising revenue, the 19th largest in the world, and the only Latin American company in the top 30 (Zenith, 2017). The group also owns three cable TV companies, a 7 per cent stake in Sky Brazil, four radio networks, four internet service providers, three magazine publishers, and a film production company. Televisa owns film, TV, radio, internet, book, and magazine publishing. Most of these conglomerates are linked or have overlapping ownerships with US-based media corporations such as Sky, Fox, and ABC.

In the English-speaking world, the names William Randolph Hearst, Viscount Rothermere, and Rupert Murdoch personify the wealthy autocrat who heads a print or broadcasting empire. Latin America has spawned its own media barons and their families: the Azcárraga family in Mexico, who founded and until recently fully controlled Televisa; the Edwards family in Chile, who controlled *El Mercurio*, *La Segunda*, and TV and radio outlets; Brazil's Mesquita family, owners until 2003 of *O Estado de S. Paulo*; and in Argentina, the Noble family, owners of *Clarín*.

For the most part these companies and their owners have been on the political right. *El Mercurio* almost certainly received some of the funding the CIA dispensed to friendly media in the 1960s to oppose the rise of Salvador Allende. Together with its sister-title *La Segunda*, it was a cheerleader for the

http://dx.doi.org/10.3362/9781909014213.010

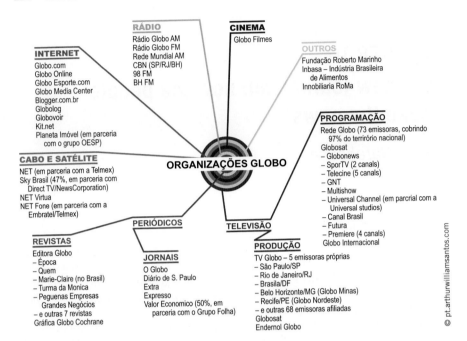

Infographic of Grupo Globo's media companies.

1973 military coup (Kornbluh, 2003). In Brazil, Globo has been a constant thorn in the side of the Workers' Party (PT) and, notoriously, edited its report of the final presidential debate in 1989 in order to present Luiz Inácio Lula da Silva in an unfavourable light, which many believe swung the election for his opponent Fernando Collor de Mello (Souza et al., 2011). Globo was also a major supporter of the 2016 impeachment of President Dilma Rousseff. *O Estado de S. Paulo* has a more mixed record: it campaigned against João Goulart, and at first supported the military dictatorship. But it opposed censorship and its editor, Júlio de Mesquita Filho, was arrested by the military in 1968 for refusing to suppress an editorial.

There have been media concentrations on the left, too. In Nicaragua, the Sandinista National Liberation Front (FSLN) and President Daniel Ortega control significant numbers of TV, radio, press, and internet outlets, but there are also lively and influential opposition media. Cuba's printed press is monopolized by the official newspaper *Granma*. Yuri Valle Roca, a Cuban blogger and fierce opponent of the government, says:

There are few printed publications in Cuba. *Granma* is the main one. It has four or five pages and is the official mouthpiece of the Central Committee of the Communist Party of Cuba. The name tells you who it is addressed to and what interests it serves. Not the people.

'People of Chile: 44 years on and *El Mercurio* is still lying!' – banner hung across the front of the Universidad Católica in Chile, during the 2011 education protests, where students caused scandal in 1967 by hanging a banner accusing Chile's august broadsheet of lying.

The Maduro government in Venezuela is accused of buying opposition news outlets to suppress criticism. The government officially controls 13 television networks, more than 65 radio outlets, one news agency, five newspapers, and a magazine (Freedom House, 2015). Carlos Correa, director of Venezuelan NGO Espacio Público, says:

> Venezuela [previously] had around 100 national and regional newspapers, several of which were very influential. The newspapers have been hit hard over the last three years, mainly because the government holds a monopoly over the supply of paper. They have used this as a means of rewarding and punishing and it has led to the closure of around 15 newspapers. Others have gone from being dailies to weeklies, and some have disappeared completely – there was one case of a newspaper that had been in print for over 80 years just disappearing. This wasn't because of the changes in the market and consumer habits, but because of state policies that have deliberately targeted and punished these publications at the same time as supporting government-owned or pro-government newspapers, subsidizing them so they can be distributed for free.

A key element in control of the media is the granting or withholding of government advertising (of growing importance for the printed press, as commercial advertising switches to the internet). In Mexico the outgoing government of Enrique Peña Nieto spent nearly US$2 bn on media advertising, more than any presidency in the country's history, according to transparency group Fundar (Ahmed, 2017). For instance, after the 2017 earthquake, full-page advertisements were taken out in many newspapers praising the schools rebuilding programme (Villegas, 2018). Patricia Mayorga, recipient of the 2017 International Press Freedom Award and a journalist with the magazine *Proceso*, describes how the same control operates at state level:

> When the new governor [of the northern state of Chihuahua] took office, he started to pay the media channels a lot of money in order to influence the editorial line. The six-year term of the ex-governor César Duarte [2010–16] was one of the worst times for the press in terms of censorship because of the excessive amount of state advertising ...
>
> Many media outlets prioritize commercial interests over journalism. They are given large sums of money in exchange for state advertising, but it's disguised. In theory, this shouldn't influence the editorial line, but it does. Government money is used to pay the companies, and this has an impact on the quality of the reporters' work. Sometimes they don't let you publish all the details, or they ask you to cover a certain topic or ask you to write about it from a certain angle, which you know isn't right, and so on. I'm not saying this is true of all companies; in Mexico now we have a very strong independent press developing. However, this does happen in the big companies, which is where most journalists work. It's very frustrating. It happens a lot in Chihuahua.

Tania Montalvo, of the Mexican news website *Animal Político*, agrees:

> Then there are other [national] newspapers such as *El Universal, Excélsior, El Sol de México*, and *La Jornada.* Their situation has been a little complicated, at least over the last six years, because people feel that what they publish benefits the political classes. This is reinforced by the vast sums of money they receive from official advertising. The same thing happens with Televisa and the big radio stations. It's hard for free journalism to exist when there are media outlets that receive such incredibly high sums of money.

Tania Montalvo.

© Animal Político 2016

Repression

Far greater control of the press is achieved by the simple expedient of threats and harassment of journalists and, if these prove inadequate, then by beatings, imprisonment, forced displacement, and assassination.

In 2017, Latin America and the Caribbean ranked as the most dangerous region in the world for journalists to work, and Mexico as the deadliest country outside a war zone – only Iraq and Syria were worse (Mioli, 2017). Out of 18 killings of journalists in the region in 2017, in eight cases the motive was confirmed; in the remainder it was uncertain. By April 2018, 17 journalists had already been killed, and it is certain that 2018 will see the highest toll on record (CPJ, 2018). These figures, for fully documented cases, are likely to be an underestimate.

Tania describes the particular dangers for journalists in Mexico:

Right now, Mexico is one of the most violent countries in which to be a journalist. *Animal Político* has not been a victim of this violence directly and we are not even close to being in a vulnerable situation, compared to media outlets out in [Mexican] states where there is a lot of violence. However, this climate of violence exists and as journalists we are all exposed to it. Also, governmental pressure has been becoming more obvious in recent months. This is something we all experience. It has affected me personally in the last five or six years. There are people in government who feel they have the right to intimidate you. They'll ring you up, telling you not to publish something, or warning you that if you do there will be consequences. There are also other tactics, like audits. All of a sudden, they'll decide to audit us, which is bureaucratic and a drain on our time and resources, especially as we're such a small organization. At least during this government, these audits have been used both to distract us from our work and to intimidate us.

When I was a reporter, they would ring my boss, saying, 'Look, I know your reporter is looking into this. What's going on? Speak to her.' Or 'How can we fix this? What does she need?' – those kinds of things.

Javier Valdez Cárdenas

Javier Valdez was co-founder of *Ríodoce*, a newspaper in Culiacán, Sinaloa. He and his paper both won international awards for their fearless reporting from one of the most dangerous areas of Mexico. Following the extradition of Sinaloa Cartel boss Joaquín Guzmán to the US in January 2017, a battle for power among and within the drug cartels ensued. Valdez was shot on the street in Culiacán on 15 May, the seventh Mexican journalist to be assassinated that year (Macqueen, 2017).

Javier Valdez Cárdenas.

Tania continues:

The authorities aren't interested. They just want to make the issue go away. They're also incompetent, something which has been clearly shown by the murder of Javier. After that happened the profession did mobilize to demand answers. There was an event at Los Pinos [the presidential residence] with President Enrique Peña Nieto and all the state governors, where they said that the case would be solved. The photographers who were there even interrupted the president, shouting 'Justice! Justice!' and at the end of the event, Peña Nieto went to speak to them and promised that the crime would not go unpunished. This doesn't usually happen when a journalist is killed in Mexico.

But what have we seen so far? They have made no progress with the case. They're completely incapable of solving the crime. Most of the time, when a journalist out in one of the states is killed, the case isn't even investigated, it gets archived immediately. Or they'll disqualify the journalist, claiming that they were a taxi driver. Or they'll claim that the victim had the number of a criminal saved in their phone and therefore they must have been involved in organized crime. Whatever it takes to fudge the issue.

The situation will not improve until there is an end to impunity for those who perpetrate the violence, as Patricia makes clear:

The rate of impunity for [all] homicides in Mexico is something like 98 per cent. The failure of the state to respond to these homicides is a green light for the criminals to keep doing what they're doing. This is another one of the risks we face ... Impunity in cases of homicide against journalists is at 99.7 per cent ... That shows how dangerous the profession is. It's a bad sign if a homicide isn't punished, but if no homicides are punished, it's even worse. It's like giving permission to kill journalists.

The threats and violence against Mexican journalists are not all related to the drug trade and its networks of corruption and political patronage. Miryam Vargas Teutle works for Radio Comunitaria Cholollan, a community radio in Tlaxcalancingo, in the state of Puebla. They campaigned against the routing of a gas pipeline from Morelos passing through their own community and dangerously close to an active volcano:

We at the community radio station were doing our best to get all these issues aired and trying to generate dialogue. People needed to know what was happening and we were like the alarm bell. But it didn't really suit the authorities to have a light shone in their direction, so that's when they moved in on us. Our station here at Tlaxcalancingo and

Miryam Vargas Teutle

© Eliana Gilet 2015

another station, Radio Zacatepec, were raided on the same day. The Federal Institute for Telecommunications came in with a full force of state officials and police. They seized our equipment and tried to make several arrests.

Tania confirms this:

> One of the biggest problems is that violence against journalists happens at different levels and takes different forms in each place. It's not the same in Mexico City as it is in the north of the country, the southeast, the Pacific, or the Gulf of Mexico. Every state, even every municipality, has a different type of violence ... Perhaps in the north of the country, journalists are being threatened directly by criminals, who tell them what they can and can't publish. In the very violent states of the Mexican Pacific, we might be talking about municipal authorities who behave aggressively towards journalists. Elsewhere, perhaps it's the state authorities responsible. Sometimes it's not even clear who's behind it. Sometimes funding for journalism dries up because pressure is applied to sponsors.
>
> It's very complicated. What little we can do at *Animal Político* is to try to create the media network I was telling you about. Because what can protect journalists is visibility. This way, your work can have greater impact. That can provide you with a network of protection, though not in all cases and it is no guarantee. Of course, it is also necessary to involve the big media organizations and ensure they take precautions like making sure their journalists know how to use secure communications. And they need to keep tabs on their reporters. At the moment, there is a journalist missing in Oaxaca. His family has proof that he worked for a certain media outlet. But the media outlet is denying any relation with him whatsoever. That's why it's important for media organizations to be involved and to take responsibility for their journalists.

Patricia points the finger beyond the crime syndicates to politicians and their parties:

> What has had the biggest impact is our exposure of political candidates with links to the drug trade. It has been life-changing for me and it resulted in the murder of my colleague Miroslava Breach. At least one party, the Institutional Revolutionary Party (PRI), fielded candidates involved in criminal groups in 2016, which we exposed in our reports. In our respective publications – *Proceso* in my case, *La Jornada* in Miroslava's – we published this report, each in our own style. This led to PRI changing at least two of their candidates, one of whom was for the municipality of Chínipas, located in the Sierra Tarahumara ... The candidate from Chínipas, who belonged to a criminal organization, got very angry, and they began to send threats and messages telling us not to publish these kinds of stories. Miroslava Breach, who was killed on 23 March last year [2017], was from Chínipas. The messages came from people who knew her. They sent us messages over the course of a year. I saw three or four of them, but after Miroslava was killed I found out that they had sent her more.

When she was killed, Javier Corral, the governor at the time, immediately provided me with a security detail for 15 days, that same morning. Eventually, I was persuaded to leave the country ... and I've not been back to Chihuahua since.

Patricia was forced to leave the country and move to Peru, supported by the Committee to Protect Journalists (CPJ). She continues to work as a journalist and has returned to Mexico for brief visits since. She specifically told LAB, 'I don't want you to mention where I am or where I'm going.' As she makes clear, she is by no means the only journalist forcibly displaced – either within the country or abroad:

A homage to Miroslava Breach: 'You cannot kill the truth by killing journalists – Justice for Miroslava'

There are around 30 recorded cases of journalists who have been displaced internally, plus all those who have fled to the United States, not to mention those who won't say where they are but who are asking for support. I meet other displaced journalists and I see their strength and determination to carry on. I think that Mexican journalism as a profession, together with the authorities and universities, must work harder to support displaced journalists. It's a very painful process and if you don't have the necessary support, it can destroy you.

Pavel Núñez, a Honduran educator, musician, and digital activist – from whom we will hear more below – has been forced to flee Honduras since we interviewed him there in late 2016. He had received death threats, his girlfriend was being harassed, and his mother was kidnapped briefly. Between 2010 and 2015, 32 Latin American journalists, mostly from Cuba and Mexico, went into exile (CPJ, 2015). It is likely that the situation has worsened since.

Elsewhere, while there is less direct violence, smears and threats are used to intimidate journalists. This is certainly true of Venezuela, according to Carlos Correa of Espacio Público:

Around 2001, those in power started to really criticize journalists. What usually started off as legitimate criticism of the press began to mutate, combining with smears and other attempts to delegitimize the press, until you got to a point where anyone practising certain types of journalism was labelled a traitor ... By 2001 or 2002 we could see it was becoming more serious ... because the government started accusing us of promoting the failed coup d'état, although they never tried to prove our liability for this in the courts.

There have also been instances of violence – our offices have been robbed twice and we have been victims of violence when we have visited public authorities. As human rights defenders we have had legal proceedings filed against us, some of them ongoing. It's an atmosphere of constant harassment, and I think it's mainly because of our attempts to incorporate a human rights perspective into the national public debate ... Our bank accounts, our online communication, and our movements when we leave the country have all been targets for surveillance. The aim of these practices is to intimidate us.

We hope that the work we have done to document the state's behaviour, especially when it has fallen below the standards required, can help us to ensure that these things never happen again. We're looking to the future and thinking about how our work can help achieve freedom of expression in Venezuela. Freedom of expression is like a thermometer that can be used to measure a country's state of health.

In Cuba, meanwhile, Yuri Valle Roca was beaten up in the street, and later charged with affray and prohibited from leaving his home province:

My partner Eralidis Frometa (of the group Ladies in White) and I were on our way to the Santa Rita church, a space won by these courageous women, when we were stopped by a volunteer employed by state security. He told me I couldn't go any further. I asked him for identification, but he didn't have any. When we decided to continue on our way, this thug attacked me. Others arrived and beat me in the middle of the street. They abducted me and took me to the police station in Santiago de las Vegas, on the outskirts of the city, to make it difficult for my group to find me.

I was charged with affray and public disorder. The investigating officer told me I was free, but a few months later, before I was due to travel to the United States, she turned up at my house to notify me that the courts had changed the penalty to a fine of 1,500 pesos, which I refused to pay because I hadn't committed any crime.

For Yuri, the role of the journalist is to speak out 'on behalf of those who are oppressed', even if doing so entails personal risk. It is this sense of social commitment that motivates many of the journalists interviewed for this chapter, as we will see ahead.

Journalism and social commitment

Most of the journalists we interviewed began by working on conventional print newspapers. Patricia, for example:

[I worked on] *El Heraldo de Chihuahua*, in the state capital. It was a daily newspaper. It still is. I only intended to work there for a year before going back to university, but I ended up staying there for 10 years.

My contact with different kinds of people allowed me to learn more about the reality of the state of Chihuahua. It also gave me the opportunity to get involved in helping people. I became passionate about telling people's stories. My first reports were about health; education, religion, and civil associations. That's where I cut my teeth. Then, around 2003, Gloria Trevi, a Mexican singer who had been arrested in Brazil, arrived in Chihuahua [to stand trial on charges of sexual abuse, kidnapping, and corrupting minors]. I was assigned to cover the story. For that case I spent hours in the courts and I began to investigate other stories too. I began to specialize in court reporting and before I left Chihuahua, I was covering trials and hearings. That's how I got hooked on journalism.

In 2010, I left *El Heraldo* and started working for another local media company called Omnia, which was a digital publication [which] also had a weekly printed paper and a TV news channel. So that was a big challenge, and I was assigned to cover the governor's political campaign. While this was going on I noticed the levels of violence and started meeting people involved in the so-called drug war. I was made head of information and I had a team of very young reporters. In the beginning we had quite a lot of freedom. My team were very enthusiastic and we worked well together.

We reported on human rights violations, disappearances, homicides, and femicides. We covered the Sierra Tarahumara in particular, because from 2011 to 2012 the level of violence began to increase and has continued to do so ever since. That's what we were working on when they broke us up. Then, in 2012, I started working for *Proceso* magazine as a correspondent. I worked for both outlets for a while, but soon I had to leave the local outlet because of increasing pressure for me to do so. I still work for *Proceso*.

Before she came to *Animal Político*, Tania Montalvo took a degree in journalism in Monterrey, worked at CNN Mexico, and then 'in very traditional media outlets at first, like the newspaper *El Universal*. This is a newspaper with enormous impact; it has the highest circulation in the country. However, the freedom to write what you want is very limited.' But her interest in journalism started much earlier:

I learnt how to read at a very young age ... As I was still too young to start school, I would sit down with my grandfather to read and what he read were newspapers. Obviously, there were a lot of things that I didn't understand. I remember reading headlines when I was very young, maybe five or six years old. There was one which read: 'The devil appeared to them and he killed them'. I took this literally and I got very frightened. When I told my grandfather what had happened, he introduced me to the idea that the press lies. The press has to attract readers, so not everything you read in the newspapers is true. I remember he told me that there are newspapers that lie and deceive people because they want to sell more.

As I got older, I continued reading in the afternoons with him. He would point out good headlines, bad headlines, but always maintaining the notion that the newspapers lie. This idea influenced me when I was at school and when it came to choosing what I wanted to study. I knew of other publications that were concerned with things beyond Mexico, publications from other countries that did things differently. That was when I said I wanted to be a journalist. I told my grandfather I felt sure it was possible to do good journalism; you shouldn't have to lie all the time. It was possible in other countries, so why not Mexico? With the internet, I had access to columns and other materials by various Latin American journalists. I showed them to my grandfather and said, 'Look, the press can be interesting, see? It's not just *notas rojas* [a sensationalist genre focusing mainly on violence] and lies.'

Brazilian journalist Renata da Silva Souza, by contrast, grew up in poverty, reached university via a community outreach project, and came to journalism later, combining her work at the community newspaper *O Cidadão* with her life as a local activist:

[I was] born and raised in [the favela complex] Maré. I live in the favela Nova Holanda, which was one of the first favelas to emerge in Maré. My grandfather came from the countryside, with a wave of people looking for work in Rio de Janeiro, and they started occupying some swampland, which is what Maré stands on. He took part in the first occupation of Maré, reclaiming land, installing electricity, basic sanitation, water, and so on. My grandfather was part of this process, this journey, and my mother and aunts were born in Maré.

We were very poor; we suffered great hardship. Often there'd be nothing to eat so we'd go really early to the lines outside churches, places handing out bread and milk. It was a tough childhood. But I have good memories ... My mother and father really valued our access to education, and I went to local schools in Maré.

To get into university, I took the Maré community *pré-vestibular* [preparatory course for the university entrance exams] in the year 2000, the first of its kind, which was at the Maré Study and Solidarity Action Centre (CEASM). They also founded the Maré Museum. To begin with, CEASM organized the community *pré-vestibular* – together with Maré inhabitants – with help from the Church, followers of liberation theology who saw the Church more as a place for the democratic transformation of society than as a strictly religious space. It was a group of young people who had succeeded in getting into university who had this idea of creating the community *pré-vestibular*, so that others from the favela might do the same.

There were psychologists and social workers present on this course, and they gave you vocational tests. I did one, and one of the exercises was: 'What do you want to be?' There was a list of professions, all sorts, not just from the world we knew. 'Doctor', lots of others. And the last profession on the list was 'journalist'. Well, I really laid into them. I said that all they do is tell lies, distort everything that goes on in the favela and don't listen to the locals. I was young, not yet politicized, but I was already so angry at the press for their portrayal of the favela. But they told me, 'No Renata, go and research what journalism is, to see what it's about.' I did so and fell in love with it! I said, 'I want to be a journalist.' ... I decided to study journalism and came across *O Cidadão*, so those things came together ... I started as a photographer, and soon afterwards I realized I wanted to write articles, and so on. That's how I discovered I wanted to do journalism.

'We could no longer remain silent': evolution of a community newspaper

O Cidadão was launched in 1999 by CEASM as a tabloid weekly community newspaper. At its peak, it achieved a print run of 20,000 copies, with 24 pages in colour, and converted to magazine format, because local people liked to collect the issues. It relied on advertising, says Renata, while the paper was printed by the big magazine and book publisher Ediouro, which is based in Maré:

> I started learning on the job, things like community communication, how to research articles. We did some great things as photographers; we published photo-comics in the newspaper ... I was living something more than just the everyday goings on; I was learning how the favela really operated, which was something very important to me. I visited all the favelas of Maré because of my work with *O Cidadão*. So many people in Maré don't know other favelas which are right next door, sometimes divided by just a street, but I had the chance to get to know the whole of Maré. I know every last alley.
>
> The first article we printed about violence wasn't about Maré specifically: the context was more general and it addressed the war in Iraq. I can't remember what the headline was, but something like 'Lines Crossing Maré and Iraq'. We wrote about guns, the arms trade, the whole spectacle of the Iraq war. That was 2003, I think. We started this debate, a difficult one. The article had a photo of a lamp post riddled with bullet holes, which stands right on the border between two favelas with rival factions. Unlike other favelas in Rio de Janeiro, Maré doesn't have just one faction, there are several. Often the border between them is a single street. There's constant tension; the possibility of conflict is always present. It can happen anytime, it's not something which can be controlled. We chose this lamp post on what we call the *divisa*, the border separating the turf of one faction from another.
>
> Our editorial policy to begin with was to talk about good things, strengthening our local identity, history, culture, the daily lives of the inhabitants. Later we realized that we had to talk about public safety. It was a difficult moment, there was a lot of resistance within the newspaper itself.

But we had no choice, because the *caveirões* [armoured cars] became part of Rio de Janeiro's public security policy. These vehicles were supposed to bring peace but did nothing of the sort. Rosinha Garotinho, who was state governor at the time, said that the *caveirões* would only patrol the favelas at night, whenever there was fighting between drug gangs. But they used to patrol at midday, when there were children around, coming out of school. We published a photo showing a *caveirão* at midday, near a school. It was taken by Bira Carvalho, a great photographer from Maré who took a lot of the photos we printed. We ran a big article about this, and on the cover there was a *caveirão*, something we got from an Amnesty International campaign which was critical of these vehicles. It was a postcard of a *caveirão*, with some cops beside it, though after discussions we decided to remove them. I was the editor at the time, and I wanted it to be very clear that the company manufacturing the *caveirões* was Ford. There was a giant Ford logo on the front. I said, 'Make the Ford logo really big so that everyone knows it's Ford helping to kill people in the favela. Or don't you think people should know that?' We had a really big fight at the paper. 'What about the Ford Foundation?' People said. 'They sponsor so much research … ' But that wasn't what mattered to me. What mattered was that Ford was helping with public security policies which were killing people in the favelas. So it needed to be on the cover. We put 'Ford' really big, and the caption read: 'Who's going to take your soul?'... That day, everyone went out distributing the paper. It sold out completely. Everyone wanted to talk about it. After all, they [the *caveirões*] were killing us.

The use of *caveirões*, excessive police and military force, and the frequent killing and wounding of innocent bystanders are all features of the so-called Police Pacification Units (UPPs) (see Chapter 8). But, as Renata argues:

The big drug dealers aren't in the favela. The drug dealers in the favela are just doing the retail. What's really behind this pacification, which claims it's the drugs that cause the violence? That's a big lie. The 'War on Drugs' is a lie. It's really a war on the poor.

Though *O Cidadão* is a printed publication, Latin America's journalists are increasingly turning to new forms of communication in order to denounce state violence of this kind and make their voices heard.

The new forms of journalism

The internet

The internet has transformed journalism, in Latin America as much as in Europe and the US. With the development of smartphones, even remote communities with no landline phones have acquired internet access. Unlike

236 VOICES OF LATIN AMERICA

printed newspapers, news websites can be created and maintained at minimal cost, and bulletin boards and blogs have given a voice to almost anyone
who chooses to express an opinion and report on what they witness. Amateur
video posting on platforms such as YouTube and Vimeo provides infinite free
or very low-cost opportunities for citizen and amateur newsreel coverage of
current events as they occur. And social media, in turn, have come to supple-
ment and replace both newspapers and news websites.

In 2015, 55 per cent of Latin Americans went online, a 20 per cent rise
from 2010. Of all households, 43 per cent were connected, a figure which
almost doubled from 2010, and will certainly have increased considerably
since. Access to mobile broadband connections increased even faster, surging
from 7 per cent to 58 per cent of the region's population in the same period
(Corona, 2016). The countries with highest access to the internet are Chile
and Uruguay, with more than 70 per cent, followed by Argentina, Puerto Rico,
Ecuador, Colombia, and Costa Rica (61–70 per cent). The countries with poorest access are El Salvador, Guatemala, and Honduras, at less than 40 per cent
(Tendencias Digitales, 2017). However, this still lags well behind, for example,
the UK, with approximately 90 per cent of households connected.

Despite this, Latin America has the highest social media usage in the world.
An average user spends four hours a day on social media (Komar, 2017).
Surprisingly, Paraguay has the highest social media penetration in the region
(83 per cent). Costa Rica was in second place (78 per cent) and Uruguay third
(74 per cent). However, 57 per cent of those social media users in Latin America
did not have enough to eat 'occasionally or often' in 2016, and 51 per cent did
not have running water in their homes (Marcial Pérez, 2016).

Honduras is one of the poorest countries in Latin America. Yet the educator, musician, and digital activist Pavel Núñez sees the same trends:

> From a historical and philosophical perspective, paper is becoming
> obsolete at the global level. It's become a sentimental thing. The reality
> is that all our young people inform themselves digitally, read digitally,
> write digitally. Nobody uses diaries or notebooks any more. As a teacher
> I see it myself, in my classes. It's much easier to set the students a task
> on Facebook than ask them to make photocopies. There's the issue of
> poverty as well, which is very serious amongst young people. So the dig-
> ital alternative has been taking over and we think it will only increase.

In Cuba, however, the state controls internet access and the high cost of time
online severely restricts usage, as Yuri Valle Roca reports:

> The internet brought positive changes. The government had to accept
> its introduction as it is considered a human right by the United Nations.
> But the Cuban government did not consider internet access to be
> a human right and so it controls it with an iron fist. It uses a Cuban
> server to control the flow of information and the websites that Cubans
> can access. It also uses it to hack and steal the personal information

Pavel Núñez, Honduras.

of opponents and independent journalists. The connection is very expensive and so is not accessible to people on low incomes; that is, the general public. The average monthly salary in Cuba is 350 pesos and an hour online costs 75 pesos. So either you connect or you eat.

News websites

The two most visited news websites in Spanish in the world are *El País* and *El Mundo* (both Spain), followed by *Clarín* and *La Nación* (both Argentina). *El País* also has a strong presence in Latin America and competes with local media there (El País, 2016). By number of webpages viewed, *Clarín* tops the list, with *El País* in second place and *Infobae* in third (Hadad, 2017).

With the internet has arrived a plethora of digital-only news websites: *Animal Político* (Mexico); *Agência Pública* (Brazil); *CIPER* and *The Clinic* (Chile); *El Faro* (El Salvador); *IDL Reporteros* (Peru); *La Silla Vacía* (Colombia); and *Plaza Pública* (Guatemala), to name just a few. These websites all belong to the ALiados network of independent digital media, formed in 2013 at a meeting in Buenos Aires (Animal Político, 2013).

Tania Montalvo describes the Mexican website she works for, *Animal Político*:

> *Animal Político* is a digital publication, the most important one in Mexico currently. It was one of the first to practise real journalism; it's not just a web page containing information or repeating what was published

in the newspapers. We started doing investigative work and it carries original information and content. It was born eight years ago on Twitter as @Pajaropolitico and a year later animalpolitico.com was born. Why did it first appear on Twitter? The founders – Daniel Eilemberg and Daniel Moreno, who is still our general director – wanted to create a digital media outlet.

Their first step was to exploit the social networks. This allowed the creation of a community, which remains a fundamental pillar of *Animal Político*, along with citizen dialogue. So, when the site was born, there was already a specific audience. Obviously, it was people with internet access who were interested in a political dialogue. What @Pajaropolitico started to do on Twitter was provide news but also to dialogue with the citizens. To respond and answer questions. This was the first Twitter account of a Mexican media outlet that wasn't automated. We have never automated our Twitter account, which is what most of the Mexican media do, especially the bigger outlets. It's now very common to have a community manager. When *Animal Político* started the job was called something else, but it's never been just some kid or student who does nothing but write the headlines. It's always been a journalist who understands the importance of citizen dialogue, and that's still the case today.

Social media and Facebook newspapers

In addition to news websites, activists are increasingly creating Facebook 'newspapers' dedicated to a particular country or issue. Libre, the political party created by supporters of the deposed Honduran president Manuel Zelaya, achieved the second-highest vote share in the 2013 first presidential election, the first in which it stood. Much of this success was down to innovative use of social media, as Pavel describes:

> Our problem was that in the run-up to the elections we didn't have any means of communication with which to do publicity and raise people's awareness. We had nothing. So the party realized that a social media campaign was the solution. Luckily, we had already created a platform. There was already a page for Libre and one for Xiomara Castro [Zelaya's wife and the Libre candidate in the 2013 elections], who was going to be the leader because she had led the movement in the streets ... I think it was the first political campaign of this type in Honduras, maybe even in Latin America, according to the measures and statistical indicators of social media use.
>
> In Honduras it's already spoken about philosophically as a fifth power, the fourth power being the traditional media, which are capable of installing and removing a president. But on social networks, for now, people are free and can protest. What level have we taken political activism to? Well, the level of educating people, teaching young people not

only how to use social networks technically, but how to communicate. They're learning about political ideology, in a country where university courses in political science don't exist, or at best it'll be a module on a social sciences course. Young people are now specializing. They are the specialists in this technology, not us in Generation X.

Young people are also starting to create their own newspapers, like *Notibomba* – which is on Facebook – with larger audiences than any current radio or TV programmes in Honduras. A single Facebook page. At my university we have seven newspapers, all on Facebook. Everyone in this country is in training, because they know how poor the traditional media is. Everyone has been trained to take out their phone immediately when they see something, some injustice, an instance of police brutality. People have lost their fear; they report it immediately on their Facebook page. More than a digital activism, I am talking about a new form of digital journalism born in Honduras, much faster than contemporary or traditional journalism. People know they have to record, report, edit. Not only is there no digital journalism degree at the National University of Honduras, there aren't even any classes on digital journalism on the journalism course.

The key, Pavel insists, is 'virality' – studying and understanding how and why certain news items on social media 'go viral':

This is not something that you can control; it happens spontaneously, like when someone posts a picture of a drunk or something and it suddenly becomes viral. It's not something that we can control, but it is something that we can study, find out what its characteristics are so we can recreate it.

How? It's easy. It depends on people who'll replicate it. We had people who were experts at this [in the media campaign for Libre] and we were able to make things go viral immediately. You just have to make sure they realize that [a particular piece of] news is important and they do the rest. When an activist is killed, it'll be all over social media and no one can say anything to anyone. [Libre's] was a hugely successful campaign, bearing in mind that this was done without any money, exclusively on social networks and despite all the censorship and the whole political and media apparatus of the right. Because they had hundreds of TV channels, radio stations, and newspapers, all fighting against this 'weak' social media strategy. So it was very successful.

In Brazil, in Rio de Janeiro, Renata da Silva Souza has researched the way young people from the favelas are using Facebook to chart police violence:

One example is called Maré Vive, a Facebook page created by young people from Maré. Some of them were already involved with communication in the community, and others with culture. They created this page in 2014 and in principle it was to cover the military occupation of

Maré [in 2014 and 2015, before, during, and after the World Cup] and resistance to it. It ended up showing how the occupation was actually much less successful than the newspapers were reporting. It became a page of counter-information – counter-hegemony, as it were – showing a different version of events, a different point of view of the occupation.

In Cuba, Yuri Valle Roca lists the social media he uses: a blog, YouTube, Tumblr, Twitter, Facebook, Google+, Instagram, and Flipagram. But because of the limitations on internet access, much material has to be distributed on memory sticks passed from person to person:

It's the only way of doing it. If the political police catch anyone doing it, they are punished and taken to prison. They are accused of terrorism, sedition, or whatever the police feel like. They charge them with criminal offences so that they are not recognized as political prisoners.

Twitter and 'fake news'

However, it is not only progressive political parties and social movements who are taking advantage of social media. In Chile, Sebastián Piñera used social media to devastating effect in the 2017 election campaign, to warn voters of the dangers of 'Chilezuela' if they voted for his centre-left opponent.

In Honduras, as Pavel reports, there has been a sophisticated use of call centres, 'fake news', and Twitter accounts aimed at discrediting Libre and progressive policies. This is digital warfare:

The oligarchy and the right know this [the power of the internet and digital media], which is why they're getting involved in this world. Not in the professional way that we are, but by playing dirty. There's the issue of the call centres, which here aren't used by companies, they're used by bad politicians to discredit, attack, and run hate and smear campaigns against communicators and political activists.

They hire 100 people, but instead of answering the phone they have a computer with internet access 24 hours a day. Each employee creates up to 50 false accounts. They then write a single tweet, and using software, these 50 false accounts immediately retweet it. This creates a chain reaction which ensures that the president is always the most discussed topic in the country. They steal photos of people from other countries for these fake accounts. We've contacted people from Venezuela who have had their photos stolen; there are people from Mexico who have denounced the government of Honduras. They use these accounts to pose as impartial people and to hack the accounts of the opposition. You can see that they don't agree with what we're doing. We did a study a year and a half ago with a group in Barcelona called Hondurans in Spain, who do work on cybernetics. We discovered more than 5,000 fake accounts on Twitter. Today we think there are more than 10,000 …

And now on Facebook they're creating a lot of fake newspapers. One example is *Nos Queda Claro*, which, thanks to advanced IT techniques, we know is the work of these same call centres. That's where they launch all the hate and smear campaigns against communicators and activists. What type of hate campaign? Well, they publish photos of people like me and say, 'We ask all nationalists, if you see these people in the street, then give them a beating, give them what they deserve – even kill them.' This is what we're up against in the digital war. Or articles in newspapers where we're accused of being terrorists – media terrorists – for reporting this type of thing and for being in the vanguard of digital educative and political processes that really work. Not because we have call centres, because we don't have the money to pay even two people to do that.

Pavel is quite pessimistic, seeing the present moment as a relatively brief phase before powerful state and commercial actors take control of the internet and digital media:

But now that they've passed the Stop Online Piracy Act (SOPA) in the United States, the internet's not the same. It's not the infinite universe it used to be, to which we had access for a couple of years. Pages can be closed down now for copyright infringement and that kind of thing. And I think that right-wing governments, the oligarchies, the enemies of the people, now understand that these are areas they have to control. I predict that within two or three years there'll be a new beginning – social networks will become traditional media. In other words, social networks will still be places 'where we can all talk', but there will be five media outlets which produce all the viral news. The rich aren't stupid. Right now, [the social networks] are free for us, but it's a universe of potential for advertising and political marketing. So I don't think we have much time to make use of this tool.

YouTube is such a powerful tool. I call it the great free university the world has right now, collective too, like Wikipedia. In the case of Wikipedia, it destroyed Oceano, Microsoft Encarta, and all the other encyclopedias written by an individual or a group of people. Wikipedia is written, corrected, and censored by the whole global community. It won't last forever, which is why I insist that we use these tools immediately and make use of this great weapon that our generation has. We're the first generation in the history of the world that has access to global knowledge, but since SOPA it's been increasingly restricted. They're going to privatize YouTube, it's going to become like Netflix, where you have to pay for a subscription. Facebook will go the same way and we'll have to look for other solutions. That's evolution, things change, things are never static.

Community radio

Latin America has a long tradition of independent and community radio stations, a vital tool with which to reach remote communities where printed media has little penetration, given that levels of literacy are often low and local people sometimes speak indigenous languages. Community radio stations combine well with use of smartphones and social networks, both for collecting and transmitting news, as Pavel describes:

I've been working a lot with community radio stations in the interior of Honduras since the coup d'état. There are areas with indigenous villages which use community radio a lot. To overcome the obstacle of the traditional media, what we're trying to do is to unite these two communications, so information on social networks somehow reaches community radio stations and can be replicated. It's the social networks that are the primary source of information. There you have the direct words of Xiomara Castro and not what some press baron is saying about her in his newspaper.

We train someone up in a community and help them at least to get a mobile phone, so they can replicate news taken from Facebook, or from someone in a neighbouring community. We try to establish links with these people, so they can then broadcast this news on the community radio stations. We are trying to bring this fifth power to areas where there may not even be any access to electricity or drinking water. The oral tradition in Honduras is very powerful and this is something we're conscious of. Getting a piece of news to one person is enough to ensure that the whole community is informed.

Radio is still the most popular form of communication. In every village in Honduras someone will have a battery radio. I can't say that we reach 100 per cent of the population, but we do at least cover a decent part of it. We've reached something like three million people through social networks. There are politicians who travel out to those places to inform people. We also hold assemblies, which people from these communities can attend and then take the news back home with them.

Miryam Vargas Teutle describes the evolution of Radio Axocotzin in Tlaxcalancingo, Puebla, south-east of Mexico City:

I was born in a small village with a close-knit community. This changed dramatically when the Periférico Ecológico was built: a bypass going right around Puebla and straight through our neighbourhood … The whole neighbourhood had a completely different feel – it wasn't safe any more: kids couldn't play in the street, people didn't go out as much and there wasn't any land to grow crops.

The idea of community radio started around this time. You see, in the early nineties we still used loudspeakers set up in public spaces to spread important news across the neighbourhood. When the Zapatista uprising happened in 1994 there was some support for them, especially amongst indigenous people. They played Zapatista songs on the loudspeakers in the barrio San Diego here in Tlaxcalancingo and there was some graffiti saying 'VIVA EZLN!' ['Long live the Zapatista National Liberation Army!'] Then the state army turned up. Everyone was shocked because it seemed like a total overreaction, but it did get people thinking about community radio and about our right to express ourselves. We wanted a voice.

The problem was we didn't really know anything about starting a radio station. There was an FM transmitter in the community centre where the project was based so we thought we'd use that. In the end, though, we decided against it and opted for a combination of an internet broadcast that was repeated through loudspeakers – one in each of our six barrios – it was only later, in 2011, that we finally transferred to FM.

My main job was sourcing the basic equipment for our radio studio: a computer, speakers, anything technical like that. I was involved in the programmes too. I loved getting out into the community to report on stories about local traditions. *La Revista* was really important for stories about everyday life in the community. It ran lots of social interest features and it was also where any problems in the community could be highlighted and talked about.

'Air, Land and Freedom' demonstration about broadcasting freedom for Radio Axocotzin and sister station Radio Zacatepec.

Three thousand people gathered in the town's main plaza for our inauguration in January 2009. Of course, we needed a name to open with, and originally we were Radio Tlaxcalancingo, but we wanted the community to give us our name. In October, when Xochipitzahuac [the Festival of Indian Peoples] came around, we did a poll and the people chose the name Radio Axocotzin. The festival was started by our community to reassert its indigenous identity and Axocotzin is one of the four *cerritos* [small volcanic peaks] that surround Tlaxcalancingo, so this is how our community radio station was born: by a popular vote, naming it after the land it represents.

Collaboration

Digital communication relies upon – and has multiplied opportunities for – supportive collaboration between journalists within countries and abroad, as Tania Montalvo of *Animal Político* emphasizes:

Doing collaborative journalism is very important in Mexico. La Estafa [La Estafa Maestra – The Great Fraud – an investigation into a US$450 m corruption scheme in the granting of public contracts], for example, was a collaborative project. We worked with another organization called Mexicanos Contra la Corrupción, and in addition, it was published in at least 10 different outlets in the local, national, and international media, including the Spanish newspaper *El País*. At the moment, I am coordinating a media network. The aim is not just to do collaborative work, but to create a network of different outlets which can all publish simultaneously. The reason for this is that if any outlet – including *Animal Político* – publishes an investigation alone, the authorities normally manage to ensure that it gets ignored, and they can count on the complicity of the big national media outlets. The strategy is to silence it. But this media network ... means that there are lots of us all publishing the same investigation, and as a result it reaches more people, it reaches different audiences, and of course it makes more noise.

This is what the Estafa Maestra achieved. It was published by *VICE News*, *Huffington Post*, *Buzzfeed*, and *El País*. I gave them the entire investigation – word for word – four days before publication. It was up to them if they wanted to publish the whole thing or just some of it. The Estafa Maestra was published on the front page of the *Diário de Yucatán*, which covers the Yucatán Peninsula in the south-east of the country. It was published in the newspaper *ABC* in the north of the country. From north to south, we had allies that published it. We've done the same thing with other investigations and we realize this strengthens us as a profession. That's why I'm creating this network, and we hope to build on it in 2018 and make it stronger still.

But journalists also need to work together for their own protection, Tania says:

> We are seeing violence and aggression against journalists increase
> and this is a direct result of the culture of impunity in Mexico, which
> includes not just homicide but all crime. It's very difficult to change this.
> On the other hand, I also believe that within the profession, journalists
> are making alliances and working together to improve things, across
> the board. This is something we are doing at *Animal Político*, but so are
> local organizations in the states, of which there are more all the time.
> Seriously, working together protects you a lot.

Patricia Mayorga agrees:

> In Mexico and Latin America we are seeing the emergence of collectives
> and more investigative journalists, which is very encouraging. There are
> more and more young people involved as well as others who aren't so
> young. Independent collectives of journalists in several states with hori-
> zontal structures have also formed, for protection. This has been critical.
> In my case and for a small group of us, though this is by no means true
> for everyone, the support of the profession has been crucial. It gives us
> hope, it gives us strength, it gives us direction. We know that if some-
> thing happens, others will carry on after us. After what happened to
> Miroslava, Javier Valdez, and other journalists, we are stronger, and we
> will carry on with their work. Journalism is unstoppable.
>
> The support of networks has been critical in combating the individ-
> ualism of the profession. It can be very lonely. Bringing about more
> collaborative journalism in Mexico has been a big step. It's happening at
> a global level too, with the publication of the Panama Papers and other
> collective journalistic projects. I think that this is crucial for journalism,
> not just in Mexico, but in Latin America and other countries too.

The Panama Papers are a vast tranche of financial and legal documents from
offshore legal firm Mossack Fonseca, leaked and published simultaneously in
2016 by newspapers in a number of countries, coordinated by the International
Consortium of Investigative Journalists (ICIJ). The papers revealed details of
tax evasion, corruption, and money laundering by leading politicians, their
families, and wealthy associates in more than a dozen countries.

For many journalists, however, international recognition and collaboration
is even more vital because it affords them a degree of protection. Patricia was
helped by the New York-based Committee to Protect Journalists (CPJ):

> They intervened when I didn't want to leave Chihuahua, when I had the
> security detail. They got involved in investigating the risk, and tried to
> make that as clear as possible, so that I would decide to leave. I wanted
> to keep working. I didn't want to be defeated. They sorted everything out
> with *Proceso*, took all the necessary security measures and gave me all the
> psychological support I needed. They took care of everything. CPJ has

given me total and unconditional freedom in my decisions. They were the ones who paid for my ticket to Peru and supported me over the six months I stayed there. I had the opportunity to recover, thanks to them, because they created the platform for me to do so and provided me with the basic support I needed. I carried on working. I went with my daughter and we were safe. I got stronger: emotionally, mentally, professionally.

Now it's the people who are making the news

News websites, blogs, community radio: all make use of social media to collect and disseminate information, to use untold numbers of 'citizen reporters', and to attract vast audiences. Hand in hand with smartphones, which provide internet access where telephone landlines may be lacking, social media have revolutionized access to information and social and political activism. Latest-generation smartphones provide every user with a camera that can take good-quality photos and video. A quick search on YouTube will provide video footage of almost every social movement action and event in the region, most of it filmed and uploaded by demonstrators, strikers, and community members. As Pavel Núñez says:

> The problem isn't the media, who has access or not. It's about who is telling the news ... The popular voice, the oral tradition in Honduras and Latin America, is still very powerful and will expand. In social media this is a great advantage ... The analysis of social media goes beyond just possession; it's about the first-ever breach of the media monopoly. Now it's the people who are making the news, we are communicating between ourselves.

About the author

Mike Gatehouse lived in Chile in 1972-3 and worked for 15 years in London for Latin America solidarity and human rights organizations. Co-author of LAB's *Soft Drink, Hard Labour - Guatemalan workers take on Coca Cola* and *In the Mountains of Morazán - Portrait of a returned refugee community in El Salvador*, he is an editor at LAB.

Interviews

Carlos Correa (Espacio Público): interviewed via Skype on 1 February 2018 by Tom Gatehouse. Translated by Matty Rose.

Patricia Mayorga (*Proceso*): interviewed on 23 February 2018 by Tom Gatehouse. Translated by Theo Bradford.

Tania Montalvo (*Animal Político*): interviewed via Skype on 26 January 2018 by Tom Gatehouse. Translated by Shareen Patel.

Pavel Núñez (Honduran educator, musician, and digital activist): interviewed in Tegucigalpa on 24 October and 2 November 2016 by Louise Morris. Translated by Louise Morris.

Renata da Silva Souza (former journalist at *O Cidadão* and communications specialist at the Universidade Federal do Rio de Janeiro (UFRJ)): interviewed in Rio de Janeiro on 1 February 2018 by Jennifer Chisholm. Translated by Hugo Moss.

Yuri Valle Roca (Cuban blogger): interviewed via email on 19 February 2018 by Louise Morris. Translated by Chris Whitehouse.

Miryam Vargas Teutle (Radio Comunitaria Cholollan): interviewed in Tlaxcalancingo, Mexico, on 2 March 2017 by Francesco di Bernardo. Translated by Hebe Powell.

References

NB: All web references were checked and still available in May/June 2018 unless otherwise stated. All references are listed, with web-links, on the page for this chapter on the Voices website www.vola.org.uk

Ahmed, A. (2017) 'Using billions in government cash, Mexico controls news media', *New York Times*, 25 December, <https://www.nytimes.com/2017/12/25/world/americas/mexico-press-government-advertising.html>

Animal Político (2013) 'Nace ALiados, red de medios digitales de América Latina', 20 June, <https://www.animalpolitico.com/2013/06/nace-la-red-de-medios-digitales-independientes>

Corona, S. (2016) 'Latin America and Caribbean see sharp rise in internet use', *El País*, 13 September, <https://elpais.com/elpais/2016/09/13/inenglish/1473774348_614340.html>

CPJ (2015) '452 journalists forced into exile since 2010', Committee to Protect Journalists (CPJ), <https://cpj.org/exile>

CPJ (2018) 'Explore CPJ's database of attacks on the press', <https://cpj.org/data/killed/?status=Killed&motiveConfirmed%5B%5D=Confirmed&type%5B%5D=Journalist&start_year=1992&end_year=2018&group_by=year>

El País (2016) 'EL PAÍS, el periódico digital en español más leído del mundo', 23 November, <https://elpais.com/elpais/2016/11/22/actualidad/1479853627_478107.html>

Freedom House (2015) 'Freedom of the Press 2015: Venezuela', <https://freedomhouse.org/report/freedom-press/2015/venezuela>

Hadad, D. (2017) 'Infobae en el podio de los medios en español más leídos del mundo', *Infobae*, <https://www.infobae.com/noticias/2017/02/06/infobae-en-el-podio-de-los-medios-en-espanol-mas-leidos-del-mundo>

Komar, M. (2017) 'Why Latin America is the "next great advertising ecosystem"', PerformanceIN, 3 July, <https://performancein.com/news/2017/07/03/why-latin-america-next-great-advertising-ecosystem>

Kornbluh, P. (2003) *The Pinochet File: A Declassified Dossier on Atrocity and Accountability*, National Security Archive, The New Press, New York, NY.

Macqueen, A. (2017) 'Javier Valdez: brave, brilliant casualty of Mexico's dirty war', *The Guardian*, 20 May, <https://www.theguardian.com/commentisfree/2017/may/20/javier-valdez-murdered-journalist-mexico-dirty-war>

Marcial Pérez, D. (2016) 'Half of social media users in Latin America have gone hungry in last year', *El País*, 30 December, <https://elpais.com/elpais/2016/12/30/inenglish/1483103018_460394.html>

Mioli, T. (2017) 'Despite global decreases in journalists' murders, press advocates report record numbers of journalists killed in Mexico', Knight Center for Journalism in the Americas, <https://knightcenter.utexas.edu/blog/00-19120-despite-global-decreases-journalists%E2%80%99-murders-press-advocates-report-record-numbers-jo>

Souza, A., Oliveira, G., Pinto, P.C., Conceição, W. and Mattos, S. (2011) 'Análise do debate editado pela Rede Globo no segundo turno das eleições presidenciais de 1989', Intercom – Sociedade Brasileira de Estudos Interdisciplinares da Comunicação, XXXIV Congresso Brasileiro de Ciências da Comunicação, Recife, 2–6 September 2011, <https://www.scribd.com/doc/65964376/Analise-do-debate-editado-pela-rede-globo-nas-eleicoes-presidenciais-de-1989>

Tendencias Digitales (2017) 'La evolución de los usos de Internet en Latinoamérica', <https://tendenciasdigitales.com/evolucion-usos-de-internet-latam>

Villegas, P. (2018) 'Mexico moves to regulate government ads. Critics say it's a sham', *New York Times*, 15 April, <https://www.nytimes.com/2018/04/15/world/americas/mexico-government-advertising-enrique-pena-nieto.html>

Zenith (2017) 'Top 30 global media owners 2017', Zenith ROI Agency, 9 June, <https://www.zenithusa.com/top-30-global-media-owners-2017>

CHAPTER 11
Cultural resistance

Louise Morris

Abstract

Art is flourishing in Latin America and has increasingly engaged with struggles for equality, group identity, justice, and memory. Music, graffiti, and memorial art provide alternative means of expression to those mandated by mainstream media, rescuing the past and helping people to construct identities for the future. Culture also provides a space for thought and discussion of some of the most contentious social issues.

At the 10th Havana Biennial (2009), Cuban artist Tania Bruguera invited audience members to speak freely for a minute each. One said she wished freedom of speech in Cuba did not have to be a performance. When Bruguera attempted to restage this performance in Havana's Revolution Square in 2014 she was arrested before it could take place and held for three days.

It is shocking that in Cuba people cannot freely and openly discuss the issues that affect their lives. Even worse is that when, in a performance, an artist provides them with the opportunity to do so, she should be targeted. But it highlights the important role subversive art plays: providing a means of expression, a lens to hold up to society, and a language in which to denounce inequality and injustice.

Latin American culture, in all its forms, is world famous for its richness and diversity. It is no wonder that, given the intense social injustice across the region, art has stepped up, filling the gap that the often more elite-controlled mainstream media has left, to critique, provide alternative perspectives, and ensure more equal representation. Closely related to activism and campaigns for social justice, art is a vital conduit for political expression and is prominent in strikes, occupations, and other forms of political action.

Engaged art often works on the periphery, avoiding the prescribed narratives of its time. This explains why artists have been singled out for repression by those in power. Chilean theatre director and folk singer Víctor Jara was executed by the Chilean Pinochet dictatorship within days of the military coup in September 1973. The similar military dictatorship in Uruguay (1973–85) imprisoned multidisciplinary artist Clemente Padín, from August 1977 to November 1979. More recently, Salvadorean performance artist Víctor 'Crack' Rodríguez was threatened with six years in prison for eating half of

http://dx.doi.org/10.3362/9781909014213.011

his ballot in front of polling station onlookers during the country's 2014 elections, before casting the remaining half. News of his action, designed to question the relationship between power and hunger, went viral within hours. He avoided prison but was placed under house arrest until after the elections.

Nevertheless, Latin American governments often promote art and support artists. Chilean artists were sometimes given minor diplomatic postings to enable them to travel abroad. The poet Pablo Neruda, for example, was Chile's consul successively in Burma, Buenos Aires, Madrid, and Mexico, which did not preclude him being made an outlaw after 1948 by the government of Gabriel González Videla.

Some of the region's most famous examples of socially critical art are those that became mainstream, nationally supported art movements, such as Mexican muralism in the late 1920s and the Cuban music style of *nueva trova* in the late 1960s.

Whether art that is state-supported can ever be truly critical or free is a contentious issue. Cuban artists have been allowed access to the international art market and to travel, at least since 1993, but can art maintain its power to protest when it is supported by the very regime it serves to criticize? If the artists are given opportunities and freedoms not available to the average citizen, this tends to alienate them from the people they wish to represent and defend.

This chapter focuses on four strands of socially and politically engaged art: music, graffiti, memorial art, and theatre of memory.

Music

There is a rich tradition in Latin America of music which expresses the critical voices of the people. The best-known examples are *nueva trova* in Cuba and Nicaragua, *nueva canción* in Chile, Peru, Bolivia, and Argentina, and *tropicália* in Brazil, as well as other protest rock and punk bands of the 1960s and 1970s. Café Guancasco in Honduras became popularly known as the 'band of the resistance' for their activism and central role in the opposition to the 2009 coup in Honduras (see box in Chapter 2).

Of course, it is not only through lyrics that music can be dissident – simply creating something to dance to as a release during difficult times could be considered a political act. The Mexican dance genre of *ruidosón* emerged from the crime-torn Tijuana of the late 2000s, blending traditional sounds with techno and a gothic aesthetic, which expressed the horror and violence of this dark period in the city's history.

Socially engaged music is found in every genre, with ever more intriguing fusions of styles, from reggaeton to samba to dubstep. There has also been a recent increase in the representation of Afro-Latin, feminist, queer, transgender, immigrant, and indigenous identities through musical reinventions and fusions, as well as lyrics which explore topics such as environmentalism, corruption, and organized crime. The Colombian fusion band Systema Solar even has a song 'Yo Voy Ganao' in praise of local fishing culture in the village of Tapanga, which is threatened by an influx of tourism to the Caribbean coast.

Recently Latin American musicians have been looking back through musical history, to recognize or reinterpret genres that were previously over-looked by society because they were associated with marginalized groups: in Colombia, for example, *cumbia* was the music of the poor, *champeta* that of groups of African descent. Music labels are releasing compilations of forgotten gems (sometimes provoked by international interest), contemporary bands play older rhythms or create new fusions, and DJs and producers sample classic vinyl. Aside from the love of 'discovering' new music and giving great older artists their dues, this trend is perhaps motivated by the nostalgia of Latin America's vast diaspora. As the legendary Afro-Colombian singer Totó la Momposina states about cumbia:

> In Colombia we don't hear this kind of music on the radio. When people leave our country and hear this music, they start crying because it's like a call. In that moment they recognize this type of music and rhythm and develop a love for it. Sometimes [they] ask why people from other countries accept cumbia more than we do.

There were times when popular pan-Latin genres such as cumbia expressed the social reality of the working class. Peruvian *cumbia chicha*, a blend of cumbia with psychedelic guitars, Andean *huayno* melodies, bittersweet lyrics, and rock and roll swagger, was created by the Andean immigrants who flooded Lima in the 1970s. These indigenous migrants faced extreme racism and were pejoratively referred to as *cholos*. The quintessential *cumbia chicha* song, 'Soy provinciano', by Chacalón y La Nueva Crema, says:

> I am a boy from the provinces,
> I wake up very early
> to go with my brothers, ayayay,
> to work ...
> seeking a new life in this city, ah,
> where everything is money and there is evil.
> With the help of God we will triumph.

Later, in a Buenos Aires crippled by the economic crisis of 1998–2002, a more brash cumbia fusion exploded from the *villas miseria*, the city's poorest neighbourhoods. It was characterized by brassy keyboards and social realist lyrics about people shoplifting food, taking drugs, and going to prison. Of course, the genre's association with the working class meant that it was frequently considered tacky and of no cultural value by the mainstream and was censored by some broadcasters.

In the past decade or so there has been a cumbia renaissance, with a wave of bands fusing the genre with everything from dancehall to rock to electronic music, assisted by strong interest from Europe and North America. Cumbia can now be heard in some of Latin America's most exclusive clubs, and it remains a staple at weddings. Yet a tension exists between the adoption of cumbia by the privileged and its humble origins. In the genre's supposed birthplace, Colombia, there are only a few bands actively promoting cumbia. Urián Sarmiento, musician and founder of Sonidos Enraizados, who promote and rescue traditional Colombian music, explains:

> The cumbia movement exists more outside the country than within it. Here there are some special cases, mainly in Bogotá and Medellín. Los Piranas, Meridian Brothers, Ondatrópica, they are the cumbia fighters here. You also have Pernett and Systema Solar in the Caribbean cities. You can't generally find cumbia nights here in Colombia. It's only this local hipster movement in Bogotá who put the word 'cumbia' on their flyers, CDs, vinyl, and social media.

In Argentina, *cumbia villera* has been widely embraced by the mainstream: glamorously dressed youth dance under ultraviolet lights to *villera's* keyboard stabs in the fashionable Buenos Aires neighbourhood of Palermo. Yet a different type of socially engaged cumbia is currently being created in the *villas*. Villa Isla Maciel is a neighbourhood clustered around the docks in Avellaneda, in Greater Buenos Aires. It is separated from the city proper by the Riachuelo river, over which there is a formidably high metal bridge, from which the local band Los del Puente (Those of the Bridge) take their name.

> My name is Iván Brasil. I'm in a cumbia band called Los del Puente, who are from here, La Isla Maciel. I've lived here my whole life. We've been playing together for eight years. We make cumbia fused with rock and the lyrics and themes of the songs are social issues, the social reality in which we live. You've noticed there's a lot of poverty, a lot of drugs in this area; we try to solve this a little. For example, we play songs that talk about the reality of the *cartoneros* – the people who collect cardboard in the street – the reality of the politicians who rob indiscriminately, the police who don't act and rob indiscriminately. We're in a place where the police guard the doors of the drug dealers – I know, because I've seen it.
>
> We make our music for people to identify with. We aim to create rich songs with positive lyrics but also to transmit the happiness that is cumbia. I think that nowadays cumbia is bypassing some barriers – it is reaching people of much higher social class. But it belongs to the poor. When this music reaches the upper classes, they just dance for joy, nothing more; it doesn't seem to me that there's a change in perspective, or only occasionally.
>
> Prejudice against cumbia has always existed and continues to exist. I've experienced it a lot. For example, I was talking with the mayor of this Villa, and I said I have my cumbia band and I want to play in a plaza, or something like that, and he said, 'Cumbia – no, it will attract a lot of vagrants.' Towards rock bands they don't have this prejudice, but cumbia is a genre that comes from the humblest barrios.

Like cumbia, rap, hip hop, and *baile funk* have, at times, faced prejudice for their supposed association with the urban poor or crime. Reggaeton, which was once a stigmatized and persecuted genre for its identification with Afro-Latin culture (Cepeda, 2018), is now being appropriated by pop stars like Justin Bieber. Reggaeton's immense popularity in Latin America ensures that its distinctive 'bom-ba-da-bom-ba' rhythm is never far away. Now, a huge pan-Afro-Latin music movement is gaining ground, with artists like Brazilian rapper Rincon Sapiência and labels like the Cuban Guampara promoting black solidarity and the reclamation of African roots.

Meanwhile, genres like hip hop, rap, and reggaeton continue to express marginal identities and discourses, from feminist, to indigenous, to queer. In Brazil, transgender singer Linn da Quebrada reclaims Brazil's popular urban music *baile funk* for marginalized groups, her songs and provocative performances promoting a radical queer perspective and trans rights. She teases and mocks the audience in 'Enviadescer', with her lyrics: 'I'll speak more slowly to see if you can understand / If you wanna be with me, boy / You'll have to get faggier!' This is courageous in a country where the average life expectancy of a trans woman is half that of a cis person.

In Guatemala hip hop remains a relatively underground musical genre, yet it has been used to encourage young people to learn or retain their indigenous languages and to take pride in their indigenous identity by infusing it with contemporary popular culture. Hip hop groups such as Balam Ajpu rap in the Mayan language of Tz'utujil and reference Maya spirituality in their lyrics. Similar efforts have been made by artists like the Mapuche hip hop star Luanko in Chile, Los Nin in Ecuador, who rap in Kichwa, and the Tzotzil-Maya rock band Vayijel in Mexico.

Although not Maya herself, Guatemalan Rebeca Lane has been a champion for indigenous rights, as well as feminism and LGBTI rights, through her infectious, critical raps. She is a central figure in the Guatemalan hip hop scene and has also gained international recognition. In Rebeca's track 'Bandera Negra' she riffs on *tener huevos,* the Spanish slang for being brave or 'having balls': 'Tengo millones de huevos en cada ovario / No me hace más mujer ni a vos te hace menos macho' ('I've got millions of eggs in each ovary / It doesn't make me more of a woman or you less of a man'). She explains her motivation:

> I started doing poetry and spoken word several years ago. I realized I was a feminist, so my poetry related a lot to my experience as a woman becoming liberated in a conservative society. Hip hop as a culture caught my attention when I started getting involved in street activism, because it was a music that expressed what we wanted to express politically through art. I joined a hip hop radio station with a programme called 'Politically Incorrect', and there I began to interact more with rappers. Then I started writing poetry with a rap basis. I never really thought that people would like my songs so much. I started writing about what moves me – my rap is feminist because I am a feminist. Along the way,

I saw the need for rappers to organize and think about our rights
as women within a culture that is
dominated by men. Recently I've
been working with other women
in hip hop in Central America and
Mexico.

© Rebeca Lane

Rebeca Lane.

I consider myself an 'artivist',
that is, my activism is through art,
in this case music. It is a powerful
tool because it enters the body and not just the mind. The power that
music has to mobilize us is fundamental for struggles, especially for
young people.

Currently I consider myself bisexual; however, I have some differences between the theory and my way of living and experiencing it in
the Latin American context.

Women who make rap in Central America and other parts of Latin
America are not part of commercial music culture because we use this
musical genre to criticize patriarchy and we deliberately avoid sexualiz-
ing our bodies to express ourselves and get attention.

Another rapper who promotes gender and sexual rights is the Argentine
Chocolate Remix, who has subverted reggaeton's frequent homophobic and
macho content and uses it instead to confront taboos of lesbian sex and
female pleasure. Costa Rican rapper Macha Kiddo recently reacted to an
increase in right-wing and discriminatory rhetoric by dropping her single
'Jony (La Romi)', aiming to skewer 'the societal insecurities that drive people towards hatred' (Villegas, 2018). The 2018 election campaign of defeated
conservative evangelical pastor Fabricio Alvarado Muñoz 'mocked and condemned abortion, same-sex marriage, and secular sex education in schools'
(Villegas, 2018). The song, which describes the quest of a trans woman (La
Romi) to survive and maintain dignity in her daily life, condemns prejudice
and stereotypes.

Music can also play a direct, visible role in protest. In demonstrations in
Venezuela, young violinist Wuilly Arteaga bravely stands and plays, to ease
tensions, in the no man's land between protesters' barricades and heavily
armed riot police. His violin has become a symbol of peace in the often violent
protests: 'When I play for the national guard, some of them listen to me, some
of them cry. And when I play for the protesters, it gives them motivation to
keep going ... I know my music creates a climate of peace, which is why I'll
continue playing on the streets of Venezuela' (Sanchez, 2017). Of course he
does not always succeed: in May 2017 a national guardsman on a motorcycle
dragged Wuilly to the ground and broke his violin. The video of him crying
over his instrument went viral, and violin donations came flooding in, including one from Colombian pop star Shakira.

Musicians remain determined to challenge the most contentious topics and prejudices in their societies. Their critical lyrics and stances prove that celebrating and enjoying music can itself be a form of protest.

Graffiti

Political graffiti is everywhere in Latin America. Mass demonstrations leave an echo reverberating across the walls – slogans that inform the public of current struggles and grievances – while criticisms and statements furtively scrawled up at night confront passers-by the next morning. But they have competition: walls are also painted by political parties, commercial advertisers, and simply for aesthetic effect.

Graffiti is usually defined as aerosol-sprayed slogans and tags, often associated with gangs and vandalism, and it is contrasted with street art, which is considered more aesthetic – paintings, stencils, and paste-ups that do not usually convey political messages, or do so in less obvious ways. Yet many artists who create what is termed 'street art' choose to define their work as graffiti. In this chapter the terms are used interchangeably.

Popular in Latin America for at least 25 years, street art has really exploded in the last decade, with several countries and cities gaining international reputations: in Brazil, São Paulo and Rio de Janeiro; in Chile, Santiago and Valparaíso; in Argentina, Buenos Aires; in Colombia, Bogotá and Medellín; and in Mexico, Mexico City, Monterrey, Guadalajara, Tijuana, and Mexicali, among many others. In fact, graffiti is everywhere in Latin America and the virtuosic talent of its practitioners attracts visitors and fellow artists from around the world.

Street art's legal status seems porous and varies widely from country to country, city to city, and with each ruling political party or mayor. In Quito, graffitiing can result in a week in jail and being ordered to pay the costs of repairing the damage. In contrast, in Bogotá, graffiti was decriminalized after the police shot dead Diego Felipe Becerra, a 16-year-old street artist. In Mexico it is generally legal with the permission of the building's owner.

Recognizing the positive potential of graffiti and street art, many cities have legalized spraying in designated areas. However, this is seen by many artists as an attempt to control and neutralize something which relies on defiance. This issue is similar to the question raised earlier: can art that is state-supported ever be truly critical? Run-down neighbourhoods are becoming gentrified partly because upmarket buyers are attracted to the street artists' vibrant work, as in Barrio Puerto and Polanco in Valparaíso, Chile. The most blatant example is the fashionable, upmarket neighbourhood of Palermo in Buenos Aires, where many businesses pay for street artists to paint murals on their façades.

In spite of this, graffiti remains a powerful tool for social change. Street art projects across the continent have been founded in some of the region's poorest neighbourhoods and have achieved impressive transformations. These projects often have several main objectives: beautifying poor, violent, and subsequently marginalized neighbourhoods to improve public perception; generating local pride and identity; and providing an alternative activity to gang membership, crime, and violence by teaching locals to work together on community projects.

One of these community projects has been operating in Comuna 13 in Medellín. The infamous Comuna was once one of the most violent places in Latin America, the battleground of narcotraffickers – most famously Pablo Escobar – the military, and paramilitaries. Perched on a hill overlooking the city, it was a settlement largely of families displaced by violence elsewhere in the country due to the civil war. Majestic views from the Comuna's highpoint take in Medellín's sprawl, while the cultural centre Casa Kolacho sits below. Rapper and graffiti artist El Zorro describes their work:

My name is Manuel Carrasquilla, they know me as El Zorro [The Fox] and I'm part of Casa Kolacho, an artists' collective which is working not only to present an alternative image but has also been trying to do something different for various years in communities affected by violence like Comuna 13. The media for many years spoke about the level of violence in the city and always pointed the finger at Comuna 13. People from outside the barrio would accuse us of being guerrillas or militia because we came from Comuna 13, even though we were living peacefully. We're trying to foster hope and our dream is to make social transformations.

Graffiti started as something with a low profile. Graffiti has been here since the 1980s – I grew up seeing this and it got me into hip hop. When the violence was very heavy, it had a big impact on the art and disrupted it, as well as the movement. It can be very dangerous and risky. There have been times when we've received threats or some *compañeros* have been murdered – but it wasn't enough reason to stop.

A lot of people – not just the rappers – left names of armed groups on the walls. If you crossed out the name of an armed group you risked death. But the beautiful thing was that when we started doing graffiti about it, drawings and paintings, people started asking for it. The armed groups didn't bother us because the letters were pretty. There's a wave of super-happy people because the graffiti beautifies the neighbourhood. We also paint murals which recognize and record our history and what happened in Comuna 13 – so it's not repeated. But we don't do this just to remember the pain, the sting of history and its sadness. We do it to look at how people learned how to overcome their circumstances. All of this generates a mentality of change and creates something positive – which is attitude and action.

Now, in this tense moment of peace that we are implementing in the city, many people can now go out of their neighbourhoods, women are happy their kids can leave the neighbourhood and not be murdered. There isn't a stigma about being from Comuna 13 like before, now it's

Manuel Carrasquilla.

like a status symbol, like 'Look, that guy is from Comuna 13!' It's a neighbourhood where people work very hard, on the minimum wage, and
[people will say,] 'Look at this worker who is managing to lift himself
and his family out of miserable circumstances.' There's still narcotrafficking, delinquency, extortion, but we've now earned some respect on
the social level – because they've seen that our work isn't just words, it's
deeds, and that we have done things that benefit the community. So the
mother of a gang member will explain to her son the benefits of living
in a pleasant neighbourhood, and the tranquillity – it touches them, it
touches them!

A similar initiative is being undertaken in Villa Isla Maciel on the outskirts of
Buenos Aires, home of the singer Iván Brasil we spoke to earlier. Artist Brian
Sánchez helps to run a project called Pintó La Isla (We Painted the Island),
which he says has renewed the face of the neighbourhood he comes from,
which at one time was dangerous. The project aims to give tools to future
generations, to create artists, and promote the concept of the neighbourhood
Isla Maciel. Brian adds:

Learning to paint a wall is just the start, because you can learn a lot of
things through art. You can meet other types of people, you can see life
in another way, that it's not just what happens here in the barrio, it's to
see that the world is much broader.

In a certain way, art transcends the barrier between rich and poor. It
breaks down these divisions because although people are poor they can
make a beautiful piece of art and it's the same art that can be appreciated
by someone with money.

The good thing about painting a humble house is that it's a present from the artist to the occupant, which generates trust in the artists,
because my parents' generation thought that to be an artist was to be
a slacker. Now the same people have realized that artists do the most
work! Because they have to do their regular job and then use the weekends from 8 a.m. to start painting. To be an artist is to be strong. There is
a new identity that we are creating in Isla Maciel, it has stopped being a
marginalized neighbourhood and has started to be a place where there's
a type of urban art gallery that is open for everybody.

These two voices demonstrate graffiti's positive potential, especially in marginalized communities with experiences of violence and crime. Graffiti empowers
the most marginalized by inscribing their presence on public space, helping
them to reclaim the city. It is also a powerful means of political communication, being accessible and visually exciting, while making use of familiar
cultural symbols to convey meaning.

Yet some people question whether explicitly political graffiti is a fair and
appropriate use of public areas, as it intrudes on the viewer's space and can
be deemed intimidating and aggressive. Juan Gabriel Gómez Alborello is a

professor at the Institute of Political Studies and International Relations at the public Universidad Nacional in Bogotá:

> Plaza Che is one of the main plazas here on campus, where you can see painted the figure of Camilo Torres, who joined the ELN guerrillas and was assassinated. There's a picture of Camilo holding a rifle and to me this is unacceptable. It's a way in which people who support the ELN have imposed their view on all of us on campus. I would like to see a referendum on this issue – are we going to accept symbols that legitimize the armed struggle here on campus?

Other people believe that walls are simply not the right place for political discussions which should instead be had in person or online. Bogotá-based, socially engaged graffiti artist DJLu disagrees:

> Every wall for me is a way of discovering the city, what is underneath the infrastructure and the solid matter. You see the different tensions, cultures, passions, and struggles on the surface of the wall and I believe that's good, as it's taking the tension and violence to the wall and not to the real arena ... Everyone's heard of violence in Colombia, but pointing these issues out in art is another way of making a call for peace, and I think it's very worthwhile because it could change society in some way. I hope and believe that we can build a better country through what I do, which is art ... If you don't want to listen, take out a bucket of white paint and buff it out.

Dexpierte street art collective is a group of former sociology students who dedicate themselves to making political graffiti about Colombia's decades-long civil conflict and its repercussions. The flat where they meet is covered in graffiti-stencilled protest posters, and aerosol cans neatly line the shelves.

> **Ana:** Dexpierte is a people's street art collective. There are three of us: the two boys and myself. We've been working for about six years. We use the technique of stencilling to place the theme of memory in public spaces; memory, that is, of the armed conflict that Colombia has experienced, but also memory more broadly, in defence of the social struggles both in Colombia and as part of a shared history in Latin America. We believe that murals, stencils, and the practices of street art are a medium of communication. They offer alternative ways to express a political discourse in the street that is a bit more accessible for people and, to a certain extent, transgressive, because people will come across it whether they want to or not.
>
> We know that it's made some groups uncomfortable because the topics we talk about generate a lot of disputes. There is one case in particular of a mural that we painted a while ago on an important avenue here in Bogotá, on the corner of 19th and 7th [streets]. We depicted the faces of three people who belonged to a political party called Unión

Patriótica, which came about through negotiations with the guerrillas around 1985. There were three faces: one of someone who was assassinated and the other two of people who suffered enforced disappearances. In the days after we painted this mural, one of the far-right groups here painted over it and wrote 'terrorists'. It was a reaction and also a dialogue, demonstrating the political positions that exist on both sides. There was no physical confrontation, nothing like that, but a symbolic confrontation took place there.

There are the risks that the public take every day in the street, and then there is the risk that comes when we engage in political discourse. Any graffiti artist who paints in the street runs the risk that the owner of the wall won't like it or that the police will turn up. In a country like Colombia, though, it's risky to put the topics that we work with out on the streets, but nothing has happened so far that has been too traumatic. It's risky for several reasons. Society is very polarized because of political and ideological forces that are extremely antagonistic. This means that using certain narratives can lead to repression. It doesn't just come from the state but from other sectors too, including the paramilitaries, who are a special phenomenon in Colombia. Their ideas and logic are anti-communist or anti-leftist – which goes against what we do – and their actions are aimed at maintaining control. Obviously, when you are involved in a practice like graffiti, which is outside their control and their idea of a clean city, it generates these clashes. In Colombia, they assassinate leaders of social movements and people who discuss human rights or denounce crimes committed by the state.

Mauricio: We came to use painting as the language through which we could reach spaces and spheres we wouldn't have been able to access with a clear and convincing message except via artistic means.

Ana: Historically, graffiti has been associated with politics all over the world, and that's true in Colombia too. In the 1970s, various groups of graphic designers, mostly from the Universidad Nacional de Colombia, started to create a graphic style that was focused on the people and concerned with the struggle of Colombian workers. One example was the group Taller 4 Rojo, a group of artists who started to produce work in support of striking workers and their children. They did this through very simple images, using silk screen printing. These started to appear in the streets, on posters supporting marches, as well as in newspapers and fanzines.

Things continued to evolve, for example with the guerrilla movement M-19, which used various alternative communications media, including graffiti, to write slogans on the streets. That's when people started to write graffiti on the walls and it's still very common when people go out on a march to leave messages on fences and walls. The M-19 used it in a very particular way, publicly making a political statement about a trade unionist who had 'betrayed' his party. The M-19 suggested that citizens should go out and write 'Yes' or 'No' on the walls with aerosols to say whether he should be executed or not. The answer from many people in a society like Colombia was 'Yes'. And that's exactly what happened: José Rachel Mercado was assassinated. So, you can see the relationship between graffiti and politics.

Coming closer to the present day, the practice of graffiti in the city becomes more nuanced. There's the case of Diego Felipe Becerra, a young graffiti artist who did graffiti that wasn't exactly political but that many people thought of as vandalism. He was doing some graffiti and the police arrived and stopped him from finishing it. One thing led to another and the police ended up killing him. This generates a discussion around the practice of graffiti itself and how its practitioners, whether their graffiti is political or not, are subject to repression.

There isn't a law about graffiti. In Bogotá they tried to have a Mesa Distrital for graffiti [local government project providing funding for graffiti artists]. I don't know if it's in force right now. Dexpierte never participated in this initiative. It's a public policy idea that allows them to legitimize graffiti in certain zones of the city. The current mayor, for example, doesn't like graffiti, so he ignores the agreements that were made before he was in office.

Mauricio: I think that a language like graffiti tends to be diminished when it's subject to laws and permits. It ceases to be a collective construction. When the places where it can be done are restricted, the capacity for dialogue is lost. Violent and confrontational situations reappear.

Ana: In other administrations, where people are free to paint walls, dialogue and communication are much easier, including between graffiti artists themselves. People work in a more collective and collaborative way. But when the authorities or the government start repressing people, graffiti also turns to this logic of violence in response to the aggression. What I've just described reflects in part what a society like Colombia is like. When we have freedom, things might be easier, but when things get repressive we tend to respond in the same way, that is, violently or defensively. I think in many cases this has prolonged a state of violence – not necessarily with weapons – between certain actors, for example the government and the guerrillas, as well as among ourselves as human beings and citizens.

We have worked very closely with social organizations and victims' associations that are independent and autonomous. The atmosphere of peace has led people to do graffiti that is more directed towards social and community causes.

Mauricio: It's more that they are broadening the narrative and language of the debate, which is getting wider – artistically, musically, in every sense … You shouldn't see it in terms of positive and negative, but instead think, 'What's happening in this negative situation that we can say at the moment? And are we allowed to say it? Are we allowed to say

© Dexpierte Coletivo 2018

Danzante del Pochó, Tabasco, Mexico.

that Colombia is the place with the highest level of murders of trade union members?'

Ana: In moments of transition like the one we're in right now, graffiti has the capacity to say with greater freedom, perhaps, things that were impossible to say previously. Or if not impossible, then more restricted. Colombia has a number of particularities, for example the murders of union members and social leaders. Speaking about insurgency in public spaces used to be difficult. It was restricted and viewed with suspicion. Currently, people are open to putting this debate out in the streets. The power of the image and of graffiti are utilized more these days.

But people continue to get into disputes, because even though we are in a moment when democracy is opening up in favour of reconciliation and peace, not everything is so rosy. There will always be some stories in the background that continue to be repressed and hidden away. It's still not easy to talk about certain subjects – the continuation of a latent paramilitarism and the crimes of the state, stories about the multinationals that support these armed groups. Even though it's visible, out in the open, and there's a willingness to talk, [the discourse] is still very biased and restricted by this machinery that doesn't permit the whole truth but rather half-truths. We uphold certain freedoms but some of them only quietly. Graffiti has this potential right now to transform itself and take advantage of these spaces that are opening up, to put this discussion out on the street. It's a matter of seizing the moment. Maybe this is one of the few opportunities that we've had as a generation, but also as Colombians, to take on this fight and to have these discussions in such a democratic way, sharing them with the people. I think that's why it's so important to do it and get the most we can out of it. We don't know how long it will be there.

When we paint [images of] the faces of people who have disappeared, our images defend a social struggle because they pay homage to them. Some people can't understand and don't know who the person is, so it doesn't affect them. They wonder why we're painting this photograph. We almost always use grey paint so that the portrait looks good but we put colour in the background and use this relation between greys and many colours to bring it to life and show that it is an active memory. It might be from the past, but we're bringing it into the present in order to make a transformation. That's what memory is for. But there are people who don't understand it, don't like it, or don't consider it to have any significance. 'Why are they doing that? It's not going to change the country.' Graffiti isn't going to make Colombia better tomorrow, but it's one of many actions that are being done across the country. What they do is start a discussion and then keep it going.

Many other artists have used graffiti to commemorate and bear witness to the disappeared in various conflicts. The Argentine artist Nazza Stencil paints pixelated stencils of some of Argentina's 30,000 missing people from the dictatorship on the walls of the Navy Mechanical School (ESMA), a former military torture centre in Buenos Aires, and elsewhere around the city.

In Mexico, the number '43', indicating the 43 disappeared students of Ayotzinapa (see box in Chapter 8), can be found sprayed all around the country. The town of Ayotzinapa itself has become a graffiti memorial and shrine, almost submerged beneath the hundreds of images left by local and visiting graffiti artists. In San Juan, Puerto Rico, the memory of the country's bloody colonial past is sinisterly beautiful on its walls. In Venezuela, the faces of those killed in the ongoing protests against the economic crisis and Nicolás Maduro's increasingly authoritarian rule adorn the homemade riot shields of protesters. Painter Oscar Olivares' images mix the faces of victims with religious motifs. He was a friend of slain student protester Juan Pernalete, and also paints murals, although they are not always political.

Memorial art

Memory is a slippery and elusive creature. It becomes embellished, fabricated, and misremembered; trauma bores holes through it, creating repetition and unprompted and distressing revisits to the past. When married with divisive state conflicts, memory becomes a battleground: whose vision of the past is to be represented requires constant and difficult negotiation between people, political factions, and ideologies. While governments and institutions struggle to reconcile themselves with histories of violent state conflict and impunity, artists have been using their intuition to navigate the ragged past and, through their work, to demand justice and collectively memorialize those lost.

Memorial art commemorates, explicitly or implicitly, people who are lost in some way, and often has a political objective: holding power to account, calling out injustices, and providing a strong visual reminder that these unresolved pasts will not be forgotten, no matter what the dominant cultural narrative may be. Given Latin America's repeated experience of violence, disappearances, dictatorships, and criminal activity, memorial art is prevalent across the continent.

While the Peruvian National Memory Museum only opened in Lima in December 2015, nine artists have been touring their Itinerant Museum of Art for Memory around the country since 2009. From 1980 to 2000 a war was waged between the Peruvian government and Shining Path, a Maoist armed group. Nearly 70,000 people were killed, with indigenous Andean people and rural campesinos caught in the midst of the conflict, often targeted with torture and rape. The Itinerant Museum of Art for Memory showcases art made about the conflict, valuing the frequently maligned Andean and campesino victims and taking the artworks directly to them in rural parts of the country. In this way it breaks free from the confines of the capital city where the art world and national memorials are usually situated.

Jorge Miyagui, one of the founders of the Itinerant Museum, describes the differing reactions to the work showcased. 'In Lima, they insult us, they call us terrorists, while in Ayacucho or Huancavelica, people are very grateful.' Fellow founder Mauricio Delgado adds: 'In Peru, there's still this strong belief that talking about memory is subversive' (Martínez, 2013). But for Mauricio, the public's interactions with the Itinerant Museum are the most interesting part of their project:

> Often, the artworks spark heated debates or even the trading of insults, which in turn become moments for reflection. Thus, the works of art become triggers for memories ... Sometimes the public intervenes spontaneously in response to one of the pieces. The Altar, one of the pieces in the Itinerant Museum's collection, is a collective creation of artists and groups of relatives of the disappeared in Lima. Often, in Ayacucho and Huancavelica, families come forward with their photos to add to the work (Delgado, 2013).

The work of many Latin American artists, mostly female, addresses the murders and disappearances of women. Mexican Mayra Martell photographs empty rooms, to underscore the lives and characters of those abducted. In these powerful and haunting memorials to loss, the girls' families have left their bedrooms untouched, as if at any moment they could return. Stephanie Janaina is a dancer and choreographer based in Mexico City. In 2015, her close friend, the activist Nadia Vera, was raped, tortured, and murdered in an apartment just two blocks away from Stephanie's, alongside anti-corruption photojournalist Rubén Espinosa and two other women. In response Stephanie created the immersive choreography project *Pièce de Résistance: Margot*, in which she lay semi-naked and completely still in a room for three hours while snails – creatures of the underworld in some Latin American mythology – traced silvery lines over her body. She wondered how the audience would react: would she be objectified, respected, or ignored? 'I felt that at the moment, I'm surrounded by blood: what can I do? I'm trying to make art that makes a difference, and what can I do? ... We are in a very violent moment in Mexico and I believe it is urgent to talk about what is happening. For me art is about resistance.'

Guatemalan memorial art primarily focuses on the 200,000 people who were killed or disappeared in the civil war (1960–96). The war pitched the government in a vicious campaign against a guerrilla movement and indigenous Maya civilians (see Chapter 8). A United Nations commission found the Guatemalan State responsible for 93 per cent of all the human rights violations documented by the Commission for Historical Clarification (CEH, 1999).

The conviction of former dictator General Efraín Ríos Montt in 2013 for genocide and crimes against humanity was annulled 10 days later by the Constitutional Court. The retrial was beset by delays and Ríos Montt died (on 1 April 2018) before it could be concluded. Current president Jimmy Morales denies the genocide in Guatemala. Some of his backers, including the founders of his political party – the National Convergence Front (FCN) – are conservative members of the military linked to war crimes dating from the conflict (Bigda, 2015). Guatemala does not have a national memory museum as such, something which has become ubiquitous around Latin America. Memory-making in Guatemala has therefore been a non-state, private, or community-driven practice and art has had a key place in memorials. Creative expression in the country often has a memorial aspect to it.

In Guatemala City, photographer Daniel Hernández-Salazar's shouting angels serve this purpose, being a memorial to those disappeared and a call to bring the perpetrators to justice. The angel depicts a man with indigenous features, semi-naked, with wings made from bones, cupping his mouth with his hands in a silent scream. Daniel's angels are possibly the most famous images associated with memory and protest in Guatemala. During the later years of the civil war and its aftermath Daniel photographed the exhumations of clandestine graves and documented the struggle for justice. He describes his approach to memorial art:

> I was born in Guatemala City in 1956, and I've been doing photography since I was a child. For me unveiling the truth has always been very important – so that people know the real reasons for things that happened. I felt that photography was a good tool to do that because it's like proof.
>
> What is memorial art? That's a difficult question. It's art with an objective: to remember. Art has a responsibility to represent what happened

So that everyone can know/Para que todos lo sepan.

to society during a particular period. I think we can't keep quiet. If we do, tragic events will be repeated. Art has to be an awakener of conscience. If art documents tragic events then I think it can liberate society from those events.

In the late 1980s and in the early 1990s, during my time with Associated Press, I started taking photos of the exhumations. I decided to quit work and return to the exhumations as an independent photographer to work in a more documentary and artistic way, with a different point of view.

One day I was working with bones alongside a forensic anthropologist in one of the forensic labs in Guatemala. He began describing people's shoulder blades to me, and said, 'They're very thin and delicate and they look like butterflies' wings'. So I began to think, they could also be wings of birds, and when I think of birds I think of flying, freedom, freedom of expression. I then connected it with my desire to make an angel, and I said these could be the wings of angels. So that's how I began developing the image.

I used the scapula bones, the shoulder-blade bones, of a person found in a clandestine grave, but in an inverse position, and then I took a picture of a model to combine with the bones to make wings. I did it in a very simple way, I sandwiched two negatives together and it worked.

It's very fleshy, it's material, not ethereal, and it's dark skinned – so it's a different angel.

I developed the first angels inspired by the monkeys who speak no evil, hear no evil, and see no evil – a convention known worldwide. I wanted to represent how Guatemalans don't want to deal with things of the past that bother them – they fear them or feel complicit. Guatemalans tend not to speak out but stay quiet, in a very hypocritical way, I think. So I developed these angels that didn't want to hear or see or talk about what happened in the war. The fourth angel was born just as they were going to break silence on what happened in Guatemala. Someone from the Human Rights Commission asked me for pictures for the covers of the report of the memory project they were working on [the 1998 REMHI report on the atrocities committed during the civil war] – and I thought of the angels. I wanted this picture to be a metaphor for telling the truth but also the proof of what happened, because of the wings. This angel was different, this angel was talking; instead of not wanting to hear or see, he does the opposite, he cries out, and denounces the atrocities.

The design was approved by Bishop Juan Gerardi, who led the project, and it took his declaration for its title: 'So That All Shall Know'. When the bishop was assassinated just two days after presenting the report *Guatemala: Nunca más!*, Daniel's angel, now irrevocably linked with speaking out about the truth post-war, was taken up by the public in a march protesting Gerardi's death, the silent demonstrators carrying placards of the shouting angel. Since then Daniel has both photographed the path of his angel and facilitated its spread as a symbol of dissent. He has pasted up giant versions on sites connected to war atrocities and Gerardi's assassination, including the US embassy. But not everyone appreciated such a strong statement:

I was waiting for reactions – I wanted them. People began to tear out parts of the poster. I knew some people didn't like the message it transmitted. [Daniel shows a picture of the slow destruction of the poster] I call it the triptych of memory. This photo was taken one or two days after we put it up, and the other a couple of weeks after, then one a month later, so it also represents memory in a way. I liked it – they were there to suffer. Some were also stolen or disappeared, so for me it was a way to remember the disappeared during the war.

Daniel revisited the project during the first Ríos Montt trial, which saw the shouting angel proclaim, 'Sí hubo genocidio' ('Yes, there *was* a genocide'), from the rear of 13 public buses that criss-crossed the streets of Guatemala City.

One of my ambitions is to install these angels in a permanent exhibition in a public space in Guatemala City, but it's difficult. We don't have a public memorial because of the lack of will and the opposition of the people who still rule Guatemala. The army has a memorial – why can't civilians have that? The state keeps memory segregated so it's not strong. The quest for justice isn't only founded on memorials, but they help as they make people stronger, I think. Their stories have been accepted, now there's a monument to prove it, so memorials support the people's struggles. Art can really help with these memorials as it can create symbols for people to relate to.

We need a national memorial so that it can become a collective memory – a place where marches could start, and ceremonies be held every year. Many people will never bury their loved ones, because they cannot be found, but at least they could have this special place where they could pay tribute and remember. So this really helps society to heal, to walk towards a different future.

The angels have become part of the cityscape – part protest, part memorial – forcing the public who witness them to process the past, countering the common desire to forget dangerous or painful memories, and inviting them to remember and speak out.

Theatre of memory

Nestled amongst the tall green stalks of maize near the village of Sololá, in the Sotz'il Jay Cultural Centre, a different type of memorial art is being practiced by Mujeres Ajchowen. They are an all-female Maya Kaqchikel theatre group who originate from and partner with a mixed theatre group called Sotz'il. Both groups perform well-researched plays derived from ancient Maya texts – stories which have often been forgotten because of the conflict, when it became too dangerous to practise their culture and Maya spiritual leaders were directly targeted. Mujeres Ajchowen add another layer to their performances by weaving messages of women's rights into the traditional legends.

These theatre groups are connected to memory in a very different way: they physically embody active cultural memory, becoming conduits through which Maya culture can be transmitted, shared, and strengthened. The theatre groups have become a defiant expression of existence and a positive force for cultural revitalization, travelling around Maya communities and abroad to perform.

While they do not explicitly refer to the genocide in their work, in the way that Daniel does, it remains an undercurrent and part of their motivation, as Mujeres Ajchowen founder Clara Alicia Sen Sipac explains:

My name is Clara Alicia Sen Sipac. I am a member of the Mujeres Ajchowen; we dedicate ourselves to theatre and Maya art made by women.

During the armed conflict that we lived through, I was still a child, so it felt to me that we were living

Clara Alicia Sen Sipac.

all the time in hiding, in fear. I think that now we are rescuing our customs because, during the conflict, we couldn't go to the top of a hill to perform a ceremony, for example, because they [the army] would think we were guerrillas. We were living permanently under threat. Now at least there exists this liberty, I can go to a hill and practise my own religion.

Grupo Sotz'il was a group which started to make art, but with a lot of political and social content, so I think it was very important that their point of view emerged after the Peace Accords [of 1996], as a way of healing and expressing, and to say who we are. We are here despite everything that's happened – we, the indigenous peoples, are here and more alive and looking forward to continuing fighting and to keep reclaiming our culture.

I come from Grupo Sotz'il but for artistic reasons we decided in 2011 to create Mujeres Ajchowen. Grupo Sotz'il trained us in many artistic disciplines – dance, music, theatre, poetry, and sculpture. Finally we decided to carry on further with Maya theatre. The truth is that in 2010 the coordinator and founder of Grupo Sotz'il was assassinated. His name was Lisandro Guarcax and he was my partner. He was also a community leader and teacher – he was my inspiration. In one of Lisandro's various activities he went to a meeting at a school and that's where the tragic event happened. They took him and beat him and murdered him. For me he is one of the fallen. There are so many who don't stop talking about what's happening in their community, their territory, or their culture. But this is what's happening in our country: if you are doing something then they watch you from afar and they may harm you. We don't have this complete liberty, I think it's still very reserved.

So my inspiration initially was him, and because he's passed across to another dimension I think it's important to continue with his legacy. He opened the path and planted the seeds and it's important to look after them so they grow. But on the path I realized there was a lot to heal, in my heart I had a lot of pain and injuries – but it's the same for every member of the group. Forming the group was a way of externalizing all of what we felt.

Mujeres Ajchowen is a cultural revindication, what we do is a consciousness-raising process. It's a fundamental way of reaching people and telling them: this is happening, this is what we're living through, and this is how we can speak out. We're not attempting to provide a solution, for we know that to find a solution to a problem of this magnitude is very complex; but we talk about how to raise consciousness. I can do this as a Maya woman. What can the rest of the society do to transform everything that is happening to us, little by little?

Mujeres Ajchowen's work is a testimony to Maya resilience and continued cultural strength. As their plays rework dominant historical narratives, they

© Heidy Cabrera

Mujeres Ajchowen perform their play Ximonïk.

present an anti-colonial visualization of Maya survival in the 21st century. Like other Mayan cultural activists, they feel compelled to reassert their culture in the wake of a conflict which sought to wipe it out. While not every form of contemporary Maya art is memorial or connected to the conflict, a Maya cultural movement has been growing across Guatemala, in which musicians, arts collectives, poets, and writers are helping to rescue and strengthen cultural practices, develop new creative expressions, and generate greater pride in a Maya identity.

* * *

Art in Latin America continues to be a radical site of political expression, where the public can make sense of and connect emotionally to controversial debates and identities. Culture provides a more intuitive, flexible, and emotive medium through which to explore dissenting thoughts and voices than is available in the political discourse of the mainstream media. The public can interact with the art in their own way. They are not being told what to think, but influenced to see things differently. The voices in this chapter have demonstrated art's transformative potential to challenge opinions and prejudices, to commemorate and call for justice, and to valorize marginalized groups and identities.

Music, in particular, has been creatively deployed to bolster recognition and respect for marginalized groups, challenging prejudices and stereotypes. The cumbia–rock fusion of Iván Brasil in Buenos Aires repossesses the genre for its original creators – the poor – and addresses the problems they face today. Guatemalan Rebeca Lane's hip hop promotes feminism, while Linn da Quebrada's *baile funk* celebrates trans rights. The subversion of genres formerly associated with misogynistic content makes their message all the more defiant. Indigenous people rapping in their own languages have also helped to engender pride in their identity and perhaps a renewed desire in young indigenous people to keep their cultures and languages alive.

Graffiti is socially transformative, both for the artists and the places they inhabit, as they inscribe their presence on public space and physically change the face of excluded communities such as Comuna 13 and Villa Isla Maciel with works of art. However, as street art collective Dexpierte point out, when graffiti is restricted by laws and permits its power is diminished, and 'its capacity for dialogue is lost'. Given its increasing commercial success, extra vigilance is required to ensure graffiti maintains its independence and capacity for dissent.

Memory, in both art and theatre, is a vital channel for art to examine unresolved pasts post-conflict and in landscapes of violence. A strong motif throughout the work of Dexpierte, the Itinerant Museum of Art for Memory, Daniel Hernández-Salazar, and Mujeres Ajchowen is a desire to retain memory as an active process so that it can transform the present. While it commemorates past sufferings, it calls for justice and an end to impunity. Stephanie Janaina's performance *Pièce de Résistance: Margot*, as well as commemorating the death of her friend, attempts to find answers to why Mexico is killing its women. She allows the audience to interpret the often dehumanizing way people relate to the female body in Mexico as a subtle warning about the country's wave of femicides.

Rebeca Lane defines herself as an 'artivist', and this intrinsic link between art and activism is coming to define increasing numbers of Latin American artists. The boundaries of art-making and activism are breaking down, emphasizing art's integral role in dissent. Art also provides powerful visual aids behind which to unite and protest, like Daniel's angels, and is used in ever more inventive ways.

Perhaps it is through art's ability to communicate emotively that its strongest potential is revealed. Art can simply express and convey things that words alone fail to. The timbre of song, a striking visual image, or the physical expression of a play – these things tap into our emotional as well as our cognitive comprehension, becoming harder to forget. Such visual or auditory experiences are a dimension of social life and can therefore help us to understand more openly the reality of the world we live in.

About the author

Louise Morris is a journalist, audio and TV producer. She specializes in women's rights and the intersection between art and politics. Louise works primarily in radio, producing and presenting documentaries for BBC R4 and producing for NPR. She previously worked producing a daily TV magazine programme. She has written for The Wire, Delayed Gratification, and BBC News Online, among others.

Interviews

Iván Brasil (Los del Puente): interviewed in Villa Isla Maciel, Province of Buenos Aires, Argentina, on 27 May 2017 by Louise Morris. Translated by Louise Morris.

Manuel Carrasquilla, aka **El Zorro** (Casa Kolacho): interviewed in Medellín on 15 June 2017 by Louise Morris. Translated by Louise Morris.

Ana, Mauricio and **Diego** (Dexpierte street art collective): interviewed in Bogotá on 8 June 2017 by Louise Morris. Translated by Matthew Kingston.

DJLu (graffiti artist): interviewed in Bogotá on 10 June 2017 by Louise Morris. Translated by Louise Morris.

Daniel Hernández-Salazar (photographer): interviewed in Guatemala City on 25 June 2017 by Louise Morris. Translated by Louise Morris.

Juan Gabriel Gómez Alborello (Universidad Nacional de Colombia): interviewed in Bogotá on 12 June 2017 by Louise Morris. Translated by Louise Morris.

Stephanie Janaina (dancer and choreographer): interviewed in Mexico City on 5 July 2017 by Louise Morris. Translated by Louise Morris.

Rebeca Lane (hip hop artist): interviewed via email on 19 May 2014 and 4 June 2018 by Louise Morris. Translated by Louise Morris.

Totó la Momposina (singer): interviewed in Norwich, UK, on 19 May 2017 by Louise Morris. Translated by Louise Morris.

Brian Sánchez (Pintó La Isla): interviewed in Villa Isla Maciel, Province of Buenos Aires, Argentina, on 27 May 2017 by Louise Morris. Translated by Louise Morris.

Urián Sarmiento (Sonidos Enraizados): interviewed in Bogotá on 9 June 2017 by Louise Morris. Translated by Louise Morris.

Clara Alicia Sen Sipac (Mujeres Ajchowen): interviewed in Sololá, Guatemala, on 26 June 2017 by Louise Morris. Translated by Louise Morris.

References

NB: All web references were checked and still available in May/June 2018 unless otherwise stated. All references are listed, with web-links, on the page for this chapter on the Voices website www.vola.org.uk

Bigda, L. (2015) 'A military-backed comedian will be Guatemala's next president. Activists aren't laughing', The Nation, 2 November, <https://www.thenation.com/article/a-military-backed-comedian-will-be-guatemalas-next-president-activists-arent-laughing>

CEH (1999) 'Guatemala: memory of silence', Report of the Commission for Historical Clarification, Conclusions and Recommendations (CEH), English summary, <https://www.aaas.org/sites/default/files/migrate/uploads/mos_en.pdf>

Cepeda, E. (2018) 'Tu Pum Pum: as reggaeton goes pop, never forget the genre's Black roots', Remezcla, <http://remezcla.com/features/music/tu-pum-pum-1>

Delgado, M. (2013) 'The museum is in the streets: the Itinerant Museum of Art for Memory', Globality-gmu.net, <http://www.globality-gmu.net/archives/3544>

Martínez, M. (2013) 'Peru's painful mirror', ICTJ.org, <https://www.ictj.org/sites/default/files/subsites/perus-painful-mirror>

Sanchez, F. (2017) 'Amid tear gas, Venezuela violinist symbolizes hope for peace', AP News, 5 June, <https://apnews.com/af915a9bffba4c439a221b044e03c344/Amid-tear-gas,-Venezuela-violinist-symbolizes-hope-for-peace?utm_campaign=SocialFlow&utm_source=Twitter&utm_medium=AP>

Villegas, R. (2018) 'This video from Costa Rican rapper Macha Kiddo is a powerful indictment of transphobia', Remezcla, <http://remezcla.com/releases/music/macha-kiddo-jony-la-romi-video>

Index of interviews

Interviewee	Profession/organization	Country	Date	Chapter(s)
Valérie Abad	Universidad Católica	Chile	2018	4
Thiago Alves da Silva	MAB	Brazil	2017	7
Leonardo Batista ('Aronor')	Ribeirinho Council	Brazil	2016	6
Iván Brasil	Los del Puente	Argentina	2017	11
Eliane Brum	Journalist	Brazil	2018	1
Jorge Cáñez ('Peatónito')	Road safety & urban mobility campaigner	Mexico	2018	9
Manuel Carrasquilla ('El Zorro')	Casa Kolacho	Colombia	2017	11
Alicia Cawiya	Huaorani people	Ecuador	2016	2, 5
Juan Ch'oc	Crique Sarco village	Belize	2016	5
Andrés Chaves	Film-maker	Colombia	2018	9
Carlos Correa	Espacio Público	Venezuela	2018	10
Marcelo Correa	CONES	Chile	2016	4
Lucio Cuenca	OLCA	Chile	2017	7
Luciana Cury	Coletivo Ocupe e Abrace	Brazil	2018	9
Marcello Deodoro	Tijuca Indiana Residents' Commission	Brazil	2017	9
Dexpierte: Ana, Mauricio & Diego	Dexpierte street art collective	Colombia	2017	11
Gabriela Díaz	HIJOS	Colombia	2018	8
DJLu	Graffiti artist	Colombia	2017	11
Ana Enamorado	MMM	Mexico	2017	8
Maria Eliete Felix Juruna	Paquiçamba Indigenous Reserve	Brazil	2016	6
Edgardo Fernández	Queer tango teacher	Argentina	2016	3
Alfredo Gallardo	CDPC	Chile	2016	7
Marcelo Giraud	Asamblea Popular por el Agua	Argentina	2016	7
Juan Gabriel Gómez Alborello	Universidad Nacional de Colombia	Colombia	2017	11
Luiz Gonzaga da Silva (Gegê)	MMC	Brazil	2016/ 2017	9

http://dx.doi.org/10.3362/9781909014213.012

Interviewee	Profession/organization	Country	Date	Chapter(s)
Esther González	CDPC	Chile	2016	7
Eriberto Gualinga	Sarayaku Kichwa community	Ecuador	2016	5
Patricia Gualinga	Sarayaku Kichwa community	Ecuador	2016	2, 5
Daniel Hernández-Salazar	Photographer	Guatemala	2017	11
Angelo Herrera	Hotel manager	Chile	2016	7
Giorgio Jackson	Former student leader	Chile	2011	4
Stephanie Janaina	Dancer & choreographer	Mexico	2017	11
Carina Jofré	CONICET San Juan	Argentina	2016	7
Fany Kuiru	Tejedoras de Memoria	Colombia	2016	5
Rebeca Lane	Hip hop artist	Guatemala	2014/ 2018	11
Camila Lanes	UBES	Brazil	2016	4
Patricia Mayorga	Proceso	Mexico	2018	10
Salvador Medina	Urban economist	Mexico	2018	9
Antônia Melo	Movimento Xingu Vivo para Sempre	Brazil	2015	6
Camila Méndez	COSAJUCA	Colombia	2017	7
Totó la Momposina	Singer	Colombia	2017	11
Tania Montalvo	Animal Político	Mexico	2018	10
Jimena Norambuena	OTD	Chile	2016	3
Pavel Núñez	Universidad Clementina Suárez/digital activist	Honduras	2016	4, 10
Ana Paula Oliveira	Mães de Manguinhos	Brazil	2016	8
Marcos Orellana	Human Rights Watch	Chile	2017	1
René Orellana	Politician and academic	Bolivia	2016	1
Rodrigo Péret	Churches and Mining Network	Brazil	2017	7
Maria Rosa Pessoa Piedade	Ribeirinha at Palhau	Brazil	2016	6
Fatima Pinho	Mães de Manguinhos	Brazil	2016	8
Michel Riquelme	OTD	Chile	2016	3
María Teresa Rivera	Reproductive rights activist	El Salvador	2018	2
Oscar Roca	CAEP	Bolivia	2016	7
Johans Rodriguez	1st Brigade of Polvorines	Peru	2016	9
Constanza San Juan	CTDG	Chile	2016	7
Brian Sánchez	Pintó La Isla	Argentina	2017	11
Eva Sánchez	Las Hormigas	Honduras	2016	2, 5

Interviewee	Profession/organization	Country	Date	Chapter(s)
Urián Sarmiento	Sonidos Enraizados	Colombia	2017	11
Clara Alicia Sen Sipac	Mujeres Ajchowen	Guatemala	2017	11
Renata da Silva Souza	O Cidadão/UFRJ	Brazil	2018	10
Raúl Sohr	Journalist	Chile	2016	1
Emília Maria de Souza	Horto Residents' Association	Brazil	2018	9
Kurt Steffens	Ciudad Emergente	Chile	2018	9
Maristella Svampa	Sociologist	Argentina	2018	1
Ayme Tanguila	Kichwa architect	Ecuador	2016	5
Javier Treviño Rangel	CIDE	Mexico	2017	8
Froyla Tzalam	SATIIM	Belize	2016	5
Rogelio Ustate	Tabaco community	Colombia	2017	7, 8
Yuri Valle Roca	Blogger	Cuba	2018	10
Miryam Vargas Teutle	Radio Cholollan	Mexico	2017	10
Ismael Vega	CAAAP	Peru	2018	6
Stefanía Vega	CTDG	Chile	2016	7
Lucrecia Wagner	CONICET Mendoza	Argentina	2016	7
Jean Wyllys	PSOL deputy, Rio de Janeiro	Brazil	2016	3

Latin America Bureau (LAB)

Latin America Bureau (Research and Action) Limited (LAB) is an independent publishing and research organization. A registered charity, based in the UK, LAB provides news, analysis and information on Latin America, reporting consistently from the perspective of the region's poor, oppressed or marginalized communities, and social movements. LAB brings an alternative, critical awareness and understanding of Latin America to readers throughout the English-speaking world.

Founded in 1977, LAB is widely known as the publisher of over 150 books and operates a website, updated regularly, which carries news and analysis on Latin America and reports from more than 40 partners and correspondents in the region (www.lab.org.uk). LAB distributes a free e-newsletter to subscribers in many countries. You can sign up for the newsletter by clicking 'Subscribe' on the www.lab.org.uk home page.

In 2015 LAB entered into a publishing partnership with Practical Action Publishing Ltd, who will distribute all LAB titles, new and old, through www.developmentbookshop.com.

Index

Page numbers in italics refer to figures.